D1601667

# THE
# POLITICS
# OF
# PRESIDENTIAL COMMISSIONS

# THE POLITICS OF
# PRESIDENTIAL
# COMMISSIONS

By
David Flitner Jr.

TRANSNATIONAL PUBLISHERS, INC.
Dobbs Ferry, New York

**Library of Congress Cataloging-in-Publication Data**

Flitner, David.
  The politics of presidential commissions.

  Bibliography: p.
  Includes index.
  1. Executive advisory bodies—United States.
I. Title.
JK468.C7F55 1986       353.09'3       86-7056
ISBN 0-941320-42-1

Manufactured in the United States of America

To David P. Flitner,
Mariam B. Flitner,
and
Emilie M. Flitner

When in man's long history other great civilizations fell, it was less often from external assault than from internal decay. Our own civilization has shown a remarkable capacity for responding to crises and for emerging to higher pinnacles of power and achievement. But our most serious challenges to date have been external—the kind this strong and resourceful country could unite against. While serious external dangers remain, the graver threats today are internal: haphazard urbanization, racial discrimination, disfiguring of the environment, unprecedented interdependence, the dislocation of human identity and motivation created by an affluent society—all resulting in a rising tide of individual and group violence.

The greatness and durability of most civilizations has been finally determined by how they have responded to these challenges from within. Ours will be no exception.

> —The National Commission on the
> Causes and Prevention of Violence

On the whole, however, I supose it is still true that commissions burst on the scene and then pass from view more or less like comets, only to appear again in the same form years and even decades later.

> —Lloyd N. Cutler,
> Executive Director,
> The National Commission on
> the Causes and Prevention
> of Violence

# Contents

# Tables and Diagrams

# A Note on Research

Research for this study involved the use of four basic types of sources. Exploration of each was seen as building upon, and reinforcing, the others. Initially, the commission reports themselves were examined. Major commissions often attach discussions of their research methods and procedures to their final reports. These discussions provided a foundation for understanding, in a general fashion, how commissions go about their work.

Second, published materials—including scholarly, popular, and journalistic writings—were studied throughout the course of research. This was an ongoing process because a number of such sources only became available once the research was under way. Some of this literature, a significant portion of which was written by commission participants, was highly useful and provided refinements and perspective on the activities of individual commissions beyond what was available in their reports, exposure to a number of theoretical approaches to the evaluation of the commission process, and anecdotal material which helped add a human, real-world perspective to the histories of various commissions.

A significant potential pitfall in the research attended exploration of some of the scholarly literature: Not only has there been relatively little analysis of the overall commission process, a fair portion of that which does exist has tended to view commissions from a pre-set theoretical perspective. Thus, there are certain limitations in the degree to which a comprehensive, fair-minded picture may be developed through reliance on this literature. It should be emphasized, however, that useful analyses have been produced and that even those with a theoretical bent offer important insights.

Fortunately, extensive hearings had been held in both the House and Senate regarding the commission process, and the records of these hearings were available as a third major resource. During the hearings many commission participants—chairmen, commissioners, and commission staff members—offered analyses of how they had gone about their investigations, what problems they had encountered, how they assessed the results of their work, and what responses they felt had been made to their reports.

The final source of data was direct contact with commission participants and others involved with the commission process. Personal interviews, telephone conversations, and sometimes lengthy correspondence were engaged in with commission chairmen, commission members, staff members, presidential aides, government figures, and scholars. These contacts provided the first-hand perspective of individuals with direct commission experience. They offered an understanding of what commissioners—and commissions—see as their fundamental tasks and goals. Perhaps most importantly, the commissioners and other participants offered their personal feelings as to the motivations that lie behind commission appointments, the validity of what commissions can accomplish, and what they see as the proper role of commissions in the American political system.

A potential problem with any interviewing is the possibility that it will yield only a narrow perspective. It may reasonably be argued that commission participants "have a stake" in how their experience is portrayed and evaluated and that they will, as a result, provide limited viewpoints. Further, since commissions involve so many people in the course of their work, it might be argued that only scores of interviews could produce an accurate impression.

In the present case, the accumulated literature of all types, combined with key interviews and contacts, provided what was felt to be a clear picture of the commission process—from appointment to investigation to report to response. Much of the available literature reveals the points of view of commission participants (at both the commissioner and staff levels) regarding positive as well as negative aspects of the commission experience. As a result, to a significant degree the task for one seeking an overall understanding of the commission process involves the arrangement of pieces to a puzzle and analysis of the whole.

Finally, while commission chairmen obviously have a stake in the subject of commissions, what is remarkable is the depth of feeling they clearly have with regard to their commission work. Many of these individuals have evidently thought deeply about this work. They are candid about what can be expected of commissions. Yet, they have no doubt that what they did was important—and the manner in which this is expressed suggests something qualitatively beyond rationalization. Many chairmen and commissioners seem to feel that they have made a genuine contribution to the education of their society. They feel that this aspect of their work, reflecting the extraordinary consensus amidst diversity which so many commissions have displayed, gives commissions a special validity in the American political process.

# Acknowledgments

This work would not have been possible without the patience, encouragement (in myriad forms), guidance, and support of many people. Chief among them are: Emilie Munyan Flitner, David P. and Mariam B. Flitner, Virginia Merrill, H. E. Harris, Betty H. Munyan, Professor Irving D. Fisher of the University of Southern Maine, Professors J. C. Heinlein and Abraham H. Miller of the University of Cincinnati, and Professor Jeffrey M. Berry of Tufts University. Each of these individuals has provided examples to follow, both personal and professional, such as to give the lie to those who would bemoan the state of the human character. I will forever be grateful to them.

I wish, also, to express gratitude to the many commission participants and observers identified in the course of the study, who shared their time, expertise, and wisdom in interviews and through correspondence. Whatever value this study may have is due, in large measure, to these individuals. Any errors of fact or interpretation are solely the author's responsibility.

Finally, my thanks to Heike Fenton, Marjorie Moore and Donna Scheeler, of Transnational Publishers, for making the mechanics of editing and publishing a more pleasant experience than any writer dares dream possible.

# 1

# INTRODUCTION

Presidential advisory commissions have become a standard tool of the presidential trade. They have been appointed to investigate every manner of subject from the standardization of screw threads and nuclear power plants to racism and population growth. At times, they have become an almost expected presidential response to national crises and volatile social issues. Commission reports represent great expenditures of time and money and the efforts of scores of individuals. Commission reports have been widely distributed to and discussed among relevant individuals, groups, and organizations around the country.

During the 1960s and early 1970s, American society faced social challenge and change on a level rivalled only, perhaps, by that of the Industrial Revolution. Change was everywhere and bewildering, sparked by new realities in international relations, domestic social conflict, mass electronic media, affluence and rising economic expectations. As a part of political efforts to respond to change and its many manifestations, presidential commissions were appointed with increasing frequency, approaching a rate of four and five appointments per year.[1] The commissions provided relatively rapid, in-depth analyses of critical problems facing the nation and offered recommendations for change. The commission reports of this period were controversial and rather consistently progressive in their findings and recommendations, a particularly noteworthy phenomenon given the generally moderate memberships of the commissions.

Despite the frequency of their use, however, commissions have suffered criticism and have often been ignored by those who appointed them. "So-called Presidential commissions do not work. They never will," said one disgruntled member of a prominent commission. "Such commissions, in my opinion, are not a valid part of the American political system."[2] These remarks suggest, in extreme form, an attitude often shared (in varying degrees) and taken for granted, particularly in journalism and academia. Cynicism and comments attributing a singular motive of presidential expediency, or declaring the inability of establishment figures to say anything meaningful about American society, often greet the appointment of a new commission or accompany discussions of commissions generally. Often, such comments emanate from individuals who are otherwise highly aware of the complex web of forces, actors, and ideas that make up the political process.

Additionally, in a phenomenon which fuels the skepticism surrounding commissions, presidents may publicly ignore the reports of commissions they have themselves appointed. Commissions, then, come to be seen, as Senator Edward M. Kennedy has put it, as "so many Jiminy Crickets chirping in the ears of deaf Presidents, deaf officials, deaf Congressmen, and perhaps a deaf public."[3] Indeed, a commission on commissions has even been suggested which, "not wholly in jest . . . should study the violence induced by the frustrations resulting from the publication of so many excellent prior reports and the public failure to respond."[4]

What sorts of intentions lie behind commission appointments? What purposes or functions are they designed to serve? Are they capable of conducting comprehensive investigations? To what extent do partisan considerations limit their performance? What are the results of commission studies? What can we reasonably expect of commissions? And, beyond all this, are commissions a "valid part of the American political system"?

This book investigates the politics of presidential commissions. It begins with a brief historical inquiry into the relevant highlights in the establishment of the commission as an institution followed by an examination of the modern commission process—appointment, investigative procedure, and the preparation of the report. The actions of the various responsive actors—the President, Congress, other government officials, concerned groups, the public—are then analyzed. On these bases it is possible to draw conclusions as to the value of commissions, their success or failure, and their burden of responsibility.

The primary focus is on the major social-issue commissions established between 1963 and 1970, although reference is made to commissions before and after this period. The commissions established between 1963 and 1970 were among the commissions of highest visibility and were therefore capable of provoking the greatest and widest possible response. They received considerable attention from public figures, journalists and, to a lesser extent, academia. Their record is still fresh, and many of those involved with them were able to be reached for discussion.

Although many other commissions have been apppointed, some within this time frame, it is the major social-issue commissions—the National Advisory Commission on Civil Disorders, the Commission on Obscenity and Pornography, the President's Commission on Campus Unrest, etc.—which have been the most heralded at the time of their appointment, attracted the most attention by their work, and stimulated the most controversy with their reports. In short, they are the commissions that have most influenced public opinion of commissions per se and therefore provide a logical frame of reference.

Through a focus on the politics of the commission process we may explore the possibility that the "failure" of many major presidential commissions has been due not to any inherent weakness, structural or functional, of the commissions themselves but to a failure of unrealistic expectations regarding the role of commissions and a failure of presidential/congressional response. When viewed from a more appropriate perspective, the commissions may well be seen as successes in performing certain functions of a democratic system deemed equally as valuable as the production of legislation: for example, education and attitudinal change.

There are genuine needs to be met in a discussion of the major social-issue commissions. One might be termed "perceptual," and it involves a lack of understanding of commission functions and capabilities. The various aspects of this misunderstanding will be explored during the course of the investigation, but they reflect beliefs that commissions are intended only as substitutes for meaningful action: that commissions are failures if they do not result in legislation; that commissions are incapable of conducting inquiries independent of presidential opinion or of status quo opinion; that commissions are simply "bad" because they have made statements with which a particular observer disagrees. More than a little, these attitudes reflect a lack of understanding not only of commissions, but of the political and social environments in which they work; the environments in which those who are expected to respond to them work; and the various personalities who have been involved. The need which must be met here involves an accurate examination of commission procedures and environments, followed by an appraisal of commission performance against accurate and realistic standards—not the criteria of partisanship or polemics.

The second need is a scholarly one. For reasons perhaps similar to the beliefs just discussed, scholars have devoted very little attention to presidential commissions as an institution worth research time. There have been but a handful of books relating to commissions published in this century.[5] Of these, fewer still have been devoted solely to analysis of presidential commissions per se.

Wolanin's book is the major work; it represents careful and respectable research. But Wolanin downplays the major social issue commissions, seemingly concerned that these will detract from his argument that low-key, procedure-oriented commissions have known some measure of success. Yet, to this extent, his argument plays into the hands of the critics. By seeming to avoid the fact that to most observers the term "presidential commission" connotes visible, volatile groups such as the Kerner Commission on Civil Disorders—upon which many opinions of commissions are based—Wolanin seems to confirm the criticism that such commissions are, indeed, failures and are best left undiscussed. The present study proceeds from the conviction that the issue of commission success or failure can be met squarely and argued on the basis of the records of the prominent social-issue commissions.

There have, of course, been scholarly articles.[6] Somewhat limited in number, these works have included: studies written by commission participants and offering either analysis and/or defense of commissions (Ruth, Skolnick, Cutler, Campbell); studies written by non-participants, offering scholarly analysis (Lipsky and Olson, Silver, Sulzner, Wilson); critical treatments (Kopkind, Derthick), the latter of which was written by a commission participant.

In short, there seems to be a critical lack of understanding, as well as mixed opinion, in the political, academic, and journalistic communities regarding the role and function of the presidential commission. An examination of the primary examples of this tool of government in a realistic manner would meet a variety of needs.

This analysis of the mechanics and politics of the commission process includes: the reasons for the establishment of commissions; the various forces and considerations which come to bear during the process of commission formation and the appointment of members; the actual organizational, decision-making, and functional procedures of the commission at work; the influences on commission members and staff from the various constituencies they represent and from the surrounding political environment; the various methods and options of presidential and congressional response to commission reports; and the responses of various other actors in the relevant social and political spheres. Finally, a vital political aspect of the commission process—education in a democratic polity—is considered: provision of factual bases for future action, education of relevant social and political groups, and general public education. This is explored as the primary function of the social-issue presidential commission. Ultimately, judgments are made as to the overall efficacy of commissions as measured in terms of functions which they are capable of performing.

By focusing on the major social-issue presidential commissions appointed between 1963 and 1970 and on their performance in a political environment, and by drawing conclusions as to the viability of the commission's role in the American system, this analysis should help to clear the air for a more realistic appraisal of the capabilities and values of this institution. A rational perspective will contribute to a more reasoned political judgment and tangible movement toward full realization of the potential of presidential commissions.

# 2

# HISTORICAL OVERVIEW

Presidential commissions are by no means a new invention. They have been used by chief executives since the beginning of the republic. A few points of history are useful in providing some perspective for the observation of contemporary commissions. This chapter, then, will examine some of the key aspects of the development of the commission as a tool of the presidency, the reasons behind commission appointments, and some of the prominent contemporary commissions.

## Early Use

One of the earliest instances of the appointment of a presidential commission occurred in 1794. In that year President George Washington was faced with the Whisky Insurrection, a revolt of western Pennsylvania farmers against the 1791 federal excise tax on spirits. Whether because he wished not to appear heavy-handed or because there existed, at the time, no national army, Washington appointed a commission, "unauthorized by law,"[1] to investigate the situation and attempt to mediate a settlement. This spirit of moderation was tempered, however, by the President's issuance of a proclamation, in conjunction with the appointment of the commission, ordering the rancorous farmers to their homes and mobilizing 15,000 militiamen from Virginia, Maryland, New Jersey, and Pennsylvania,[2] an action which may well have preordained the commission to failure.

While the commission did not succeed in its efforts at mediation,

Washington nonetheless applauded the report of the commissioners, noting that it "marks their firmness and abilities" and shows "that the means of conciliation have been exhausted."[3] He then promptly suppressed the rebellion militarily.

While Washington's motives may be open to question, his precedent of the appointment of a commission took root, and presidential advisory commissions, as well as commissions established by Congress for presidential appointment, have been used with frequency ever since. Indeed, as Elizabeth Drew has put it, "the technique of appointing a special presidential commission . . . to investigate, obfuscate, resolve, defuse, defer, detail or derail a problem has become as much an instrument of the presidency as the State of the Union Message, the toss of the ball on opening day, or the review of troops in wartime."[4]

As the presidential system of advisors and Cabinet was built, recognition of the need for rapid personal surveillance of a situation stimulated use by the early presidents of small fact-finding groups which reported directly to the President and which were without congressional statutory authority. Three early instances included President Van Buren's sending of a commission to study European post office establishments and an agent to acquire information on European armies, and President Jackson's appointment of two commissioners to investigate the Naval Department.[5]

Jealous of perceived encroachment upon its co-equal status, Congress began raising questions regarding the President's authority to appoint commissions. This point was raised specifically with regard to President John Tyler's appointment, in 1841, of a nonstatutory commission to investigate the affairs of the New York Custom House. The House of Representatives challenged Tyler to explain his basis for such action and the ensuing debate offered the first clear defense of the power to create nonstatutory commissions. Tyler replied:

> I have to state that the authority for instituting the commission . . . is the authority vested in the President of the United States to 'take care that the laws be faithfully executed, and to give to Congress from time to time information on the state of the Union, and to recommend to their consideration such measures as he shall judge necessary and expedient.' The expediency, if not the necessity, of inquiries into the transactions of our customs-houses, especially in cases where abuses and malpractices are alleged, must be obvious to Congress.[6]

Representative Wise of Virginia supplemented the argument:

> How can he [the President] perform these constitutional duties unless he has agents—the eyes and the arms of the Executive, as Mr. Madison called them—to procure information and facts for him to communicate to Congress? There is no other proper officer to perform these duties but himself, and will gentlemen let frauds and abuses go on until the President himself shall in person ferret them out? Does not each House of Congress exercise this power for itself? . . . The commissioners are not *officers,* it is true; but they are legitimately *commissioners,* standing in the same necessary relation to the Executive as *committees* do to this House.[7]

Ninety years later, Calvin Coolidge echoed these thoughts in, for him, a lengthy statement:

> The use of fact-finding commissions is again being criticized. . . . Some people are born with a complete set of ready-made opinions. Facts do not affect them. But no executive, from first selectman to President, can know everything necessary to discharge his office or be able to learn it from official sources. He must call on some body which can gather the information. Public duty requires it.[8]

It is perhaps interesting to note that while Tyler felt obliged to respond to Congress, he did not consider himself beholden to it in the matter of commissions, as he pointed out in a letter to a commissioner:

> . . . the report of the commission is now wanted, by me, *for my own information.* I do not doubt but that it will contain many suggestions . . . most worthy to be recommended by me to Congress. . . . Whether, when made, I shall deem it best to communicate the entire report to Congress, or otherwise make it public . . . will be for my own decision.[9]

An act of Congress, passed in 1842, sought to prevent public monies' being spent on commissions without statutory approval.[10] This would not be the last attempt to control presidential activity in this area. But such restrictions have proven to be of little significance in practice, as the de facto establishment of the "commission tradition" will attest.

## Theodore Roosevelt

In the early days of commission use at least two factors are likely to have prevented their achieving high visibility: one, communications were limited; two, commissions tended not to deal with problems of wide public interest. It remained for a twentieth-century President, Theodore Roosevelt, to develop the presidential commission as an institution and suggest the wide political possibilities inherent in the use of commissions. It may very well be that Roosevelt's most significant contribution to the development of presidential commissions was the national scope of the subject matter of his commissions. The importance of T.R.'s commissions was their public relevance; this was in contrast to pre-Rooseveltian commissions.

At the beginning of the twentieth century the development of the midwestern and western lands was imminent. It was clear to Roosevelt that if the government did not take the initiative in the areas of public land use and conservation a valuable and perhaps irretrievable opportunity would be lost. As a naturalist, outdoorsman, and rancher, T.R. knew whereof he spoke when he warned Congress of "the approaching exhaustion of the public ranges"[11] through unrestricted grazing and the acquisition of vast tracts of territory by big buyers. Years later, referring to this period, he would remark with striking prescience:

> The idea that our natural resources were inexhaustible still obtained, and there was as yet no real knowledge of their extent and condition. The relation of the conservation of natural resources to the problems of national welfare and national efficacy had not yet dawned on the public mind.[12]

In his Second Annual Message of December, 1902, Roosevelt urged Congress to look into these matters and suggested that:

> if the Congress finds difficulty in dealing with them from lack of thorough knowledge of the subject, I recommend that provision be made for a commission of experts specifically to investigate and report upon the complicated questions involved.[13]

Having paid proper homage to the legislative body and gotten the message that Congress was not becoming interested rapidly enough, T.R. acted and deftly reported a year later:

In order that definite information may be available for the use of the Congress, I have appointed a commission . . . to report at the earliest practicable moment upon the condition, operation, and effect of the present land-laws and on the use, condition, disposal, and settlement of the public land. The commission will report especially what changes in organization, laws, regulations, and practice affecting the public lands are needed to effect the largest practicable disposition of the public lands to actual settlers who will build permanent homes upon them, and to secure in permanence the fullest and most effective use of the resources of the public lands; and it will make such other reports and recommendations as its study of these questions may suggest.[14]

The Republican Congress did not act, but Roosevelt continued to press for reform, basing his arguments on the recommendations of the Public Lands Commission, in his fourth, fifth, and seventh annual messages.

Two aspects of presidential commissions were revealed by this experience. The first is the educational nature of commissions; in this case the President used a commission to begin a process of public information in an area not previously considered to such an extent. Early on, T.R. declared a concern for natural resources as a priority of his presidency; a commission was one way to "get the ball rolling." Second, the experience clearly pointed up a critical limitation of the commission as a policy-making tool. For, despite the most earnest support of the President and dedication on the part of a commission, there is never a guarantee that anyone will listen to its report or act on its recommendations. Roosevelt's entreaty, in his Seventh Annual Message, that Congress "take time to consider"[15] the recommendations of the Public Lands Commission was an early indication of the difficulties inherent in the implementation of commission proposals: authority is dispersed and responsibility for action does not belong to the commission itself.

Land settlement was but one part of the process of the nation's natural resource development and in March, 1907, Roosevelt turned attention to the question of conservation with the appointment of the highly visible Inland Waterways Commission. The conservation movement was growing at this time, due in part to Roosevelt's initiatives, and the commission was given a wide mandate to "consider the relations of the streams to the use of all the great permanent natural resources and their conservation for the making and maintenance of prosperous homes."[16] T.R. planned to achieve maximum exposure for the commission by participating himself in one phase of its work. He describes this activity immodestly in his autobiography:

> The most striking incident in the history of the commission was the trip down the Mississippi River in October, 1907, when, as President of the United States, I was the chief guest. This excursion, with the meetings which were held and the wide public attention it attracted, gave the development of our inland waterways a new standing in public estimation. During the trip a letter was prepared and presented to me asking me to summon a conference on the conservation of natural resources. My intention to call such a conference was publicly announced at a great meeting at Memphis, Tennessee.[17]

As Emmet John Hughes has said of Roosevelt, "his use of drama was no mere indulgence: it had impact."[18] In the case of the Inland Waterways Commission his presence and enthusiasm increased the commission's visibility and public awareness of its subject in a way the commission could not have done on its own. In his sponsorship of and commitment to his commissions, from inception to report and after, Roosevelt was perhaps unique among the presidents. Undoubtedly, he lent a legitimacy to his commissions which increased their stature as a presidential tool and which maximized their potential for stimulating public awareness in a pre-television age.

The conservation conference, which T.R. had announced in Memphis, was held at the White House in May, 1908, and further demonstrated Roosevelt's development of commission use. The conference was attended by members of the Cabinet, the justices of the Supreme Court, members of Congress, the governors of thirty-four states (There were forty-five states at this time.), and the presidents of various groups concerned with natural resources. Results of the conference included adoption of a unanimous resolution by the governors, the appointment of thirty-six state conservation commissions, and the appointment of the National Conservation Commission. Roosevelt was clearly pleased with the outcome of the conference and later wrote:

> It is doubtful whether, except in time of war, any new idea of like

importance has ever been presented to a nation and accepted by it with such effectiveness and rapidity, as was the case with this conservation movement when it was introduced to the American people by the conference of governors.[19]

The National Conservation Commission prepared, for the first time in any nation, an inventory of all the natural resources in the United States. Its work was completed in six months and was facilitated by Roosevelt's making available to it the assistance of various government departments. The commision's report provided what Roosevelt called "the essential facts . . . when facts were greatly needed as the basis for constructive action."[20] The President submitted the report to Congress with a message describing it as "one of the most fundamentally important documents ever laid before the American people."[21]

In all, Roosevelt appointed six commissions, which included those discussed above, as well as the Country Life Commission (which travelled throughout the nation gaining first-hand impressions and which distributed thousands of questionnaires to farm families for later study), the Commission on the Organization of Government Scientific Work, and the Commission on Departmental Methods.

All of Roosevelt's commissions were run on a volunteer, unpaid basis, and no appropriations were ever requested for them. In 1909, however, in the closing weeks of his presidency, T.R. requested $25,000 from Congress for printing and distribution of the report of the Country Life Commission and its accompanying materials. Presidential-congressional relations had, by this time, deteriorated to the point of near combat and Congress took advantage of what it saw as an opportunity to restrict presidential prerogative. Rather than grant the appropriation, it began considering the Tawney Amendment to the Sundry Civil Act, which forbade the expenditure of any public monies for any aspect of any commission not authorized by Congress.

T.R.'s response was to defend, unequivocally, his position:

> Congress cannot prevent the President from seeking advice. Any future President can do as I have done, and ask disinterested men who desire to serve the people to give this service free to the people through these commissions.[22]

Roosevelt declared that he "would veto the Sundry civil bill . . . and that if I were remaining in office I would refuse to obey it."[23]

The bill was passed the day Roosevelt left office and adhered to by his successor. Its intent, however, as has been the case with other attempts at restrictions in this area, has been circumvented. In practice, the proscription of the Tawney Amendment has been given a very loose interpretation by the Attorney General and the Comptroller such as to make it ineffectual. Further, Presidential Emergency and Special Projects funds have proven useful in the maintenance of commissions. In many cases, of course, presidents have found it convenient to obtain congressional approval of proposed commissions.[24]

Although Theodore Roosevelt's statements about his commissions may have approached hyperbole, his contribution to the development of the modern presidential commission would appear to have been substantive. Observation of his use of commissions may aid in the evaluation of contemporary commissions. Roosevelt was the first to use commissions to confront issues of national relevance, thereby suggesting a greater role for commissions than had previously been the case. He established the presidential commission as a tool for public education as well as policy advancement. Conservation was a case in point. Intelligent use of natural resources was a high priority for Roosevelt, and his task in developing policy was seen as twofold: the public had to be made aware of the issues, and there was a need for what Roosevelt regarded as the product of his Country Life Commission: "information so accurate and so vitally important as to disturb the serenity of the advocates of things as they are."[25]

Roosevelt promoted his commissions while they did their work and, when he had received their reports, enthusiastically sponsored them before Congress.

In these ways, Theodore Roosevelt contributed to the establishment of the commission as an important political and education tool of the modern presidency. Rates of appointments of commissions have waxed and waned in subsequent years, in accordance with various presidents' conceptions of their prerogatives and their policy interests. Further, presidents' responses to the reports of their commissions have varied considerably from Roosevelt's, as will be discussed later. But the presidential commission, as a routinely called upon tool in the formulation of policy and as a presidential response to events, is by now a political fact of life, due in large part to Theodore Roosevelt.

# The Sixties and Seventies and the Choice of Commissions

At what point then is the approach of danger to be expected? I answer, if it ever reach us, it must spring up amongst us. It cannot come from abroad. If destruction be our lot, we must ourselves be its author and finisher.[26].

————Abraham Lincoln

In his first State of the Union message, John Kennedy offered the nation a prescient challenge: "Before my term is ended, we shall have to test anew whether a nation organized and governed such as ours can endure. The outcome is by no means certain."[27] For, more than any other period in the century since the Civil War, the sixties and early seventies represented a period of profound questioning and change. The growing awareness of the poor amidst unprecedented affluence and prosperity, the revolutionary impacts of television and the bomb, urban riots, assassinations, mass demonstrations, Vietnam, Kent State and Jackson State, altered and challenging life styles, environmental crises, and moon landings—all served to set the 1960s and 1970s apart from preceding decades.

Serious concern was expressed, during this period, over the durability of the American socio-political system. This was sparked in significant degree by the violent manifestations of racial tension, assassination, and dissent against the Vietnam War. As historian Arthur Schlesinger wrote:

The murders within five years of John F. Kennedy, Martin Luther King, Jr., and Robert F. Kennedy raise—or ought to raise—somber questions about the character of contemporary America. One such murder might be explained away as an isolated horror, unrelated to the inner life of our society. But the successive shootings, in a short time, of three men who greatly embodied the idealism of American life suggest not so much a fortuitous set of aberrations as an emerging pattern of response and actions—a spreading and ominous belief in the efficacy of violence and the politics of the deed.[28]

And Michael Harrington has spoken of:

that paradox presented by the National Commission on the Causes and Prevention of Violence: that after the most prosperous decade of American history, this country is in danger of building a hate-ridden, strife-torn anti-utopia.[29]

Rioting, polarization of opinion, and shootings continued into the early seventies to the point where Richard Strout would write: "They search an airplane after a bomb threat. But for the nation as a whole we are pretty much used to the warning, 'There may be a bomb on board.' "[30]

A basic result of the unsettling and tumultuous events of this period was the need for information and ideas. Against this background the presidential commission emerged as a primary governmental tool for the investigation of national problems. The complex nature of American society and its dilemmas led to the choice, by President and Congress alike, of presidential commissions as one of the potentially most helpful instruments for lending perspective and factual bases to the national debate over approaches. The complex nature of the problems was expressed by General James M. Gavin:

> All around us the scientific revolution has created a wide gap between the world as it is and the world as we believe it to be. This distortion of our vision, this gap in our knowledge, makes it close to impossible for us to solve our problems. For they cannot be solved until they are seen and understood.[31]

It was to be hoped that commissions might see and understand.

## Reasons for Appointment

Presidential advisory commissions are investigatory bodies, generally without statutory bases, which within a defined purview are directed to seek out all relevant information, sift it, piece it together, arrive at conclusions and, on the basis of their conclusions, make recommendations for legislative and/or social action. All results and recommendations are in the form of a written report given to the President and Congress. A basic theory behind the choice of commissions has been stated by a House Government Operations Committee report:

> Access to competent advisors and good advice through sound man-

agement practice should create a wiser President, more confident and effective top executive branch officials, a Congress more knowledgeable in performing its legislative functions, and a citizenry more alert to the problems of its time.[32]

Commissions are seen as being in a position to fulfill this role at least as well as, and probably more efficiently than any other instrument of the government. Former New Haven police chief and member of the Commission on Campus Unrest, James Ahern, spoke to the value of commissions in testimony before a subcommittee of the Senate Judiciary Committee:

> They afford the President, the Congress and the public the unique opportunity to have an impartial panel examine a particular problem, its causes and its possible solutions. Because they have been non-political, the reports Commissions submit can provide an impetus for change that is free from the taint of partisan political advantage.[33]

The reasons for appointing commissions are diverse and reflect a variety of political, organizational, and presidential personality factors. Examination of the reasons for appointment should help elucidate the role commissions are intended to play in the American political system.

Broadly speaking, the reasons for commission appointment fall into four general categories: they provide symbolic reassurance; they are part of the presidential policy process; they are seen as an efficient organizational tool; they permit delay. One or all of the reasons may conceivably be involved in the appointment of a particular commission and some overlapping of categories is possible. Each category is considered more specifically below.

### Symbolic reassurance

Simply by their existence, commissions symbolize cognizance and concern over a situation at the highest level; that is, the Presidency. George Reedy has written that *"all* human communication is through symbols and the only issue is whether the symbols that are used are comprehensible to both sender and receiver."[34] Commissions communicate that the President is aware of a situation and will begin a process of directing his, and the nation's, attention to it.

In the 1960s and early 1970s a plethora of new and old problems erupted upon the national consciousness. Such issues as "law and order," "dirty movies and mail," illegal drug use, campus disturbances and the overall increasing incidence of open violence were the subjects of considerable rhetorical and literary attention prior to the appointment of their "own" commissions. In this respect, then, commissions represent the President's recognition of what the Warren Commission called "the intense public demand for facts" and an attempt to manifest in the most comprehensive way an assuagement of the "universal demands for an explanation."[35]

There is a philosophic aspect to this function. In a democracy it is desirable that the majority should not be too inclined to embrace repressive measures against those who feel excluded from the expected benefits of society and that this majority would do well, perhaps, to ask why such individuals feel as they do. Alan Silver has made the point thoughtfully:

> Men who engage in dangerous and desperate behavior—indeed, any behavior—have a certain claim to have taken seriously the meanings which they see in their own acts, and wish others to see in them.[36]

Commissions may be used, in this connection, to inform the public and its leaders as well as to reassure the disaffected that they are being "taken seriously." Of course, this will by no means suffice if those in positions of authority have no intention of acting upon the conclusions and recommendations of the commissions.

A related aspect of this reason for the choice of commissions is the imperative of inflated expectations regarding the presidential role. This can be stated a number of ways but distills to the observation of Martha Derthick that the modern President is "expected to respond to every public misfortune."[37] Commissions, in this respect, "become one of the principal techniques by which he tries to fill the gap between that which he is held responsible for and that which he can actually do."[38]

Elizabeth Drew has suggested that one makes use of commissions "Because you cannot think of anything else to do but you know you had better do *something.*"[39] This obligation that the contemporary President *do* something has grown out of, among other things, public expectation combined with presidential personality. Harry Mc-

Pherson, Special Counsel to President Lyndon Johnson, remembers the influence of this phenomenon on the creation of the National Commission on the Causes and Prevention of Violence (Eisenhower Commission):

> The Eisenhower Commission was, I think, the product of a sense of frustration and of very mixed feelings on Johnson's behalf. He had an instinctive, deep-rooted feeling that he must respond to almost any situation with *something*. And what the hell do you respond to the assassination of Bob Kennedy with? . . . [Johnson experienced] terrible waves of emotion, very much like Martin Luther King's assassination. When Johnson heard about that, King had just been making some very effective anti-war speeches saying that the Administration had lost its moral rudder and was going off the deep end. And Johnson was full of rage about that when King was killed, and his mixed feelings of recognizing the terrible thing this would mean to the country, and violence, etc. All that. So they [commisions] come out of ambiguous emotions. . . . We argued over whether he would create this commission. I thought that since there had already been a lot of criticism of commissions, that this one would be regarded as simply too much. But, at the same time, there *was* a fear, a concern, about violence in America. That concern had surfaced in a way that probably never had before because the '60s were a violent time; violence against blacks, violence *by* blacks, violence by students, the war, the assassination of three of the most famous Americans. It was a staggering period. . . . The danger with something like that [a commission] is that you get kind of windy hand-wringing that doesn't really do anything. . . . But, at the same time, I could see that if they could identify some things that seemed to be making us as violent as we were in the '60s it might help.[40]

Sometimes, as Doris Kearns Goodwin has said, it comes down to the simple question of: "What other alternatives, when a crisis occurs . . . , does the President have?"[41]

Commissions, then, can represent a symbolic tool with which the President communicates awareness of a situation that is of concern to his constituency, reassures the disaffected that they will not be ignored, and responds to the sense that he must *do something*. Commissions are one place to start doing something, especially when there may be potential danger in leaving a problem unattended any longer. As Gary T. Marx has observed, "the last time urban change was left to the Lord was at Sodom and Gomorrah."[42]

## Policy process

Commissions may be appointed as part of the presidential policy process. They may be intended to: develop factual bases upon which policy may be constructed; educate, generally; legitimize already considered proposals; represent an executive response to a particular group's request. All of these may be fundamentally interrelated.

The issues which prompted appointment of the major commissions of the 1960s and early 1970s were complex and almost uniformly controversial. Probably no action could have been taken on them which would not have aroused considerable antipathy. To the extent that disagreement rested on ignorance, commissions have been intended to provide facts. These facts were to be of use, potentially, in executive policy formation as well as in the adjustment, through enlightenment, of public thinking. Raymond P. Shafer, Chairman of the National Commission of Marijuana and Drug Abuse, saw his commission's task as threefold: a) to educate; b) to help adjust the law to new realities in our changing society; c) to focus public attention on problems that might not otherwise receive it.[43] John P. Roche, Special Consultant to Lyndon Johnson, felt that when the President appointed the Kerner Commission "he really hoped that this body would throw a lot of light" on the problems and "focus public attention on the remedies."[44] According to Associate Director Lloyd E. Ohlin, the Commission on Law Enforcement and the Administration of Justice was appointed to begin a policy process while keeping certain political constraints in mind. A commission was seen as an acceptable vehicle for a federal initiative on crime which would not seem to represent excessive intrusion into state and local areas of responsibility and which would be able to complete its study and yield legislation prior to the 1968 elections.[45]

As a part of the policy development process commissions may be intended to "provide an official source for the data needed to substantiate future policy decisions."[46] However, they may at times be appointed with a more specific hope in mind: the reinforcement of views already held or the legitimization of policy proposals already considered. Harry McPherson feels this was one goal held by Lyndon Johnson for the Kerner Commission:

Johnson was, I think, convinced that the black riots . . . Watts, Detroit, Newark . . . had sinister origins, planned origins. And he was eager to get, from the FBI and others, any evidence that they were bad fellows who were—I suppose Communist agents was one of the most obvious—who were helping to inspire them; looking for evidence of money and weapons procurement and things like that. I'm sure he told Kerner that he wanted him to look at that.[47]

Johnson aides Roche and McPherson agree that legitimization of policy already in the works was one of LBJ's aims. Roche considers this one of the offensive (as opposed to defensive) functions of commissions—"to get somebody to give you a cover on some significant policy changes"[48]—while McPherson speaks of commissions "legitimizing the Administration's role of having a broad spectrum of citizens out there . . . 'laying its hands on.' "[49] McPherson elaborates on Johnson's intentions vis-à-vis the Kerner Commission:

The Kerner Commission . . . was as carefully designed and constructed—it attempted to be, anyway—as any commission ever was. Johnson felt the need for having a group of bright and sophisticated people, respected people, saying what the country had to do—ought to do—to reduce the danger of new riots and, at the same time, to tell the black community that it ought to seek its benefits, its gains, elsewhere than in riots. In other words, to have a sympathetic, liberal, respected commission saying that we ought to go on a course which Johnson (and, I'm sure, most liberals) had already determined to go. It was important as a kind of confirmation of that policy.[50]

While acknowledging this hoped-for role of commissions, one must point out that there is no guarantee the desired result will be achieved. In fact, commissions, as often as not, deliver reports which go far beyond executive expectations. This aspect of commissions will be discussed at a later point.

Commission appointments may represent a response of the President (as pluralist actor) to a direct or perceived group request. Martha Derthick suggests, in this vein, that "the pressure to respond is greater as events involve interests with a special claim upon him or engage the attention of organizations with access to his office."[51] But the President may find a political advantage in this use of commissions which goes beyond his ties to "friends." Commission appointments can be seen as having "pacification effects:" those who favor change are encouraged that an issue is, at the least, receving attention; opponents of change are assured that, at the least, investigation will precede action taken on the issue.[52]

Commissions from two recent administrations were appointed as the result of group or individual agitation. Commissioner Martha Derthick reports on two possible origins of the Commission on Campus Unrest. In one version, an American Bar Association delegation proposed the commission in a meeting with President Nixon shortly after the deaths of students at Kent State University and Jackson State College in May 1970. The President agreed to the commission and the ABA nominated several members. According to the second version, the commission appointment represented the desire of Secretary of Health, Education, and Welfare for an impartial examination of the Jackson State incident. It was felt that the shootings were related to race and that the Mississippi judicial system would not respond to the fullest extent. Derthick feels this version is supported by the appointment of four blacks to the nine-member commission and by reports of a White House promise of an investigation to a delegation of Jackson State students.[53] An example of individual initiative carried to fruition in the form of a presidential commission was provided by singer-public interest activist Harry Chapin. Chapin personally sponsored the idea of a commission on world hunger before Congress and is credited as the "prime mover" behind the resolutions[54] which led to President Jimmy Carter's establishment of the Commission on Domestic and International Hunger and Malnutrition.[55]

Finally, the Commission on Wartime Relocation and Internment of Civilians, initiated by Congressman Norman Y. Mineta in 1979, represented an attempt to respond to the accumulated grievances of Japanese-American citizens growing out of their treatment by the government during World War II.

Commissions, then, may provide a useful tool for the President as "man in the middle" in a system of conflicting group aims and expectations of a presidential response to nearly all situations.

Commissions are frequently a product of the presidential policy formation process. They may be used to assemble a factual basis for future policy; to educate; to legitimize policy already considered; to provide a response to group requests. It should be noted that similar reasons may lie behind congressional creation of commissions for presidential appointment.[56] During the period under study, however, there existed no requirements that substantive presidential (or congressional) responses follow the issuance of commission reports.

## Organizational tool

Commissions may be used as a tool for surmounting the pathologies of organizational complexity. They may be chosen to avoid duplication of effort by a number of agencies or to circumvent bureaucratic obstacles. They may even be seen as part of the process of incremental decision making and may, at times, grow out of the imperatives of organizational behavior.

In some cases there are a goodly number of bodies ready to undertake investigations, all of which would take varying amounts of time, testimony, and taxpayers' dollars. The Warren Commission noted, in this respect, that following the deaths of President Kennedy and Lee Harvey Oswald a variety of investigative options were considered: a court of inquiry before a Texas state magistrate; a Dallas County grand jury investigation; hearings by committees of both Houses of Congress as a response to theories of foreign and domestic conspiracy.[57] Appointment of the commission represented recognition of this "too many cooks" dilemma. The commission "sought to avoid parallel investigations and to concentrate fact-finding in a body having the broadest national mandate."[58]

President Reagan's appointment, in 1986, of a commission to investigate the disastrous launch of the space shuttle Challenger was motivated in part by a desire to avoid the appearance of conflict-of-interest in having the National Aeronautics and Space Administration conduct the primary examination (in effect, of itself).

Over forty years ago, Carl Marcy noted that commissions "grow out of the inadequacies in the executive departments or in Congress, or, in some instances, they develop because of the unusual nature of the problem to be met."[59] Commissions, as ad hoc bodies, are intended to perform an investigative function more efficiently than might other bodies, avoiding some of the pitfalls of organizational behavior. Because they are of limited duration, commissions might avoid the rigidities of institutionalization and loss of originally intended purpose. In his study of organizational intelligence, Harold

Wilensky has written of the advantage of the ad hoc group. "For official fact-finding and public education," Wilensky says, it may be useful to:

> move out of conventional channels of investigation and commu-
> nication toward men of independent mind and stature—a strategy
> commonly used to overcome the pathologies of hierarchy and spe-
> cialization. . . . Whatever its political risks, as a means to counter
> the expanding influence of unchecked experts, to preserve open
> discussion of complex issues, and to mobilize elite support for
> innovations, the independent government commission has no
> peer.[60]

The conclusions reached by such a body are seen as carrying an increased legitimacy by virtue of their representing a collective, rather than individual, product; the result of "several minds stimulated by the exchange of ideas."[61]

The commission form of inquiry, then, at least in theory, can be seen as a tool for the overt circumvention of normal bureaucratic and investigative channels. A given commission may or may not be ap-pointed with this intent. It is at least possible, however, that consid-erations of efficiency lie behind the choice of a commission over some alternative vehicle of inquiry.

At least one analyst views commissions through the theoretical perspective of incrementalism;[62] that is, commissions are part of the overall process by which government adapts, in piecemeal fashion, to social change.[63] According to this analysis, commissions "define problems and initiate new responses," and "mobilize public opin-ion," and can therefore be thought of as "vehicles for problem-solv-ing and conflict-management" which aid in "pacifying the policy demands of various political interests."[64] Whether or not commis-sions play as significant a role in the process of systemic maintenance as this would suggest, this perspective offers a further explanation for the choice of commissions.

One participant in executive decision making suggests that some commissions emerge as a product of the organizational imperatives of deadlines and the demand for results. In this case, a commission was again devised outside normal channels, but for reasons other than investigative efficiency. Harry McPherson recalls that, as an aide to President Lyndon Johnson, he was once assigned the task of preparing a presidential message on agriculture. Working against a next-day deadline, McPherson concluded there was no ready solution to then-current agricultural difficulties and, in the middle of the night—because "I had to have *something!*"—devised the idea of a rural poverty commission. The commission was made a part of the presidential message which was delivered the next day, before the Secretary of Agriculture could stop it.[65]

It is probably not the case that commissions are appointed primarily for their organizational attributes. But, at least to some extent, commissions are seen as tools for the avoidance of duplication of effort and some of the more debilitating aspects of institutionalization. It is possible to view them as aspects of the process of systemic adaptation.

## Delay

Commission appointments, beyond any other intentions, may be made to delay action, to "buy time." This is not quite the cynical function it may appear, since a cooling-off period may, indeed, be an appropriate short-run response to an explosive situation.[66] John Roche has spoken of the Johnson Administration's hope that appointment of the Kerner Commission on Civil Disorders would help "defuse" the tension of racial conflict in the 1960s.[67] George Sulzner, in his analysis of commissions as an integral component of the process by which government adapts to emerging social conditions, suggests that "the ability of a national governmental study commission to channel controversy into more objective settings, which may cool heated emotions somewhat . . . promotes political pacification."[68] The commission not only affords time for "cooling off," it may facilitate the direction of grievances into channels recognized as more legitimate and likely in fact to yield greater results to those who have expressed their grievances. This is not to deny, however, that rioting may have been required in order to get legitimate authorities to take the grievances seriously in the first place.

The use of commissions for purposes of what might be termed "benign delay" raises the possibility of another, more questionable kind of delay. Because of the seeming lack of substantive results from commission studies, many observers have been moved to the cynical observation that the appointment of commissions is merely a presidential ploy to avoid concrete action.[69] This has, no doubt, been true in some cases, as in any undertaking in a democracy admirable as well as questionable aims are likely to motivate those involved. The evidence suggests, however, that while some commission appointments may reflect the sheer expediency of the moment, in general the situation is "a good deal more complicated and ambiguous than that."[70] The observations of a number of participants in the commission process support this interpretation.

A plausible case can be made that appointment of the Kerner Commission reflected a personal sense of distress on the part of the President vis-à-vis the largesse of his social policies and the attitudes of its intended recipients. "Johnson, when he appointed the Kerner Commission," recalls Special Consultant John Roche, "was heartbroken. Johnson felt heartbroken by the riots; a sense of personal betrayal, in fact. . . . He thought they'd [Blacks] be grateful."[71] The President (and he was probably not alone among the reform-minded of that period) felt genuine confusion, and the commission was chosen to procure answers as well as to provide symbolic reassurance.

James S. Campbell, General Counsel to the Commission on the Causes and Prevention of Violence, suggests a more complex interpretation of the word "expediency" than is perhaps implied in criticisms:

> I'm sure that our commission was appointed completely out of expediency in the sense that after these two terrible assassinations [Martin Luther King, Jr. and Robert F. Kennedy], his [President Johnson's] anger at television (which was a factor, I think, in appointing the commission); I think all those things were part of the expediency that gave rise to the commission. I think other commissions are probably appointed more genuinely to get information about a problem.[72]

The Violence Commission, as has been suggested earlier, largely grew out of the very real feeling that "something" must be done, a motivation to be distinguished qualitatively from a desire to avoid action.

Further corroboration of the proposition that commissions are designed for something more than evasion is provided by Lloyd Ohlin, Associate Director of the Commission on Law Enforcement and the Administration of Justice:

The pervasive feeling among all those connected with the Commission was that the President's mandate contained a serious and responsible charge. The Commission was not designed solely as an expression of Presidential concern or as a diversionary political tactic; the political realities required a much more substantial federal commitment.[73]

In this connection, it may be pointed out that Lyndon Johnson was demonstrably an activist president. In addition, the record suggests he genuinely desired substantive social change.[74] Appointment of commissions to obfuscate or avoid meaningful action would not have accorded with the assessments of his character provided by many personally associated with him. Doris Kearns Goodwin has said, in this regard:

> I don't think he would have thought of it at the moment as a way of avoiding taking action. That's not the way his mind would have worked. . . . [He was] oriented toward action. . . . He still believed in that brain trust theory, to some extent, that maybe some new ideas could be generated. He was always a believer in the possibility that there were new solutions to the same old problems.[75]

It would seem unlikely that Johnson would choose to avoid action, to avoid responding to situations of importance to him. His inclination was toward an activist, reformist response and his commissions may be seen as a part of this.

Commissions permit delay, then, in a number of senses. They may facilitate a cooling-off period during which conflict may be directed into legitimate channels. They offer a potential mechanism for the avoidance of substantive response. But, as has been seen, participants do not feel the latter function is often the case.

Presidential commissions are appointed for a variety of reasons, many of which may overlap and any combination of which may explain the appointment of a particular commission. In a general sense, commissions may be intended to provide symbolic reassurance of presidential cognizance of some situation, act as a part of the presidential policy process, gathering information for the basis of policy, educating, legitimizing already considered policy, or providing a response to group requests; perform an organizational function, efficiently developing information outside normal organizational channels with their perceived inefficiencies; permit delay.

Commissions are intended to function within a defined purview, to collect information in response to a specific request and develop whatever conclusions and recommendations seem consistent. There is no evidence that commissions are intended to enact legislation, advocate revolution, act as presidential puppets or mouthpieces (although this may be desired), or deliberate only in terms of what will be politically feasible at the moment. Commissions are not specifically scholarly in nature, not wholly pragmatically political; yet neither are they haphazard or anarchic. Commissions are collective ad hoc groups which offer advice. They are relatively free to develop whatever conclusions they see fit, yet they may be seen as restrained by factors which shape any advice-giving: a desire to be listened to; the backgrounds and values of those giving the advice; the quality of the information upon which the advice is based. Commissions probably do not meet wholly the standards of any one perspective—presidential political realities, long-range scholarly inquiry, or radical reformism. Commissions are intended to examine the current state of knowledge on a particular subject and offer advice as to how that subject might most reasonably be dealt with, based on the judgment of a group of diverse human beings. It is then the responsibility, or opportunity, of other actors in the public and private sectors to do what they will with that advice.

## Typology

Before proceeding further, I would like to suggest a simple typology of commissions. Basically, presidential commissions may be procedure-oriented, situation-oriented, or crisis-oriented. This study will focus on the latter two. Procedure-oriented commissions are likely to examine the operating procedures of existing agencies in order to recommend improvements in their efficiency or to make judgments as to their overall utility. The commissions may have responsibility for organizing some temporary activity. Generally, they can be seen as performing low-visibility, non-pressing tasks such as examining postal procedures, criminal code reform, Radio Free Europe, and the celebration of the American Revolution Bicentennial. A much larger scope for this kind of commission was envisioned in Congressman Richard Bolling's proposal, in 1980, for a Commission on More Effective Government to examine the efficacy of virtually all government in the United States. While the subject areas of these commissions may be of considerable importance in some sectors, they do not, for the most part, deal with widespread, controversial social phenomena or developments which may be perceived as immediate threats.

Situation-oriented studies are those which investigate a condition of perhaps vital concern that is spread out over area and time and may be of general importance to a large portion of the population. Commissions during the period under study which have concerned themselves with such areas have been the Commission on Law Enforcement and the Administration of Justice (Katzenbach Commission), the Commission on Obscenity and Pornography (Lockhart Commission), the Commission on Population Growth and the American Future (Rockefeller Commission), and the National Commission on Marijuana and Drug Abuse (Shafer Commission).

Crisis-oriented commissions are occasioned more by a particular event (or related events) which may or may not spark consideration of more fundamental underlying situations. Some examples include the President's Commission on the Assassination of President Kennedy (Warren Commission), the National Advisory Commission on Civil Disorders (Kerner Commission), the National Commission on the Causes and Prevention of Violence (Eisenhower Commission), and the President's Commission on Campus Unrest (Scranton Commission).

## The Major Commissions of the Sixties and Seventies

What follows is a brief description of eight of the most significant and most visible commissions of the period 1963-1973. No attempt is made to present a comprehensive picture of each commission's findings and recommendations. But as frequent mention will be made of these particular commissions, it would seem useful to explore, basically, what each investigated and what it concluded.

### The President's Commission on the Assassination of President Kennedy

One of the most crisis-oriented of all commissions, the President's Commission on the Assassination of President Kennedy was appointed in the midst of widespread speculation, national confusion and fear. The commission was established by President Lyndon Johnson in November 1963, in the wake of the murder of President John Kennedy and the killing of his alleged assassin, Lee Harvey Oswald. More commonly known as the Warren Commission, after its chairman, Chief Justice Earl Warren, the group's mandate was given by the new President:

> The purposes of the Commission are to examine the evidence developed by the Federal Bureau of Investigation and any additional evidence that may hereafter come to light or be uncovered by federal or state authorities; to make such further investigation as the Commission finds desirable; to evaluate all the facts and circumstances surrounding such assassination, including the subsequent violent death of the man charged with the assassination, and to report to me its findings and conclusions.[76]

In short, as a White House press release of the same day summarized, it was the commission's job "to satisfy itself that the truth is known as far as it can be discovered, and to report its findings and conclusions to him [the President], to the American people, and to the world."[77]

The world, indeed; for speculation and shock were by no means bound by American shores. The assassination of the popular young President caused lament and fear of possible plots in many parts of the world. James Reston has described Johnson as "disturbed by the conspiratorial speculations in Europe"[78] and in this case a commission was to play more than a domestic informational role.

After nearly a year of inquiry the commission presented its report consisting of a large body of evidence offered to support its findings that: a) the fatal shots were fired from one place only; b) the assassin was, indeed, Lee Harvey Oswald; and c) "The Commission has found no evidence that either Lee Harvey Oswald or Jack Ruby [Oswald's murderer] was part of any conspiracy, domestic or foreign, to assassinate President Kennedy."[79]

The findings were followed by a number of recommendations regarding the Secret Service and protection of the President, and a proposal that Congress make the assassination of the President or Vice President a federal crime.

From the moment it issued its report the Warren Commission was, and continues to be, steeped in controversy primarily because many people clung to the theory that because Oswald was a communist sympathizer there *must* have been a conspiracy involved in the assassination (of which Oswald was but a small part) and that for some reason of national security the commission had simply "whitewashed" its investigation and report. Numerous volumes purporting to expose this shady business were released[80] and in a celebrated investigation by a New Orleans district attorney evidence of a conspiracy was claimed. But despite much understandable publicity in the case no convictions were forthcoming.

The evidence of the commission itself, however, was quite substantial, and while the question of a plot may never be fully settled, the report of the Warren Commission remains at this time the most complete investigation available of the subject.

## The President's Commission on Law Enforcement and the Administration of Justice

In July 1965, President Lyndon Johnson appointed the Commission on Law Enforcement and the Administration of Justice (known as the Katzenbach Commission for its chairman, Attorney General Nicholas Katzenbach). As the chairman noted, one reason for the establishment of this situation-oriented commission was to be found in the President's "recognizing the urgency of the Nation's crime problem and the depth of ignorance about it."[81] Another reason was the political climate in the nation concerning the "law and order" question, an issue which had been considerably agitated by the presidential campaign of 1964 and particularly the Goldwater candidacy. One observer notes that LBJ was quick to recognize the sensitive nature of the issue and suggests that "Undoubtedly he believed that he could preempt the issue by proposing a bundle of anticrime legislation and, simultaneously, a grandiose study of the problem."[82] Further, as the President was in the process of preparing an anti-poverty program, the commission could contribute to a comprehensive approach to the subject: "He probably saw a true tie-in between the themes of poverty and lawlessness. Probably the Commission idea served the function of killing two rather large birds with a single hefty stone."[83]

Generally, the scope of the investigation was suggested in the opening statement of the commission report's summary: "This report is about crime in America—about those who commit it, about those who are its victims, and about what can be done to reduce it."[84]

The commission explored a wide range of crime-related subjects from street crimes, organized crimes and juvenile crime, to criminal behavioral motivation, victims of crime and the entire enforcement and correction system. Upon its findings as to the nature and particulars of crime, the commission based over two hundred specific recommendations, which it summarized as follows:

> First, society must seek to prevent crime before it happens by assuring all Americans a stake in the benefits and responsibilities of American life, by strengthening law enforcement, and by reducing criminal opportunities.
>
> Second, society's aim of reducing crime would be better served if the system of criminal justice developed a far broader range of techniques with which to deal with individual offenders.
>
> Third, the system of criminal justice must eliminate existing injustice if it is to achieve its ideals and win the respect and cooperation of all citizens.
>
> Fourth, the system of criminal justice must attract more people and better people—police, prosecutors, judges, defense attorneys, probation and parole officers, and corrections officials with more knowledge, expertise, initiative and integrity.
>
> Fifth, there must be much more operational and basic research into the problems of crime and criminal administration, by those both within and without the system of criminal justice.
>
> Sixth, the police, courts, and correctional agencies must be given substantially greater amounts of money if they are to improve their ability to control crime.
>
> Seventh, individual citizens, civic and business organizations, religious institutions, and all levels of government must take responsibility for planning and implementing the changes that must be made in the criminal justice system if crime is to be reduced.[85]

The report of the Katzenbach Commission encountered certain difficulties on the road to legislative implementation, but it found wide acceptance among correctional and enforcement institutions and concerned organizations around the nation and remains the only overall survey of crime, criminals, and the criminal justice system produced by the federal government since the 1930s.

## The National Advisory Commission on Civil Disorders

Probably the most visible of all recent commissions, the National Advisory Commission on Civil Disorders (known as the Kerner Commission for its chairman, then Governor of Illinois Otto N. Kerner) was established by Lyndon Johnson in July 1967. A crisis-oriented commission, the Kerner Commission was appointed in response to the wave of ghetto-racial riots that occurred in the summer of 1967.

In his July 27 television address announcing the creation of the commission, the President recognized the high-tension atmosphere in the nation and set the tone for dialogue and investigation:

> Not even the sternest police, nor the most effective Federal troops, can ever create lasting peace in our cities.
>
> The only genuine, long-range solution for what has happened lies in an attack—mounted at every level—upon the conditions that breed despair and violence. All of us know what those conditions are: ignorance, discrimination, slums, poverty, disease, not enough jobs. We should attack these conditions—not because we are frightened by conflict, but because we are fired by conscience. We should attack them because there is simply no other way to achieve a decent and orderly society in America.[86]

Of course, it may be argued that Johnson was assuming conclusions a priori and "telling" the commission what it should report (indeed, the commission chose a portion of the passage for the opening of its report). On the other hand, it may be that the President's acknowledgment of the complexity of the problems the commission was to investigate actually contributed to relieving fears the commissioners might have harbored of proceeding into controversial political territory in the course of their search.

If there was any question on this score Johnson perhaps sought to correct it two days later at the ceremonial first meeting of the commission at the White House:

> Sometimes various administrations have set up commissions that were expected to put the stamp of approval on what the administration believed.
>
> This is not such a commission. We are looking to you, not to approve our own notions, but to guide us and guide the country

through a thicket of tension, conflicting evidence and extreme opinion.[87]

In his remarks, that day, the President went on to indicate the general scope of the commission's inquiry:

> We need to know the answers, I think, to three basic questions about the riots:
> ——What happened?
> ——Why did it happen?
> ——What can be done to prevent it from happening again and again?. . .
> What we are really asking for is a profile of the riots—of the rioters, of their environment, of their victims, of their causes and effects.
> We are asking for advice on
> ——short-term measures that can prevent riots,
> ——better measures to contain riots once they begin,
> ——and long-term measures that will make them only a sordid page in our history.[88]

In conclusion, the President urged the commissioners to

> . . .let your search be free. Let it be untrammeled by what has been called the "conventional wisdom." As best you can, find the truth, the whole truth, and express it in your report.
> I hope you will be inspired by a sense of urgency, but also conscious of the danger that lies always in hasty conclusions.[89]

Following eight months of investigation and analysis the Kerner Commission offered what many considered one of the strongest and most outspoken commentaries on American society ever made by an institution of government. It included in-depth profiles of key riot-stricken cities; a history of American protests and the growth of the ghettos; descriptions of the ghetto environment; analyses of community, law enforcement, judicial, and media responses to disorders and the conditions that produce them; and recommendations for national, state, and local action and reform. The commission's message was quite explicit:

> This is our basic conclusion: Our Nation is moving toward two societies, one black, one white—separate and unequal. . . .

Violence and destruction must be ended—in the streets and in the lives of people.

Segregation and poverty have created in the racial ghetto a destructive environment totally unknown to most white Americans.

What white Americans have never fully understood—but what the Negro can never forget—is that white society is deeply implicated in the ghetto. White institutions created it, white institutions maintain it, and white society condones it. . . .

Two premises underlie the work of the Commission. That this Nation cannot abide violence and disorder if it is to ensure the safety of its people and their progress in a free society.

That the Nation will deserve neither safety nor progress unless it can demonstrate the wisdom and the will to undertake decisive action against the root causes of racial disorders.[90]

The report was received with mixed reactions, as might be expected from the nature of its conclusions. [Specific responses will be discussed at a later point.] Some reactions included shock, as a result of the report's condemnation of white America. Some felt the report did not go far enough in pointing out institutional offenders and in analyzing basic societal inequities which could only be redressed through a radical realignment of the social structure. Regardless of the diversity of response, the commission served as a basis for further policy discussion and continues to do so.

## The National Commission on the Causes and Prevention of Violence

In response to the assassinations of Martin Luther King, Jr. and Robert F. Kennedy, specifically, but to the miasma of national carnage, generally, President Johnson established, in July 1968, the National Commission on the Causes and Prevention of Violence (referred to as the Eisenhower Commission after its chairman, President Emeritus of the Johns Hopkins University, Milton S. Eisenhower). The President's mandate to this crisis-oriented commission was as broad as its title indicates:

I ask you to undertake a penetrating search for the causes and prevention of violence—a search into our national life, our past as well as our present, our traditions as well as our institutions, our culture, our customs and our laws.[91]

Where previous commissions had approached various aspects of the dilemma of social violence in America, e.g., crime and urban riots, the Eisenhower Commission faced the awesome task of investigating all phases of violence, "from robbery to murder, from civil disorder to larger conflicts, from child abuse to suicide."[92] Sounding a theme quite reminiscent of the Kerner Commission, only much broader, the commission suggested its role in an interim progress report to the President:

> An awesome complexity is concealed in such simple questions as who is violent, when, why, under what conditions, and with what consequences. Recognizing this complexity, however, may well be the first step toward understanding—and toward convincing the American people that they must be uncommonly thoughtful, open-minded, and persevering if the challenge of illegitimate violence in our society is to be met.[93]

The commission's report was released following a year and a half of study. It consisted of a historical review of violence in America; analyses of violent behavior including violent crime, group violence, civil disobedience, assassination and campus disorders; an interpretation of the roles of firearms and the media in promoting the acceptability of violence; and eighty-one recommendations including drastically increased federal, state, and local expenditures for dealing with the myriad social conditions which are conducive to violence and for containing it when it does occur. The commission further recommended extensive regulations on the procurement and use of firearms by non-law-enforcement personnel, efforts by the broadcast media and the citizenry to reduce the high presence of violence in programming, particularly children's, and diligent efforts by those in a position to make them to encourage cooperation and dialogue between students and educational administrators and to open avenues of participation in public affairs to youth.

The report was widely distributed among educational institutions and organizations and, because of the comprehensive character of its subject, it has been the object of conferences and discussions concerning violence in the United States.

## The Commission on Obscenity and Pornography

Perhaps the most tumultuous and controversy-ridden commission of recent years, the Commission on Obscenity and Pornography (known as the Lockhart Commission for its chairman, dean of the University of Minnesota Law School William B. Lockhart) was established by Congress for the President's appointment in October 1967 (the commission's first meeting, however, was not until July 1968).

In describing the dissemination of obscenity and pornography as "a matter of national concern,"[94] Congress asserted the federal government's

> responsibility to investigate the gravity of this situation and to determine whether such materials are harmful to the public, and particularly to minors, and whether more effective methods should be devised to control the transmission of such materials.[95]

To explore the issue, Congress established the situation-oriented Pornography Commission which was,

> after a thorough study . . . of the causal relationship of such materials to antisocial behavior to recommend advisable, appropriate, effective, and constitutional means to deal effectively with such traffic in obscenity and pornography.[96]

The commission's report was all the Congress had asked for—and more. Before the document had even been released, word was leaked as to the probable nature of the commission's findings and posturing, charging, and counter-charging began. The report was subjected to a hail of attacks from many who were eager, in an election year, to avoid any suggestion that they were "soft on smut." As Commissioner Otto N. Larsen put it later: "The Commission on Obscenity and Pornography was conceived in the Congress, born in the White House, and after twenty-seven months of life, was buried without honor by both parent institutions."[97] As *The New York Times'* Clive Barnes reflected, however:

> *The Report of the Commission on Obscenity and Pornography* provides all of us for the first time with data and evidence on this terribly complex subject. It seriously requires the attention of every citizen concerned with the quality of our lives. As much as any other public document it represents the United States of America, 1970. Read it. You may love it or hate it, accept it or challenge it, but you shouldn't ignore it.[98]

Basically, following extensive research into a number of phases of the subject, the commission found little scientific evidence to support the idea that exposure to pornography was somehow damaging or conducive to criminal behavior (indeed, in some cases precisely the opposite was the case) and that even agreeing on an acceptable constitutional definition of the term was highly difficult. On the basis of the evidence compiled, the commission recommended that the right to procure "pornographic" or "obscene" materials belonged to the individual rather than the state or federal governments and that, therefore, all statutes (with certain notable exceptions) relating to restrictions on the freedom of consenting adults to receive such materials should be repealed. The exceptions included restrictions on the sale of certain materials to youths (below such ages as the states might determine); limitations on mail advertising of pornographic materials; and restrictions on public display or store front advertising. The commission also strongly recommended the promotion of public sex education, particularly in schools, and a more mature and healthy attitude toward sex and discussions of it in the society generally.

Of course, a logical approach does not always appeal (nor does it always seem relevant) to those whose convictions are already set regarding such delicate issues as sex, a reality of which the commission was made unequivocally aware. The report of the Lockhart Commission, however, remains the most comprehensive study available of the effects of "obcenity and pornography."

## The President's Commission on Campus Unrest

In response to the most violent period of campus demonstrations and official responses in the nation's history, and particularly to the murder of six students within ten days, President Richard Nixon appointed, in June 1970, the President's Commission on Campus Unrest (referred to as the Scranton Commission for its chairman, former Governor of Pennsylvania William W. Scranton). In establishing this crisis-oriented commission Mr. Nixon set forth its mandate:

——To identify the principal causes of campus violence.
——To assess the reason for breakdown in the processes for orderly expression of dissent.

———To suggest specific methods and procedures through which legitimate grievances can be resolved.

———To suggest ways to protect and enhance the right of academic freedom, the right to pursue an education free from improper interference, and the right of peaceful dissent and protest.[99]

The commission's report, which met with a chilly reception at the White House, included analyses of student protest and its causes in the 1960s, the black student movement, the responses of universities and law enforcement officials to disorders, potential university reform, the role of government with regard to campus unrest, the Kent State and Jackson State tragedies, a message to the American people, and recommendations for preventing disruptions and violence in the future. The report's language was strong and its message to the citizenry was at once a warning and a challenge:

> Too many Americans have begun to justify violence as a means of effecting change or safeguarding traditions. Too many have forgotten the values and sense of shared humanity that unite us. Campus violence reflects this national condition. . . . A nation driven to use the weapons of war upon its youth is a nation on the edge of chaos. A nation that has lost the allegiance of part of its youth is a nation that has lost part of its future. . . We urgently call for reconciliation. Tolerance and understanding on all sides must reemerge from the fundamental decency of Americans, from our shared aspirations as Americans, from our traditional tolerance of diversity, and from our common humanity. We must regain our compassion for one another and our mutual respect.[100]

The commission's conclusions and recommendations echoed its intolerance of violence and its call to reconciliation:

> We utterly condemn violence. Students who bomb and burn are criminals. Police and National Guardsmen who needlessly shoot or assault students are criminals. All who applaud these criminal acts share their evil. We must declare a national cease-fire. . . . We urge that the President exercise his reconciling moral leadership as the first step to prevent violence and create understanding. . . . To this end, nothing is more important than an end to the war in Indochina.[101]

In addition, the commission recommended a lowering of rhetoric on all levels, improved training of law enforcement officials for dealing with campus disorders, more effective university responses to disruption within the purview of the First Amendment and greater tolerance on the part of the students.

The commission found that at Kent State, "the indiscriminate firing of rifles into a crowd of students and the deaths that followed were unnecessary, unwarranted and inexcusable"[102] and that, at Jackson State, "the 28-second barrage of lethal gunfire, partly directed into crowded windows . . . and into a crowd . . . was completely unwarranted and unjustified."[103]

## The Commission on Population Growth and the American Future

Recognizing the need for information as well as action with regard to the "population explosion," Richard Nixon proposed, in July 1969, a Commission on Population Growth and the American Future and offered these thoughts:

> One of the most serious challenges to human destiny in the last third of this century will be the growth of the population. Whether man's response to that challenge will be a cause for pride or for despair in the year 2000 will depend very much on what we do today.[104]

The situation-oriented commission, chaired by John D. Rockefeller 3rd, was officially established by Congress in March 1970, and was given the task, basically, of investigating:

> the probable extent of population growth and internal migration in the United States between now and the end of this century, to assess the impact that population change will have upon government services, our economy, and our resources and environment, and to make recommendations on how the nation can best cope with that impact.[105]

The commission's study ranged over many aspects of the subject, and its report included examinations of such areas as population growth and distribution, economic, environmental and governmental effects, public policy with regard to population expansion, sex education, human reproduction and methods of control, population stabilization, immigration, national migration, statistics and organizational changes. Throughout the report the commission offered its recommendations which, in essence, involved the suggestion for a national policy with regard to population growth encouraging smaller families and making the means to that end more accessible—all this in the belief that the quality of American life and the ability of the nation's institutions and resources to maintain and improve it will increasingly depend on the level of population. Among the commission's most controversial recommendations were suggestions that abortion, contraception services and voluntary sterilization be made more acceptable and available.

National debate continues on these issues (particularly on abortion, despite the Supreme Court's upholding of the right to abortion,[106] which was in basic agreement with the commission's recommendation) but the report of the Population Commission remains the basic work available for future decision making, policy orientation, and public discussion on the question of population.

## The National Commission on Marijuana and Drug Abuse

In response to national controversy and general ignorance on the subject, Congress established, for the President's appointment, the situation-oriented National Commission on Marijuana and Drug Abuse, chaired by former Governor of Pennsylvania Raymond P. Shafer. The commission was established in the Comprehensive Drug Abuse Prevention and Control Act of 1970, but funds did not become officially available for it until March 1971. In the first of two reports the commission explored marijuana specifically, covering "the nature and scope of use, the effects of the drug, the relationship of marijuana use to other behavior and the efficiency of existing law.[107] In its second report the commission looked at the broader issue of drug use and abuse in the society generally, from tobacco and alcohol to hallucinogens and heroin.

In light of its findings the commission made recommendations for action, developing what Chairman Shafer would later call a "triple approach" to the drug problem: a) do not simply cut off supply; b) do not simply punish offenders; c) do not simply rehabilitate. An effective approach must include education, law enforcement, *and* rehabilitation.[108]

The commission's first report took a "middle-of-the-road" approach to dealing with marijuana use. While it stressed the desirability of continued efforts to restrict the traffic and sale of the substance it also recommended decriminalization of it for personal use. The report investigated the historical use of marijuana and its use in various parts of the world, the characteristics of the user and its effects on him, the social effects and implications of use and society's response, and proposed policy changes.

The second, more comprehensive, report attempted to put some perspective into the public and governmental discussion and response regarding drug use. It emphasized treatment rather than penalties and pointed out, in light of the fact that a great percentage of Americans use some sort of drug on a recreational basis, that the distinction between socially acceptable and socially unacceptable drugs is rather arbitrary. The report recommended mandatory treatment programs for individuals charged with possession of narcotics, with the exception of marijuana, with no punishment in excess of a $500 fine. The commission declared that "For drug-dependent persons, the only legitimate role of the criminal justice system is to function as an entry mechanism into a treatment system." The commission called for the suspension of school drug education programs, pending their evaluation and their being made more realistic, and for the repeal of state laws which required such courses. The liquor industry was called on to publicly acknowledge that compulsive use of alcohol represents the nation's "most destructive drug-use pattern" and to undertake research into the relationship between drinking and traffic accidents, violent crime, and domestic discord. Reflecting its broad definition of "drug use," the commission recommended the cessation of advertising of "mood-altering drugs," such as sedatives, tranquilizers, and stimulants. The report called for the establishment of a single, independent federal agency to deal with all matters relating to drugs, combining the responsibilities of ten different agencies in the Departments of Justice, the Treasury, and Health, Education, and Welfare, and in the White House. The report recommended that legal restrictions on the availability of narcotics be left in place.[109]

The Shafer Commission's reports were not welcomed with open arms by the Nixon Administration, but they are the most comprehensive compilations of research on drug use and abuse ever made by the United States government and remain available as the basis for further investigation and policy formulation.

As commission use has evolved, so have the procedures by which commission investigations are conducted. Chapter 3 will examine the basic methods most presidential commissions use, from organization to report.

# 3

# BASIC COMMISSION PROCEDURE

The commission process involves a number of functions. The President and/or Congress must create, appoint, staff and fund the commission; an investigation must be conducted; a report must be made. This chapter will outline the basic procedure of commission work, up to the making of the report.

## Establishing a Commission

Upon recognition of the need for an advisory commission, establishment may be by one of two methods—presidential or congressional. First, the President may create a commission by Executive Order and appoint its members; e.g., Executive Order 11365 of President Johnson created the Kerner Commission in 1967. He may choose to involve Congress in the process by requesting appropriations, civil service staff personnel, and subpoena and immunity powers, or he may not. The President may fund his commission from his emergency fund or from the budgets of various Cabinet departments and executive agencies with an interest in the commission's study. In either case, the basic appropriations difficulties in which presidentially established commissions have frequently found themselves have stemmed from a lack of consistency in procedure, leading to unnecessary obstacles and inefficiencies in the course of the commissions' work. This situation will be explored more thoroughly later.

Second, presidential commissions may be established by Congress and given a statutory basis. An example is the Commission on Obscenity and Pornography which was created by Congress in Public Law 90-100, in October 1967. In most instances of this method, Congress leaves appointment of a majority of commissioners and, at times, top level staff members to the President and reserves some percentage of appointments for itself. In its enabling legislation Congress provides for funding and personnel, defines the legal authority of the commission with regard to the reception of testimony, may direct that interim reports and/or recommendations be made (The President may do this, as well, with his own commissions.), and sets a prospective date for delivery of the commission's final report and termination of its activities (although this may be extended if the need is recognized). Congressionally appointed commissions generally address their reports to the President, the President of the Senate, and the Speaker of the House of Representatives.

Generally, compensation is provided for non-government employees (commissioners as well as staff) on the commissions (although it is not unknown for commissioners to refuse this), and travel expenses are covered for government and non-government employees alike, involved in the commissions' work. Presidentially appointed and congressionally appointed commissions do not differ fundamentally in their methods or mandates, and except where distinctions become apparent they will be discussed together as presidential commissions.

## The Commissioners

The task of appointing all or some of the commissioners is generally a function of the establisher of the commission. When the President establishes a commission, he almost invariably appoints all members himself. Congress, on the other hand, seems to prefer dividing appointment authority among a number of sources though leaving, as has been mentioned, the largest number to the President. Three examples illustrate Congress' method. The two Herbert Hoover-chaired Commissions on the Organization of the Executive Branch of the Government, of 1949 and 1955, were created by unanimous votes of Congress. Each commission had twelve members, of which four were appointed by the President, four by the Vice President, and four by the Speaker of the House. At least two of the appointees were to come from private and two from public life. Appointments were made on a proportional partisan basis. The first commission contained an equal split of six Republicans and six Democrats; the second had seven Republicans and five Democrats. Each commission chose its own chairman.[1]

In the case of the Commission on Population Growth and the American Future, Congress specifically designated the membership composition:

> (1) two members of the Senate who shall be members of different political parties and who shall be appointed by the President of the Senate;
> (2) two members of the House of Representatives who shall be members of different political parties and who shall be appointed by the Speaker of the House of Representatives; and
> (3) not to exceed twenty members appointed by the President.
> (b) the President shall designate one of the members to serve as Chairman and one to serve as Vice Chairman of the Commission.[2]

In the case of the President's own commissions, almost all commissioners have been presidential appointees. The President may also, if he chooses, select the General Counsel, Executive Director or Research Director of the commission, but this is generally left up to the commissioners or chairmen themselves. In the case of congressionally appointed commissions, instructions in this regard may be found in the statute of appointment.

The number of commissioners has varied with the scope of the area to be investigated, and backgrounds of commissioners are as diverse as the topics of study. Table I indicates the number of commissioners in each of the eight major commissions under study. Table II lists the various fields from which the commissioners were recruited and the number from each field.

### Table I: NUMBERS OF COMMISSIONERS BY COMMISSION

| | |
|---|---|
| President's Commission on the Assassination of President Kennedy | 7 |
| President's Commission on Law Enforcement and the Administration of Justice | 19 |
| National Advisory Commission on Civil Disorders | 11 |
| National Commission on the Causes and Prevention of Violence | 13 |
| Commission on Obscenity and Pornography | 18 |

| President's Commission on Campus Unrest | 9 |
|---|---|
| Commission on Population Growth and the American Future | 24 |
| National Commission on Marijuana and Drug Abuse | 13 |

## Table II: NUMBERS OF COMMISSIONERS BY PROFESSION

| | |
|---|---|
| Attorney | 15 |
| Professor | 14 |
| United States Representative | 10 |
| United States Senator | 10 |
| Clergy | 7 |
| Medical | 6 |
| University President or Dean | 5 |
| Business | 4 |
| United States Judge | 4 |
| Police | 3 |
| State Government (not Governor) | 3 |
| Cabinet Member or Official | 2 |
| Former Governor | 2 |
| Housewife | 2 |
| Labor Leader | 2 |
| Newspaper Publisher or Editor | 2 |
| Political Action Group | 2 |
| Private Foundation Official | 2 |
| Race Relations Group | 2 |
| Research, Research Institute | 2 |
| State Judge | 2 |
| Student | 2 |
| Governor | 1 |
| Civic Leader | 1 |
| Author | 1 |
| Mayor | 1 |
| University Fellow | 1 |
| Cannot Be Determined | 5 |

There are two points not revealed by Table II. First, twelve of the commissioners were women, there being five on the Population Commission alone, which may indicate an increase in the number of women who will be appointed to commissions. Second, youth has not gone unrepresented: two of the commissions had student advisory panels, one had a youth consultant panel and, as the table indicates, two commissioners have been students and one a university fellow.

It might also be pointed out that some commissioners might easily qualify for placement under more than one heading. For example, some are M.D.s serving in different roles; some may be involved in more than one field at the same time. The list, then, should not be taken as a description of the full range of commissioners' activities but rather as an indication of the basic diversity of commission membership.

How is a commissioner chosen? It would seem that many of the same attributes of "availability" as apply in the selection of candidates for political office apply in the selection of commissioners. For the most part, prospective commissioners are men who have distinguished records of public and/or private service, who may have some connection with the area under study (although this, more often than not, may be outweighed by leadership and administrative abilities or a prestigious name), and who may or may not be predisposed strongly in one direction towards the area of study. Bringing in "blue ribbon" members can potentially add prestige, credibility, and visibility to a commission.

Evidence suggests that commissioners are thought to be persons of "predictable moderation,"[3] persons of "action" rather than of "thought,"[4] and, generally, persons of open mind. On the latter point, Otto N. Larsen, a member of the Pornography Commission, has written:

> When I was called from the White House and asked to serve on the Commission, I pointed out that I had not been involved with any research specifically concerned with obscenity and pornography. I was told that the President was looking for qualified people who had experience with research that would be relevant, but that he did not want persons who had already made up their minds about the subject. I responded by asking if this meant that the Commission was free to move with the data and was not being formed merely to provide information to support a given policy position. The answer was an emphatic yes, and I was given some names of prominent persons who were not being put on the commission because they had publicly committed themselves to a particular view on the issue. Thereupon, I accepted the appointment.[5]

Commissioners are chosen in what appears to be a somewhat ad hoc manner, involving presidential designation of certain names and staff development of others.[6] The commissioners are often chosen for the groups they represent (or are thought to represent). The concept of commissioner-as-representative has taken on some complexity. At times, in fact, a commissioner may serve a multi-representational role, as is illustrated by a description of the make-up of the Kerner

Commission on Civil Disorders. Massachusetts Senator Edward Brooke was present as both a Black and a Republican. Otto Kerner, as Governor of Illinois, brought some of Mayor Richard Daly's Chicago "clout." Atlanta Police Chief Herbert Jenkins was seen as both a "good cop" and a modern southerner. Kentucky Commissioner of Commerce Katherine Graham Peden was to provide some conservative balance on the commission.[7]

In an attempt to balance a commission—ideologically, geographically, racially—the President may seem to be setting the stage for irreconcilable conflict in which commissioners become "hot potatoes in a no win game."[8] This does not, however, appear to be the usual result. As Frank Popper reports, commissioners "believe that clashes between the opinions they represent are constructive: they consider the collective advice of a commission valuable to the President and the public because such advice, even if not particularly innovative, represents an honest synthesis of varying opinions."[9] "You know who you're supposed to represent as soon as you see who the other commissioners are," a participant on a number of commissions has said. "The commissioners are a deliberate cross section of people with lines into other people. But even if you're a delegate, you try to relate to broader interests, including the general public's and the President's"[10]

The process of commissioner selection may potentially affect the process of commission work. A number of observers have pointed up aspects of this possibility. Martha Derthick, noting that commissioners "tend to come from urban locales and to be cosmopolitan rather than parochial,"[11] suggests what amounts to a class bias theory. In this view, commissioners who are chosen by agents of the President and represent the presidential constituency," tend to share an outlook which is "cosmopolitan and urbane and which favors seemingly sophisticated and tolerant explanations of events to intolerant and simplistic ones." The commission's political function is to "organize expression on behalf of this body of opinion," which will compete with other viewpoints.[12]

Lloyd E. Ohlin, Associate Director of the Katzenbach Commission on Law Enforcement, refines and expands upon this theory with regard to a specific commission. Ohlin feels that the nature of his commission's membership—primarily lawyers—made it clear that the President was not looking for radical proposals for change in the criminal justice system. These individuals' methods would involve "carefully documented, feasible proposals for making the *existing* system work more effectively. . . " Ohlin suggests that such a commission's recommendations "could be expected to carry great weight and gain wide acceptance."[13] A practical result, then, might be increased legitimacy of commission findings among various relevant groups. Commissioners, at the outset, may seem unlikely to advocate revolutionary change in a system of which they are a part, yet the facts of their backgrounds may lend legitimacy to that which they ultimately *do* advocate.

Another potential aspect of this "bias" is raised in the charge that "commissioners are disinclined to indict politically important figures, or programs or agencies identified with the President who selected them."[14] One participant in the presidential decision making process holds that this phenomenon is not quite so devious as it might appear: "There's an automatic skewing in favor of the guy who thinks you're important enough to put . . . on a commission. It's not necessarily dishonest."[15] Further, the thrusts of many major commission reports—whether directly or by implication—can reasonably be seen as having actually involved indictments of incumbent administrations and their policies. The Scranton Commission, to name one example, offered a considerable number of recommendations which challenged President Nixon's policies regarding campus disturbances and the Vietnam War.[16]

Another phenomenon with regard to the appointment process is the practice of appointing a former commissioner to a new commission. In the eight major commissions in this study, three of the commissioners were on two commissions each. Dr. Milton Eisenhower, chairman of the Violence Commission, served on some twenty commissions.

## The Chairman

As with many endeavors, a leader's role may be what he chooses to make of it and this is the case with the commission chairman. Whether appointed directly by the President or by his fellow commissioners, the chairman has various options as to his exercise of leadership. He may take the initiative and place himself firmly in a position of authority through his direction of full commission meetings and the commission staff. He may, conversely, take a back seat and let the staff navigate. Or, he may take a position somewhere in the middle. In any case, no matter what extent of authority he perceives as his to be used, the chairman is the centerpiece of a presidential commission; indeed, most major commissions are referred to by the name of their chairman rather than by their official name.

The chairman must, ideally, exhibit the integrity and fairness of a judge, the administrative skills of an executive, and the intellectual abilities of a scholar. In his memoirs, Lyndon Johnson illustrated the role of these qualities as he related the selection of a chairman for the Commission on the Assassination of President Kennedy:

> The Commission had to be bipartisan, and I felt that we needed a Republican chairman whose judicial ability and fairness were unquestioned. I don't believe I ever considered anyone but Chief Justice Earl Warren for chairman. I was not an intimate of the Chief Justice. We had never spent ten minutes alone together, but to me he was the personification of justice and fairness in this country. . . . We had to bring the nation through that bloody tragedy, and Warren's personal integrity was a key element in assuring that all the facts would be unearthed and that the conclusions would be credible.[17]

The basic prerequisite is what Lyndon Johnson said with regard to his appointment of Milton Eisenhower as chairman of the Violence Commission: LBJ said he needed "someone with a national reputation for objectivity."[18]

In addition to a reputation for fairness, the chairman frequently brings an atmosphere of prestige to a commission and, ergo, visibility.

As one former executive director put it, "I think the Chairman really sets the tone of a commission."[19] Some evaluative observations on the performance of some chairmen should illustrate the chairman's role. Lloyd N. Cutler, Executive Director of the Violence Commission, has described the unique (within the commission context) leadership function of the chairman:

> Our chairman was Dr. Milton Eisenhower, an able and devoted man who . . . was the key to the success of the entire commission. Dr. Eisenhower was a man with whom all of the commissioners

were ready to agree even though they might disagree a great deal with one another. It was his presence and his continuing force on the commission that I think led to the largely unanimous reports that were filed.

He is also quite a draftsman in his own right and . . . every word in this report was at least reviewed and edited by Dr. Eisenhower and a very large number of those words were written in the first instance by him.[20]

Otto Larsen has described the role of William Lockhart on the Pornography Commission:

Chairman Lockhart, a recognized authority on constitutional law, brought his experience both as a scholar and as a leader in academic, church, and civic affairs immediately to bear on the work of the Commission. The significance of this goes beyond style to the direction of his commitment. Even with social scientists on the Commission, it was unlikely that we could have stayed on an empirical track . . . without his reasoned support and vigorous leadership. He resisted all effort to use money for public relations types of activities, in the interest of allocating funds to research. He read every article, research proposal, and report. He even labored on some of the questionnaires. By his example, it became clear that this was to be a working commission, not one that merely reviewed the work of others. . . . The chairman . . . reports that he shifted policy grounds because of the research on effects.[21]

Of Otto Kerner, *The New York Times* has written:

In 1968 he seemed the appropriate leader to tell American whites that their discrimination had created and maintained the black ghettos that had been exploding with violence each summer.

His record as Governor had been solidly liberal with no hint of scandal; he had a good record on civil rights and came out of Chicago, one of the troubled cities that the commission was to examine.[22]

One critic of the Kerner Commission said, nonetheless, that "Chairman Kerner did very little substantively, except to steer a course between the political 'sides.' "[23] It might plausibly be argued that such a function would be considered intrinsically worthwhile in a high-level body of diverse individuals examining inflammatory social issues. As has been suggested, on more than one commission this proved to be a quite necessary role.

A final point might be made with regard to the chairman. Apparently, once the President (Lyndon Johnson, at least) has decided upon an individual to chair a commission, this individual does not always have much time or latitude regarding his acceptance or rejection. (Of course, the press of events which led to the decision to appoint a commission in the first place may be a strong factor here.) Lyndon Johnson deftly described the manner in which he put such an offer to Earl Warren:

> I knew it was not a good precedent to involve the Supreme Court in such an investigation. Chief Justice Warren knew this too and was vigorously opposed to it. I called him in anyway. Before he came, he sent word through a third party that he would not accept the assignment. He opposed serving on constitutional grounds. He said that if asked, he would refuse. He thought the President should be informed of that. . . . When the Chief Justice came into my office and sat down, I told him that I knew what he was going to say to me but that there was one thing no one else had said to him: In World War I he had put a rifle to his shoulder and offered to give his life, if necessary, to save his country. I said I didn't care who brought me a message about how opposed he was to this assignment. When the country is confronted with threatening divisions and suspicions, I said, and its foundation is being rocked, and the President of the United States says that you are the only man who can handle the matter, you won't say "no," will you?
>
>   He swallowed hard and said, "No, sir."
>
>   I always had great respect for Chief Justice Warren. From that moment on I became his great advocate as well.[24]

A similar instance occurred with the selection of Milton Eisenhower to chair the Violence Commission. The President called Dr. Eisenhower and asked if he would serve. When the educator asked for a bit of time to consider, Mr. Johnson replied that he had already scheduled a television address for that same day announcing the appointment of the commission. Acceptance was hard to avoid.[25] Some might call this browbeating. LBJ might have called it persuasion.

The chairman becomes the personification of the commission. His name, which may be well known and respected, attaches to the group. The effective chairman must be fair in facilitating balance among, and open expression of, the diverse backgrounds and opinions represented by the commission members and the staff. He will strive for the pursuit of objective inquiry and will not be seen as overtly partisan. He will demonstrate a commitment to the commission and its task. More than any other individual, he can set the tone of the commission to sustain it through months of research, meetings and deadlines. Finally, his very name and presence may bring visibility and legitimacy to the commission and, ultimately, to its findings.

## The Partisan Temptation

A serious consideration in the appointment of commissioners (and commissions themselves) is the issue of partisanship. Presidential commissions are intended to provide analyses of situations from a position outside the subjective realms of parties and government agencies and institutions. It would be perhaps unrealistic, however, to ignore the potential desire on the part of the President (or that of anyone else concerned) for a favorable assessment of his policies—or at least not an unfavorable one. This "partisan temptation"—the desire to affect results for reasons other than those of inquiry—can manifest itself in a number of situations: in the area of maintenance of a proper distance between a commission and its subject of study, e.g. when this is a government institution; in the commissioner appointment process; and in the behavior of commissioners themselves. It must be remembered, as well, that until 1972 presidents were under no obligation to respond to commission reports (see Chapter 6 on the Federal Advisory Committee Act), a situation which conceivably could have contributed to the temptation of partisan meddling.

### Independence of inquiry: maintaining a proper distance

An example of the question of independence from the subject under study is provided by the experience of a commission which did not enjoy it.

"Commissions can be very valuable," Howard Shuman, Executive Director of the Douglas Commission on Urban Problems, has said, "provided they are independent. They must be independent of the agency being examined. . . . They can examine programs in a critical way which no agency can do for itself."[26] The Douglas Commission is a case in point. The Commission on Urban Problems grew out of the 1965 Housing Act. It was intended to study national housing policies, particularly those under the Department of Housing and Urban Development, and report to the Secretary of HUD. When asked by the White House to head this group, Senator Paul H. Douglas of Illinois made his acceptance contingent upon independence from HUD (in other words, the commission would report directly to the President rather than the Secretary) and a wider scope of inquiry including codes, zoning, and taxation. The White House agreed, but the Secretary and the HUD bureaucracy never accepted what they feared would be an embarrassing exposé of policy mismanagement; they repeatedly attempted to circumvent the commission's work by blocking staff efforts to set up the commission apparatus and by attempting to control the group's investigatory process.

According to the White House, the commission was to "work *with* but not *under,* the Secretary of HUD,"[27] and the department lost little time in sending budgetary and study instructions to the commission, along with a directive that an HUD official be present at all meetings; all of which was, to the commission, a declaration of dependence. The commission refused HUD's conditions, with the exception of the last, and even this concession was later seen as "a mistake because every criticism of HUD during both our private sessions and our public hearings went to the Secretary from his inside agent."[28]

The commission went about its work, but it became increasingly evident that much was wrong with HUD policy and that this would have to be reflected in the commission's report. HUD officials went to the White House with claims that the commission had exceeded its mandate and was in disarray from lack of unity. By the time the commission had completed its report, however, HUD's claims were suspect at the White House. Still, sufficient misinformation had been spread and an open response seemed too awkward to make. The White House was caught between a desire to reform housing policies, a strongly critical report regarding a Cabinet department, and fears aroused by that department that the report would put "the administration in a bad light."[29] It was decided that the commission should deliver its report to President-elect Nixon. Chairman Douglas refused this, however, and the commission released its report to the press. The White House offered no response and HUD omitted portions of the report when the document was forwarded (as the original legislation had required) to Congress.

Sometimes the reverse of the Douglas Commission case has been true; not only has a proper distance been maintained, but the President or Congress will appear to have forgotten that a particular commission even exists. Representative John Monagon, of Connecticut cited the example of the Commission on the Standardization of Screw Threads. The commission was organized in 1919 with a promise that less than one year would be required for its work. The commission's life was continued for three more years, at which time its members took a trip to Europe. In 1922, the commission's life was extended for three more years. In its first eight years of existence the commission spent $150,000.[30] A phenomenon perhaps related to simply continuing the life of a commission, unexamined, involves authorizing a commission and never appointing its members. This occurred with regard to at least three commissions in 1968 alone, as was discovered at a 1970 House Government Operations Committee subcommittee hearing. The three included: 1) The National Commission on Fire Prevention and Control. Public Law 90-259 provided for twenty members, including the Secretary of Housing and Urban Development and the Secretary of Commerce. The remaining eighteen members, including the chairman, were not appointed; 2) The National Commission on Consumer Finance. Six members, without a chairman, were appointed; the commission was not activated; 3) The National Advisory Commission on Low-Income Housing. Only eight of the commission's twenty-one members were chosen and the commission was not funded.[31] All three commissions had been authorized by Congress and, following the subcommittee disclosure of neglect, the President appointed members and activated the groups.[32] But the question remains as to why the commissions were not fully appointed when they were authorized.

## Appointments

The partisan temptation may extend to the appointment of commissioners and staff personnel. One critical observer has suggested that when the Kerner Commission conspicuously avoided mention of the Vietnam War as a contributing factor, directly or indirectly, to urban unrest, it was at least partially a result of President Johnson's personal appointment of the executive director. This observer suggests, further, that there were questions as to the acceptability to the administration of academics who agreed to participate in preparing the commission's report.[33]

With regard to the appointment of commissioners the question reaches new levels. In some cases, it is said, the President may be "able to pay off friends and allies with commission appointments, or help some . . . in their careers, or (if it came to that) implicate potential enemies in an administration production."[34] This does not, of course, guarantee anything.

The basic problem comes when the President appoints extremists, demagogues, or anyone with his or her mind obviously set on the subject to be pursued. It would seem, as commissioners are quite human, that different opinions will be inherent and quite in evidence without the President's making biased appointments. The commissioners have a responsibility in this to "give up some of their self and occupational role interests and develop orientations toward the commission as an organization with a life of its own,"[35] which simply means they must avoid becoming apologists for their own areas of interest if the investigation begins to move close to home for them.

In the case of the Commission on Obscenity and Pornography, President Johnson, contrary to the mandate of Congress' authorization bill stating that "the Commission shall elect a chairman . . . from among its members,"[36] designated a chairman himself.[37] Commissioner Charles Keating argued that the chairman was biased regarding the subject under study, by reasons of his being associated with the American Civil Liberties Union and his having written on the legal aspects of the question.[38] Commissioner and sociologist Otto Larsen has written, however, that:

> Johnson's appointments did not, with one exception [Commissioner Rev. Morton A. Hill], have an apparent vested interest one way or the other in obscenity and pornography. . . . If the other Commissioners had a pre-existing commitment concerning obscenity and pornography, it perhaps more closely resembled disinterest than anything else. To some extent, Public Law 90-100 required this, and President Johnson made his appointments accordingly.[39]

In fact, prior to his appointment to the commission, William Lockhart favored controls on the distribution of pornography.[40]

## Commissioner behavior

Perhaps more to the point, with regard to the Pornography Commission and the partisan temptation, was President Nixon's action upon gaining an opportunity to affect the commission. What occurred provides perhaps the most blatant example in recent history of disruptive commissioner behavior.

Members of the Pornography Commission had been appointed by Lyndon Johnson. The commission's work, however, continued after the Nixon administration took office. The commission had been at work for one year, its work divided among four panels, and a rule of confidentiality agreed to, when President Nixon appointed Commissioner Kenneth B. Keating Ambassador to India. Thereupon, the President was presented with the opportunity of filling a vacancy on the commission. His choice was Charles H. Keating.

As Otto Larsen has put it, "The two Keatings were not related in any fashion."[41] Indeed, it would appear that Mr. Nixon, in his appointment of Mr. Keating, was unaware of Carl Marcy's reassurance, twenty-five years earlier, that

> the importance and prominence of the President make it difficult
> for him to select a body of fact-finders who are obviously unfit for
> the job either by reason of ability or preconceived ideas about the
> facts to be found.[42]

Charles Keating is a Cincinnati lawyer and founder of an antipornography organization well known in that city—Citizens for Decent Literature, Inc.—which has spread to include 300 chapters, nationwide.[43] In short, Mr. Keating's mind was already made up on the subject of the commission's inquiry and, as he has observed, "the White House knew when I was appointed my interest was to control pornography. . . . They didn't send me in as an objective observer."[44]

From the time of his first meeting with the commission, Keating refused to abide by commission decisions. His primary activity in this regard concerned the previously agreed-to rule of confidentiality which the commission had adopted to protect freedom of inquiry and discussion during the deliberative stages of its work.[45] Commissioner Keating stated bluntly that he would not abide by the rule.[46] At one point, several commissioners stated that Keating's position was restricting their participation in commission work. Further, Keating refused to serve on any one of the commission's four working panels, preferring to act in an "at-large" capacity and participate in any panel activity at any time. When this was refused and Keating was assigned to a panel, he sent a substitute to participate in his place and sought to send representatives to monitor other panel meetings. Again, these practices were seen as unacceptable by the commission. Lengthy discussions via the mail and at commission meetings were unable to resolve these difficulties.[47] As the commission prepared to finish its work and release its final report, Mr. Keating began leaking the commission's findings and recommendations to the press.[48] On at least one occasion, as well, Commissioner Reverend Morton Hill was responsible for an unauthorized leak.[49]

The reception accorded the commission's report was hostile and will be discussed later. At this point, it is perhaps enough to note that a single commissioner, sufficiently determined, has it within his power to disrupt commission procedure and, potentially, to affect its deliberative process.

## The Staff

Upon appointment, the chairman or the assembled commission takes its first important action: staff selection. Among the first to be chosen, if they have not already been designated by the President, are the Executive Director and the General Counsel. The Executive Director hires, oversees and coordinates the all-important investigative research staff with its task forces and large number of personnel involved in activities ranging from polling to secretarial work. At times, the Executive Director may be referred to as the Director of Research, although these may be separately filled positions. Frank Popper offers a sense of the Executive Director's job:

> above all, he must infuse both the commissioners and the staff with
> a sense of urgency. The short life of a commission, rather than

simplifying the director's job, complicates it. Much of his work is administrative, unconnected with the substance of the commission's topic. While the staff does the research and writes, he recruits, mediates, reassures, badgers, negotiates for secretaries, and argues with the Government Printing Office about how long it will take to print the report. He has little to do with writing the report, and his detailed grasp of the commission's topic—for which he was hired in the first place—is only rarely used.[50]

The General Counsel may be consulted on legal questions raised in connection with commission work. Because many commissions contain large numbers of attorneys, on occasion a General Counsel may not be appointed, but this is rarely the case. Also, while it is normal for one General Counsel to be appointed, a commission may, due to the nature of its particular area of investigation, appoint an entire legal staff. This was the case with the Warren Commission. In addition to its regular staff, the commission appointed a fourteen-member legal staff to work for its General Counsel.

The next order of business is to hire the remaining members of the staff, procure office space, and organize the operation. These initial steps alone can consume valuable commission time. Lloyd Cutler, Executive Director of the Eisenhower Commission, is said to have spent ten weeks of the commission's eighteen-month life in assembling a staff.[51] Delay is not always for lack of available personnel, however; the Kerner Commission, for example, received literally hundreds of applications and recommendations for employment.[52]

Staff positions may include: Deputy or Associate Director, Administrative Officer, Editorial Officer, Public Affairs Officer, Director of Research, and myriad assistants. In addition, numerous research groups and consultant panels may be included and a good deal of research work may be contracted out to universities, foundations, and corporations. Staff members may be chosen for their competence, recognized expertise, connections with higher staff personnel or commissioners, or for their ties with various constituencies of relevance to the work of the commission.[53]

Office space may be provided either by the White House or the General Services Administration.

The staff, composed primarily of lawyers and academics, may be either quite large or rather small in number. This may, to some extent, reflect the scope of a commission's subject of inquiry. For example, the Warren Commission, which investigated a narrow range of events, had a staff of 27. The Kerner Commission on Civil Disorders, however, had a much broader scope and used a staff of 115. There is no hard and fast rule about this, as is suggested by the fact that the Eisenhower Commission, which studied the phenomenon of violence generally, required a staff of only 31. Table III indicates staff sizes for the eight commissions under study, arranged according to the years in which the commissions issued their final reports.

### Table III: STAFF SIZES BY COMMISSION IN CHRONOLOGICAL SEQUENCE

| | | |
|---|---|---|
| 1964 | President's Commission on the Assassination of President Kennedy | 27 |
| 1967 | President's Commission on Law Enforcement and the Administration of Justice | 63 |
| 1968 | National Advisory Commission on Civil Disorders | 115 |
| 1969 | National Commission on the Causes and Prevention of Violence | 31 |
| 1970 | Commission on Obscenity and Pornography | 22 |
| 1970 | President's Commission on Campus Unrest | 139 |
| 1972 | Commission on Population Growth and the American Future | 40 |
| 1973 | National Commission on Marijuana and Drug Abuse | 70 |

As was suggested above, commissions may hire outside consultants and researchers—at times, literally hundreds—to conduct particular studies and make reports. While not considered full-time participants on the commission, these individuals do contribute to the number of persons involved in the business of commissions. Often, this is the maximum degree to which persons holding academic positions can participate in commission activities. The temporal limitations of commission work, combined with the fact that commissions may be appointed after commitments for the academic year have been made, frequently preclude academic participation.[54].

The commissioner-staff relationship is an important one. Obviously, a generally smooth working relationship must exist if the commission is to fulfill its mandate. Yet, one observer has suggested that the "relationship between the commission and the staff is usually one of mutual contempt."[55] Lipsky and Olson have elaborated upon the nature of this relationship:

> an important point of tension is the commissioners' need to feel reassured that staff members are free from bias and are presenting their work free from ideological distortion. . . . The dangers of fail-

ure to allay commission suspicions that the staff is overzealous or partisan are two: The commissioners may reject staff work and in the end develop conclusions independent of staff analysis; or, in anticipation of commission antagonism, staff work may be screened to provide commissioners with only "acceptable" material. In either case, the commission runs the risk of staff revolt, the erosion of organizational loyalty among the staff, and divisive public debate inspired by discontented staff.[56]

Some conflict is probably inevitable, not only because commissions are groups of diverse human beings who must work together on a common project, but also because of the often-controversial nature of commission topics. It is worth noting, however, that Milton Eisenhower, who served on nearly twenty commissions, argued that he never experienced commissioner-staff conflicts that proved inhibiting.[57]

## Time Constraints

One of the first and most basic realities that a commission and its staff must consider as they begin their work is the limitation of time. Relative brevity of existence can be an asset to commissions in terms of resistance to the constraints of institutionalization. At the same time, it can cause great pressure and lead to less than ideal working conditions. The limitations of time, along with the vastness of subjects, necessitate efficient use of staffs.

Amitai Etzioni has said that, "More than anything else, commissions are part of government by fire-brigade."[58] As a result, commissions must usually work toward a deadline, whether self-imposed, pre-set by President or Congress, or necessitated by events. An example is provided by the experience of the Kerner Commission. President Johnson called on the commission to present an interim report in March 1968, and a final report by August 1. Executive Director David Ginsburg and Deputy Executive Director Victor H. Palmieri determined, however, that the commission should produce but one report—and rather quickly. "We absolutely had to come out in March with the whole report," Lipsky and Olson quote Palmieri as saying:

That premise developed in August and September and it grew and grew until it became inevitable that we *would* come out in March. It would have been silly to come out with a report on the summer of 1967 in the middle of the summer riots of 1968. But nobody, literally nobody, knew of our decision. It was never explicit between Ginsburg and me, or between either of us and any commissioner.[59]

The commission was successful in meeting its self-imposed deadline.

Some observers have discussed potential drawbacks to the imposition of deadlines. Lipsky and Olson, for example, feel "One consequence is that generalists, such as lawyers, may be hired over specialists, since staff directors may not know precisely what they want to do."[60] Futher, "the staff is almost obliged to develop (or simply accept) a general working theory of riot causation to guide the research."[61] Added to this are suggestions that conclusions may rest on inadequate foundations or be incomplete. James F. Short, a sociologist and Co-Director of Research of the Violence Commission, has spoken of these latter possibilities with regard to the commission's study·team report on the activities and violence surrounding the 1968 Democratic National Convention in Chicago:

> high-level involvement and decision-making were not systematically documented or researched at the "eye-witness" level. The police—surely culpable in view of what happened—bore the burden of responsibility just as surely shared by their civilian superiors. Thus, the pressure of time and the focus and methods of investigation led to an incomplete picture of those who participated in the violence (police and demonstrators) and of those who, in a larger sense, were responsible for the confrontation.[62]

Lloyd E. Ohlin, also a sociologist and Associate Director of the Commission on Law Enforcement, writes:

> One of the most difficult problems was the slow pace of research sponsored by the Commission—so out of phase with the inexorable timetable of writing deadlines, Commission meetings, and approval procedures for recommendations. Most recommendations had to be drawn in anticipation of research findings, rather than from final reported results.[63]

While the perspectives these observers offer would seem significant, we still might ask: Does the pace truly pose a problem? Interestingly, interpretations of the effects of time constraints may depend upon one's background and professional training. For example, all the above observations were made by scholars, the latter two of whom actually participated in commission work. When the question of pace is raised with James S. Campbell, a lawyer and General Counsel to the Violence Commission as well as Co-Director of its Task Force on Law and Enforcement, a quite different interpretation is offered:

> In the case of commissions there is, I think a natural euphoria, in a sense of doing a defined task for a limited period of time; nobody's going to make a career out of it, anyway. People are not usually in it for the glory, particularly. I think the motivations are in many ways simpler and purer in the case of working for a commission than they are working for a government agency. . . . I think the pace *is* very hectic. But I don't think people should be under illusions about how that pace compares with policy making levels in the Executive branch. The pace, after all, is a pace that is carried on by people who are deliberating, who are compiling, writing, researching, thinking. And it's a very hectic pace but at least one is doing those things; at least one is thinking, deliberating, researching, and so on. You have the same kind of pace in the Executive branch to "put out fires," and to meet budget deadlines, and to get something up to the Hill. The pace is just as fast there and there's no *time* for thinking or deliberating or writing or researching. . . . At least with commissions one is "hectically thinking" . . . I think that, by and large, it's stimulating. . . . I don't think that we ought to apply scholarly standards, as such. A scholar couldn't, I suppose, work for very long at the kind of pace the commission people work at. But this is not an exercise in pure scholarship. There's some research that goes with it. Mainly, it's a matter of public education; a collecting, a sifting, comparing, thinking about, disseminating. It's not pure, original research, in most instances.[64]

James Short, quoted above, supplements these points:

> While all of this activity seemed to occur more-or-less continuously in a frenetic melange, it was not unstructured. Staff contact with Commissionsers, individually and collectively, was handled through

the executive director, often with the assistance of the general counsel [James Campbell] . . . there was much direct contact among all
parties.[65]

Time constraints would seem to affect some more than others.
They are a continuing aspect of the commission process which, to
some degree, shape the commission's final product. Table IV indicates the "lifetimes" of the eight commissions under study.

### Table IV: COMMISSION "LIFETIMES"

| | |
|---|---|
| President's Commission on the Assassination of President Kennedy | 10 months |
| President's Commission on Law Enforcement and the Administration of Justice | 24 months |
| National Advisory Commission on Civil Disorders | 8 months |
| National Commission on the Causes and Prevention of Violence | 18 months |
| Commission on Obscenity and Pornography | 36 months |
| President's Commission on Campus Unrest | 3 months |
| Commission on Population Growth and the American Future | 24 months |
| National Commission on Marijuana and Drug Abuse | 26 months |

## The Investigation

Once a commission has been appointed and staffed, it begins its
investigation. The investigatory process involves staff and commissioner research, meetings, and, when appropriate, hearings, travel,
and contracts for outside research. Various problems may arise at
different times throughout this period.

### First steps

The very first steps in the investigation may include: development
of a working outline; consultation with former commission participants and experts; establishment of liaison with relevant governmental agencies from whom informational support may be needed;
decisions regarding norms of communication, delegation of responsibility, the advisability of scheduling hearings, and rules of procedure; reviews of the current state of knowledge in the field under
investigation and determinations as to the need for new research.[66]
There may be decisions of a qualitative sort, such as that reported

by James Short, Co-Director of Research for the Violence Commission: "at its first meeting, the Commission unanimously agreed . . . that more was needed than compromise of our preconceptions."[67] There may be fundamental decisions about what the commission hopes to accomplish. James Campbell, General Counsel of the Violence Commission, has discussed this point:

> One way to evaluate the commissions would be to look at a commission in terms of the goals that it set for itself. It may not have done that explicitly but you can see by the way it went about its work what its goal really was. I think if you look at the Eisenhower Commission you would see that it really did not intend to be a body that would generate legislative proposals that would go straight from the White House to the Congress; one reason being that we knew perfectly well when we started that we would report to a President other than the one who appointed us. And we didn't know which party he would be from, at that point. We also knew some of the problems that the Kerner Commisson had had, and some of the others, and we were very anxious to be free from, particularly, Johnson's political pressure and influence. We made a real effort to be independent. And the cost of that, or a necessary concomitant of that, is that you separate yourself from the power center in the White House. Your independence is gained at a price of not being able to drop legislation in the hopper.
>
> The other thing you can see about the way the Commission worked was that it decided, early on, it was going to commission very wide-ranging research and publish as much of it as it could. . . . I think you'd have to say the Eisenhower Commission saw itself in a more academic way and set public education, really, as its goal. And I think we were very successful in that.[68]

## Study areas and task forces

Some commissions find it useful to divide themselves into areas of study, each area being presided over by a group of the commissioners and developing its own staff assistance. For example, the Pornography Commission organized itself into "four working panels": 1) Legal, 2) Traffic and Distribution, 3) Effects, and 4) Positive Approaches.[69] The Katzenbach Commission on Law Enforcement also divided its work into four areas: police, courts, corrections, and assessment of the crime problem. Each area was the responsibility of a task force made up of commissioners, full-time staff members, consultants, and advisers. This basic working structure was supplemented by special task forces and workings groups which focused on subjects which arose during the commission's investigation.[70] Assignment of commissioners to task forces, it was hoped, would assure "that at least some Commission members would be fully informed about the work of each of the task forces."[71] Task force work may be overseen by the Executive Director, with task force directors making preliminary decisions regarding research contracts and consultants.[72]

Other commissions choose not to divide into study areas or to assign commissioners to task forces. Executive Director Lloyd Cutler has explained the theory behind this approach, with reference to the Commission on the Causes and Prevention of Violence:

> They [Katzenbach Commission] had their commissioners take part in the work of task forces. We decided at the beginning, after considering that possibility, not to do that but to give scholarly freedom to the task force scholars themselves and reserve the commission for reviewing all of this work and then reaching its own conclusions.[73]

Task forces may still be used, then, only without the participation of the commissioners themselves. There is nothing to suggest that one method of commission organization is necessarily less effective than the other in permitting commissioners to become familiar with their subjects.

Whether or not commissioners are assigned task force duties, it may be pertinent to ask whether the commissioners themselves actually participate to any significant degree in the work of commissions. The evidence suggests they do. The commissioners do not play the same role as staff members, in terms of research, but this does not mean they are idle figureheads. James Campbell has suggested that, although commissioners do not necessarily work as hard as staff, "they're not intended to: it's a part-time kind of thing,"[74] and he reports that, on the Eisenhower Commission:

> a majority of them at least did their homework rather faithfully. . . . We had plenty of people who read what the staff prepared and thought about the problems. . . . We never had the feeling we were

giving them a lot of material they never read. . . . Some people, like Dr. Eisenhower, were faithful beyond anyone's reasonable expectations.[75]

Raymond Shafer agrees, with regard to his Commission on Marijuana and Drug Abuse. He argues that he chaired "a working commission," not simply a group of notables rubber-stamping the product of a staff, and that its members were experienced in various facets of the field of study.[76]

Some commissioners work not at all.[77] As in any collective human undertaking, the depths of commitment may not be the same in all participants. There may be conflicting demands on some commissioners' time, and a few commissioners are likely to feel that commission work is not worth much of their time. Among those who do work, however, there may be degrees to their efforts, as was suggested by Campbell. Frank Popper observes, in this regard, that a sense of urgency about a commission's subject is likely to motivate many commissioners who make the most useful contributions and that these individuals have often been Blacks. Popper cites a moving presentation by Technology Commission member Whitney Young, at an early meeting, as having had a decisive influence on all subsequent commision proceedings and on its report.[78]

On balance, then, it would appear that commissioners perform their commission-related duties and take an active part in commission work.

## Organizational needs

With areas of inquiry delineated and task forces appointed, the commission's work has begun. The staff begins compiling information and developing research. The commission begins to function as an organization, but it may lack the rewards and penalties needed for internal discipline that are available to more structured organizations.[79] Some sense of order may be established by the Executive Director. Lipsky and Olson have described the role of David Ginsburg, Executive Director of the Kerner Commission:

> Ginsburg's role in inducing commissioners' confidence in staff work was considerable. According to all accounts, Ginsburg conducted

himself without regard for partisan concerns. Ginsburg fully embraced the commission as his client, creating an atmosphere of openness which was simultaneously tough-minded. He would invite suggestions, while demanding that commissioners be specific in their criticisms. He would show patience in debate, but was willing to cut it off with exclamations that the staff had discussed the subject at great length. He relieved Republican anxieties by avoiding positions which could be interpreted as particularly favorable to the president.[80]

Scranton Commissioner Martha Derthick notes that bargaining may facilitate agreement and maintains that a trade settled the commission's key division.[81] Although commissions do not possess all the tools of order normally at the disposal of an organization, then, modes of operation do emerge, as well as internal protections against partisan influences.

It is perhaps interesting to note an unusual organizational situation faced by the Violence Commission. The commission desired active scholarly participation yet wanted lawyers to perform administrative functions. It was decided, therefore, that commission task forces would be co-directed by a lawyer and a social scientist.[82] Commission participants agree that this combination led to some unnecessary disharmony but was, overall, productive.[83]

## Contacts with other agencies

Early on, in the investigative process, contacts may be established between a commission and other governmental agencies in order to supplement commission informational sources. Frank Popper feels that, for the most part, "agencies feel threatened by commissions, resent them, and tend to give them little help in their work."[84] Nonetheless, some cooperation is possible. In its notes on investigative procedure, the Warren commission cites a variety of governmental informational sources. The commission first received reports from the Federal Bureau of Investigation and the Secret Service, both of which, undoubtedly, can be perceived as having had an interest in cooperating. The Department of State reported on Lee Harvey Oswald's defection to and subsequent return from the Soviet Union. Reports were also made by the attorney general of Texas, which included Dallas police reports. The commission then requested all information on the assassination, and the background and activities of Lee Harvey Oswald and Jack Ruby, from the ten major departments of the federal government and fourteen of its independent agencies and commissions, as well as from four congressional committees. Additional reports were handled by agencies of the Internal Revenue Service, the Department of State, and military intelligence. Contributions were made by the Central Intelligence Agency. The FBI itself conducted 25,000 interviews and submitted 2,300 reports, totalling 25,400 pages, to the commission. The Secret Service conducted 1,550 interviews and submitted 800 reports, totalling 4,600 pages. Finally, the secretaries of State and the Treasury, and the directors of the CIA, the FBI, and the Secret Service, were asked to testify before the commission.[85] Leaving aside questions of factual accuracy and organizational motivation, it would seem that agency cooperation can be obtained.

## Job evolution

As the commission work pace intensifies, personnel responsibilities may change. James Campbell of the Eisenhower Commission reports that although he was hired as General Counsel, "I did an awful lot of writing . . . and an awful lot of administering and rather little lawyering."[86] Campbell also indicates that an esprit de corps existed on the commission: "we had a good share of squabbles. . . . But we had a policy of openness. We didn't try to suppress research—quite the contrary. I think there was a spirit of collegiality and shared inquiry that was really very good."[87]

## Information evolution

An evolution of information occurs during the commission process. Information is gathered from a variety of sources and "gaps in information and understanding . . . [are]identified and new knowledge-generating processes [are] undertaken."[88] Thus, as this commission participant suggests, "as the work of the commission progressed, reformulation and refinement of its mandate took place continually."[89] Consultation may take place, on an informal basis, between staff and colleagues in their own fields and with cabinet personnel.[90] At least one high-level staff member reports that his commission's generation of information led to the discovery of facts "too embarrassing and difficult for the Commission to handle."[91]

Lipsky and Olson identify a problem which they see as having emerged during one portion of the Kerner Commission's development of information:

> the commission staff, driven by a need to impress the commissioners with the reliability of their findings, fashioned parts of the report by a process which we may call "incremental concretization." This involves the gradual adaptation and molding of initial analyses based on admittedly shaky data into increasingly "harder" analyses by ignoring the qualifications and caveats upon which the original investigations and conclusions were based, even though no new evidence is introduced to make the findings more reliable. . . . At the very least, incremental concretization results in the appearance of certitude when uncertainty better characterizes the state of knowledge.[92]

This implies the question of the quality of commission research, generally. Lipsky and Olson argue that there were scientific weaknesses in the Kerner research methods.[93] In addition, in at least one later study, a body of Kerner data was recalculated to show that rioters were among the least advantaged ("riff-raff") and not, as the commission had found, among the more socialized groups.[94] Perhaps the best known example of criticized research is the case of the Warren Commission, where large numbers of people continued to believe in a conspiracy theory after the commission's report was made. This was supported by a special House committee's reinvestigation of the Kennedy assassination, years later (see Chapter 7). Commission research is subject to time constraints. Protracted social scientific inquiry is difficult to conduct under commission work conditions and the resultant product may reflect hurried preparation. The fact is, however, that most commissions do not attempt to conduct too much original research. On occasion they have successfully stimulated original research, particularly through the use of surveys (see below). Yet they must rely largely on the work of experts in the field who have already engaged in relevant research or who can summarize the current state of knowledge in their area. The quality of much commission research, then, reflects the quality of research in the field. Some commission research is, no doubt, weakened by the pressure of time. However (again, with the possible exception of the Warren Commission), it has not been demonstrated that basic commission conclusions have been to any significant degree erroneous. Overall, the widespread acceptance of commission reports for use in classrooms, training programs, and administrative settings would seem to attest to the fundamental acceptability of the quality of the research which underlies commission reports.

The role of the staff is integral to the commission process; as John P. Roche has said, the staff provides continuity, "fills the vacuum."[95] Harry McPherson has observed: "The strongest force on the commissions that I knew—and I think it would probably be generally true—was the staff of the commission . . . they are giving pretty busy men the options."[96] This raises the question of the susceptibility of commissions to having their results dictated by ideologically zealous staff members. James Campbell suggests an alternate hypothesis:

> I think it's unlikely. I think that a lot of the unhappiness that some staff people express with commissions, or some academic people express with commisions, is that the commissions don't adopt their views *enough.* I'm not sure you can really have it both ways. I tend to think that the commissioners realize that they're the ones who are on the line and they're going to have to make up their own minds. I'm sure they're heavily influenced by what the staff puts in front of them. But they're also influenced by their constituencies. . . . So, there are a lot of different forces pulling on the commissioners.[97]

The contribution of social scientists to the generation of commission information seems to have a mixed record. In their study of the Kerner Commission, Lipsky and Olson suggest that, "Like the chef who sprinkles paprika on a dish, the social scientists on the team contributed color but little substance."[98] Two social scientists who participated in the work of two other commissions see things differently: "The list of social scientist consultants to the [Violence] Commission is impressive in both its quality and its length;"[99] "the Commission on Obscenity and Pornography, on all its levels, had more input from sociologists and other social scientists than any other commission in government history."[100]

The gathering of information by a commission, then, can suggest new avenues of inquiry, further define the commission's mandate, and begin to shape the commission's report. A discussion of some specific tools of information-gathering follows.

## Task forces and outside reports

Commissions appoint task forces and outside study groups and contract for special reports in order to meet specific informational needs. It may be that a particular incident requires an investigation too detailed for the commission staff to conduct efficiently. It may be that commissioners have specific needs for understanding which require further study. An example of the latter case occurred during the work of the Kerner Commission. When some commissioners expressed the view that Blacks should be able to advance in American society in the historical manner of other urban immigrants, sociologist Herbert Gans was asked to prepare an essay on the subject which became the basis for Chapter 6 of the commission's final report.[101]

A celebrated example of a contracted report emerged from the Violence Commission. The commission had, as one of its duties, responsibility for making an inquiry into the violence in Chicago during the 1968 Democratic National Convention. The commission contracted with Daniel Walker of Chicago for the study. Beginning with the FBI-trained staff of his Chicago Crime Commission, Walker constructed an investigative team of 90 full-time and 121 part-time interviewers and researchers.[102] Many of these persons were made available through law firms and banks, at no cost. Fully 3,437 statements were collected. Of these, 1,410 were taken by the Walker group and 2,017 were taken and supplied by the FBI. Other statements were supplied by the United States Attorney's office in Chicago and other sources. The interviews totaled 20,000 pages. In addition, the staff viewed 180 hours of motion picture film provided by television networks and stations, the Chicago Police Department, and private sources. More than 12,000 still photographs were examined. Official records of the National Guard and the police were reviewed. And, while they were not compiled as facts, journalistic accounts were considered. The Walker report, which caused considerable controversy with its condemnation of the behavior of the Chicago police, was completed in fifty-three days.

In addition to providing information, outside reports may serve political functions. They may be useful for exploring a subject deemed too sensitive for the commission to handle directly. Then, as one observer has remarked, "The task forces could publish their reports without acceptance or disavowal by the commission, and the public could draw its own conclusions about the validity of the task forces' material."[103] A different political function may be performed by the contributions of consultants from the academic, professional, and technical communities. Beyond any intellectual value their work may have for a commission, the very fact of the consultants' participation may be useful in mobilizing the support of specialized groups for the commission's recommendations.[104]

Occasionally, outside or task force reports may themselves be too hot for a commission to handle. The Violence Commission's Task Force on Group Violence, headed by Jerome Skolnick, produced a report to which the commission objected, both on ideological grounds, and because it was felt "the task force report presented an interpretation and a series of conclusions, instead of carrying out its assignment to provide the facts necessary to reach a conclusion."[105] The commission did not prevent publication of the report,[106] but it made little reference to it in its own final report.

The Kerner Commission experienced considerable difficulty with a staff report entitled "The Harvest of American Racism." Produced under great pressure and with less than totally scientific data, the report was rejected by staff superiors. This was followed by the demotion or dismissal of nearly 100 persons. Although portions of the report later appeared in the commission's final report, certain of its subjects—such as police provocation of riots and the beneficial results of riots—were not included.[107]

Task forces, consultants, and outside reports provide supplemental information for commission scrutiny, perform political functions and, on occasion, become issues themselves.

## Surveys

Some commissions deem survey research a necessary aspect of their investigations. In some instances this may represent original research. The Pornography Commission's largest study consisted of a national survey of 2,486 adults and 769 youths. The survey's intent was:

(1) to identify the amount, frequency, and circumstances of the

public's exposure to erotic materials; (2) to describe community standards and norms pertaining to distribution, consumption, and control of erotica; and (3) to collect other relevant data concerning the correlates of exposure to erotic materials.[108]

The survey's results indicated little support for a presumption of socially undesirable effects and majority sentiment in favor of unrestricted adult access to erotic materials.

The Commission on Law Enforcement and the Administration of Justice undertook original survey work. The commission's Task Force on Assessment of the Crime, in cooperation with the Office of Law Enforcement Assistance, contracted with the National Opinion Research Center for a national survey of unreported crime, the attitudes of victims and the general public toward crime and criminal justice, and self-defense measures. The Bureau of Social Science Research, in Washington, and the Michigan Survey Research Center received contracts to conduct studies of high-crime precincts in Washington, D.C., Chicago, and Boston. Another survey, conducted in cooperation with the National Council on Crime and Delinquency, developed information on the nation's correctional facilities and personnel. Finally, questionnaires regarding the effectiveness of field procedures in combating crime were sent to more than 2,200 police departments. These various surveys yielded data which had not previously been available.[109]

The survey, then, provides an additional tool for commissions in the development of specific types of information.

## Travel

Commission investigations may be facilitated by travel. This may involve staff alone or the commissisoners. Travel to areas of specific concern to a commission enables participants to examine conditions in a first-hand manner and gain insights perhaps otherwise unattainable. As the final report of the Douglas Commission on Urban Problems put it, "One has to see and touch and smell a slum before one fully appreciates the real urgency of the problem."[110] In addition, travel facilitates speed of procedure, which is significant in that investigations must often take place quickly, while memories are fresh.[111]

The Kerner Commission sent staff teams of six persons each to twenty cities. Upon arrival, these groups broke into teams of two, which conducted interviews with mayors, city officials, judges, residents of areas affected by disorders, community leaders, businessmen and labor leaders. Fully 1,200 interviews were conducted and a digestive report was made to the commission. Although this information was subjected to what Lipsky and Olson see as "incremental concretization" (see above), the commission noted that these investigations resulted in information regarding both the chronologies of various urban disorders and the tensions leading to them.[112]

In addition to this staff work, Kerner Commission Vice Chairman John V. Lindsay and Executive Director David Ginsburg made an unannounced visit to Newark. On the same day, commissioners Kerner, Peden, and Thornton made an unannounced visit to Detroit and commissioners Wilkins and Abel toured East Harlem and Bedford-Stuyvesant in New York City. Eight riot cities were surveyed in person by commission members.[113]

Law Enforcement Commission Associate Director Lloyd Ohlin reports that field observers from the commission rode with police and reported on citizen-police interactions. These observers also examined procedures in the lower criminal courts. Commission staff members met with a variety of people—groups of slum residents, professional criminals, ex-offenders—in an effort to construct a more complete picture of the criminal justice system and its impact.[114]

## Hearings

Perhaps one of the more visible aspects of commission work involves the holding of public hearings. Hearings serve a number of purposes, both informational and political, and represent yet another means by which commissioners become familiar with their subjects in a manner which may surpass examination of literature. Hearings may be open or closed. In addition, commissions may accept sworn written testimony.

Hearings are, first of all, intended to inform. To this end, the staff must decide "what kinds of witnesses representing what kinds of points of view will bring the most enlightened position with the greatest effect both on the commissioners and on the general public."[115] Witness lists may be compiled and "carefully balanced ideologically, although to the public this may not have appeared to be the case."[116] The commissioners are then presented with a variety of perspectives, viewpoints, and experiences which may, as much as anything, make clear the seriousness of the issues they are considering.

Numbers of witnesses and the subjects of their testimony are many and diverse. The Warren Commission notes that in closed hearings it heard direct testimony from 94 witnesses, that its legal staff heard from 395 others, and that 61 sworn affidavits were supplied along with two further statements.[117] In closed sessions, the Kerner Commission heard from mayors and their assistants, police and fire chiefs, leaders of human relations commissions, federal, state, and local officials and governors, ghetto residents, civil rights leaders, authors, journalists, sociologists, historians, psychologists, economists, officials of the Department of Justice and the FBI, army officers who commanded riot control forces, and academic and police experts in police-community relations. During twenty days of hearings, from August to November 1967, the commission heard from over 130 witnesses.[118] The hearings covered: Black history; employment and ghetto conditions; police-community tensions and community relations; action programs and citizen participation; manpower and job training; the employment service and ghetto employment; the role of business and labor; rural-urban migration; education, youth, welfare and consumer protection problems and programs; the ghetto family; and the administration of justice during civil disorders.[119]

The Pornography Commission concluded that, at least during the early portions of its work, public hearings were not likely to produce much accurate data or to be a wise expenditure of the commission's limited resources.[120] The commission used, instead, what might be termed the "indirect hearing" whereby nearly 100 national organizations were invited to submit written statements of their views on obscenity and pornography. In addition, the commission asked for the views of those in law enforcement, experts in constitutional law, and the legal profession in general.[121] Public hearings were held, eventually, in Los Angeles and Washington, D.C. Fifty-five witnesses were invited, representing law enforcement agencies, courts, government at many levels, civic organizations, writers, publishers, distributors, film producers, exhibitors, actors, librarians, teachers, youth organizations, parents and other interested groups.[122] Thirty-one persons accepted. The commission heard, in addition, the statements of a number of private citizens in attendance at the hearings.[123] Commissioner Otto Larsen feels that in this particular case hearings did not reveal much that was new to the commission: "the four-day forum was at least an interesting review of arguments, all of which had been revealed in reviews of the literature or in earlier discussions."[124]

In a series of hearings and conferences, the Commission on the Causes and Prevention of Violence heard the testimony of "more than 150 public officials, scholars, educators, religious leaders and private citizens from media executives to young students."[125] Fully six days were devoted to hearings on mass media.[126]

It would seem clear, then, that the holding of public hearings can provide commissioners with substantial exposure to perspectives on their subjects of inquiry. James S. Campbell, of the Violence Commission, has compared the commission investigative process to "a very intensive course of study."[127] And Frank Popper suggests: "there is general agreement, even among commissioners, that hearings inform commissioners so that, by the time the report is being written, their knowledge of the commission's subject is often comparable to the staff's."[128]

Beyond factual and statistical education, however, there is another aspect to the learning which may take place during hearings. This involves the sheer drama of poignant statements or incidents. The effects of such events can be significant. Executive Director Howard Shuman has discussed the particular effects of hearings on members of the Douglas Commission on Urban Problems:

> Among the best things the Commission did was to hold hearings in the ghettos of the major cities of the country. . . . The best testimony received was from the ordinary citizens. It had a fire and a spirit which was unmatched by the experts we heard. . . . The hearings and inspections provided a common experience for the members of our commission and united them as no other action could have done.[129]

Jerome Skolnick agrees with this potential of hearings: "Commissioners are used to hearings, are used to testimony and probably cannot be moved in any new direction unless emotionally engaged. Commissioners are culturally deprived by the privatized life of the man of power."[130] Lipsky and Olson, in their examination of the Kerner Commission, suggest that "Witnesses with dramatic testimony were particularly instrumental in creating a sense of commission urgency."[131]

At times, the object of attention may become a commissioner, as much as a witness. During hearings held by the Eisenhower Commission, an angry exchange erupted between a black witness and Commissioner Eric Hoffer. Jerome Skolnick reports the result:

> That day, I think it is fair to say, was the most emotional day of the hearings for the Violence Commission. Eric Hoffer was an exemplary witness for the depth of racism existing in this country. No wealth of statistics could have conveyed as well to the other commissioners and to the public in general what racism meant to the black man.[132]

In a lighter vein, Skolnick's observation that "Hearings are a form of theater"[133] was perhaps supported by an incident during Pornography Commission hearings in which a vehement anti-censorship witness placed a cheese pie in Commissioner Otto Larsen's face.[134]

Hearings may serve political functions. They may be useful in reassuring various groups that their views will be heard, that they will be "given their day in court."[135] Further, hearings may help a commission establish its legitimacy. In this regard, Martha Derthick observes that members of the Scranton Commission "knew that by making hearings open, whatever value they might have as sources of information would be lost," but that the commission "held public hearings in order to demonstrate that it would listen to diverse opinions."[136]

Hearings are a method of information-gathering for commissions. They may provide statistical as well as qualitative enlightenment for commissioners. They may serve political functions in terms of providing a forum for representation of group opinions and in terms of helping to establish commission legitimacy.

## Conferences

Commissions may sponsor conferences on specific aspects of their topics. This investigative tool can not only provide information, it can involve in the commission's work various groups, professionals, and officials who may have some opportunity for acting on commission recommendations.

The Commission on Law Enforcement and the Administration of Justice sponsored conferences on riots and riot control, correctional standards, mentally disordered offenders, plea bargaining, the federal role in crime control, and the legal manpower problems of the criminal system. Scientists and businessmen were brought together, in another conference, to consider cooperative measures against crime. In response to a presidential request, many governors established state committees for the reform of state laws and criminal systems. Representatives of these committees attended a commission-sponsored conference in October 1966. In a related effort, the commission's staff consulted with state and local criminal justice personnel to collect information on the functioning of the state and local systems and to judge the ways in which commission recommendations would be likely to affect them.[137]

The Kerner Commission, also, made profitable use of a conference and stimulated others. In November 1968, representatives of the media industry attended a commision-sponsored conference in Poughkeepsie, New York. The commission's final report contained a recommendation from the conference that the black community receive greater media coverage during "normal" periods. The recommendation was widely adopted. In addition, in response to commission suggestions, the Justice Department held conferences for police administrators on riot-control techniques. When riots erupted after the assassination of Martin Luther King, Jr., these latter conferences were given credit for having limited the loss of life.[138]

## Commissioner growth

An aspect of the commission process which is rarely if ever mentioned in the literature, yet which would seem of fundamental importance, is a collegial intellectual growth among commissioners. More than one high-level commission participant has reported that during the commission work members may go through a process of learning which leads to their advocacy of positions they would once have opposed. Coupled with this may be an esprit de corps which unites the commissioners with a sense of common purpose.

The explanation most frequently offered for this phenomenon is that exposure to facts dispels preconceptions. The commissioners study a situation in depth, and "people's views *do change* as a result of that."[139] Dr. Milton Eisenhower, whose Violence Commission propounded eighty-one recommendations, nearly all of which were unanimously agreed upon, said later: "I want to tell you it was a revelation to me . . . We freed our minds of all preconceptions. When we started we couldn't have agreed on anything."[140] Governor Raymond Shafer has said: "We had a *real* esprit de corps on our commission," and maintains that it was a diverse group which produced the unanimous report of the Commission on Marijuana and Drug Abuse.[141] Associate Director Lloyd Ohlin has discussed how this process evolved on the Commission on Law Enforcement, a group not given a radical mandate:

> I have encountered a conspiratorial explanation of how Commissions are formulated and their activities directed toward certain predetermined ends. My own experiences and observations of the Crime Commission were quite different. Many of the participants held strong views about particular problems of crime and criminal justice and how they should be dealt with. However, no one that I knew held a clearly formulated agenda of either problems or recommendations for the Commission in its early days. Instead, there emerged informal groupings of persons who shared similar, but non-specific ideological views . . . these informal ideological factions generated strong motivation to produce persuasive factual and theoretical support for the arguments and recommendations proposed to the full Commission. . . . Commission members became articulate spokesmen and advocates for their task force recommendations before the full Commission. Other Commission members, unable to dig as deeply into the background data and theories on which these recommendations rested, were inclined to defer to those Commission members who had done so. Task force staff were therefore encouraged to involve sympathetic Commission members in their work, especially those likely to be most persuasive as advocates of their recommendations. As a consequence, this process led to far more liberal recommendations by the Commission than one would have thought possible at the outset, given the conservative cast of its membership. For many Commission and staff members, the task force work was a general learning experience, bringing together issues, facts, and theories in a systematic

way to address problems which they had not been forced to consider in such depth before. Many of them became advocates of policies that they might not have thought feasible at the beginning.[142]

Martha Derthick, a member of the Scranton Commission, feels that progressive results are more the result of presidential appointments, organizational imperatives, and "intensive exposure to a social condition or an alarming set of events."[143] The evidence suggests, however, that commission service offers many commissioners a genuine learning experience which may significantly alter their perceptions.

This phenomenon, it might be added, may add legitimacy to commission reports. As Amitai Etzioni has put it, "If 10 wise men drawn from such a cross-section of the nation support a set of conclusions, the country is more likely to go along with them than if these conclusions are advocated by 10 experts."[144]

At least on some commissions, then, a process of intellectual growth may lead commissioners to new and common positions on issues on which they might never have previously agreed. This may be stimulated by strong advocacy, deference to expertise, or organizational pressures. More often, it would seem, commissioners' views evolve because of in-depth exposure to facts.

## Difficulties

Commissions may encounter special difficulties during the course of their work beyond the normal pressures of deadlines and personality clashes that may attend any organized undertaking. One difficulty consists in what Michael Lipsky and David J. Olson have termed "competing for legitimacy."[145] This involves the fact that, while a presidential commission may be the most prestigious or highly visible group examining an issue, it may not be the only one doing so. During the Kerner Commission investigation, for example, the Senate Permanent Subcommittee on Investigations, of the Committee on Government Operations (McClellan Committee), conducted a riot investigation of its own, with the aim of substantiating the views that conspiracy lay behind urban riots. Although the committee and the commission formally agreed to cooperate, the "aggressive and abrasive" investigators of the McClellan Committee "sometimes made it difficult for Kerner field researchers to win the confidence of informants, who had difficulty distinguishing between the two investigative bodies."[146]

Another difficulty for commissions regards funding of commission activities. Haphazard and unpredictable appropriations processes afflicted many of the commissions under study. The testimony and observations of a number of commission participants illustrate the nature of the problem:

> Judge Kerner. One area that I think took up too much of the staff's time and frankly too much of my time when we considered what our major purpose was—financing. There was hope at the time that we would have an appropriation. This was discarded. So that actually we begged and borrowed from Presidential funds . . .
> Senator Kennedy. Didn't you have some idea prior to the time the Commission was set up that you would be able to receive funding and financing for the Commission?
> Judge Kerner. No; I am afraid we did not.[147]

> the [Kerner] commission cost several millions of dollars—"You'll never know how much," [Executive Director David] Ginsburg said . . .[148]

> Mr. Scranton. . . . When I first went to the White House . . . I asked how much money we would have. And, at that time, they said they didn't know.
>
> After considerable deliberation, I said to them, I will try to do this job in the period of time you have given us, and I would like to keep the amount under a million dollars.
>
> And they indicated to me that if I could do that, that would be satisfactory.
>
> And then shortly thereafter, we were able to obtain, first, $500,000 from HEW, which was the first appropriation they gave us, and then another commitment of close to $200,000. And, . . . the Commission financed its work with, I believe, a total fund of $685,000, which I think was an alltime low. And it did all come from HEW.[149]

> Mr. Cutler. [Executive Director, Violence Commission] . . . When the President created our commission, he went to Congress forthwith to obtain the subpena power for the commission . . . He did not initially request congressional appropriations for us, thinking that he could find the money within various executive branch ap-

propriations already made. . . . In the beginning . . . we had a budget approved by the Budget Bureau and cleared by the President. The White House staff then attempted to obtain block grants of that money from various executive branch agencies such as HEW, Department of Justice, et cetera, and they did obtain a certain amount in that manner out of funds that had already been appropriated to them for work in fields that were related to our work. Ultimately it became necessary because of the budget constraints on each agency for the President to seek an additional appropriation . . . So, some of our budgeted funds were eventually covered by a direct congressional appropriation to HEW with the legislative history making clear that the money was intended for us.

Mr. Clesner. [Subcommittee Counsel] What you are really saying, it might have been wiser when he asked for subpena powers to have asked—

Mr. Cutler. To get money as well.[150]

Not all commissions have faced this problem and, indeed, all the commissions were able to complete their work. It goes without saying, however, that some efficiency is probably sacrificed if a commission must spend appreciable amounts of energy seeking funds, or if it must conduct its investigation amidst financial uncertainty. (Funding procedures for commissions were reformed with passage of the Federal Advisory Committee Act of 1972. See Chapter 6.)

The commission investigative process involves a variety of procedural steps and options designed to facilitate the collection and processing of information. The commission itself must be officially established. Members must be appointed, along with top staff personnel. The bulk of the staff must be hired. Key organizational decisions must be made regarding definition of the commission's task and delineation of study groups, if any, and task forces. Decisions and actions must be taken regarding the utility of investigative tools such as contracted research, surveys, travel, hearings, and conferences.

The commission must work against a deadline and may encounter intra-staff conflicts, competition for legitimacy in the interpretation of events, or financial difficulties. Nonetheless, the investigation proceeds and, often, a process of intellectual growth may stimulate commissioners to abandon preconceptions and entertain new ideas about their subject of inquiry.

Once the investigative steps have been completed, the commission is ready to write and release its report.

# 4

# THE REPORT

As America gets worse and worse, its reports get better and better.

—Murray Kempton[1]

The raison d'etre of the presidential commission is the production of a report which includes investigative findings and recommendations for action. In pursuit of this goal the various elements of the commission are to have harvested as much evidence as possible, sifted and processed it, and brought it to the full commission for consideration. Ideally, the commission will follow Lyndon Johnson's philosophical entreaty to the Kerner Commission: "Let your search be free. Let it be untrammeled by what has been called the 'conventional wisdom.' As best you can, find the truth, the whole truth, and express it in your report."[2] This chapter will examine the process by which commission reports are written, full commission meetings, the release of reports, and some of the forces and considerations that come into play at various points in the process.

## Interim Reports

Commissions may issue interim reports. This was done in one form or another by the Kerner Commission, the Eisenhower Commission on Violence, the Shafer Commission on Marijuana, and the Commission on Population Growth. Interim reports may be isued in response to legislative or presidential directives or as a strategic move by the commissions themselves to gain attention.

The Kerner Commission sent public letters regarding riot control to President Johnson and other officials during the course of its study. Ironically, although the commission's final report focused on social programs and reform, Frank Popper feels that the recommendations described in the four public letters were the only ones which Presidents Johnson and Nixon sought to adopt. Popper reports that some members of the commission came to regret having released the prearranged letters, feeling that "their desire for publicity led them to be manipulated by the White House" while the latter appeared to be responding to the commission in a significant way.[3]

The Violence Commission deliberately issued its Walker Report on the 1968 Democratic National Convention in Chicago—thereby invoking presidential displeasure—"in order to establish their credibility with anti-Johnson and anti-Nixon groups."[4] This was considered a successful maneuver to the extent that subsequent commission activities were well-publicized. One commission staff member is quoted as saying, "The Walker Report put us in business."[5] In addition, the Violence Commission issued a progress report to President Johnson after six months of work.

Both the Commission on Marijuana and Drug Abuse and the Commission on Population Growth issued interim reports after one year of work, in accordance with their legislative mandates.

## Full Commission Meetings and the Preparation of the Report

As bodies, commissions do not meet very often. During a lifetime of two years, the Commission on Law Enforcement and the Administration of Justice met but seven times, for two or three full days at a time.[6] The Kerner Commission met for forty-four days in the course of its eight-month existence.[7] In apparent contrast, a staff member of the Scranton Commission on Campus Unrest has noted that "The Scranton Commission" may very well be the hardest-working commission ever to carry out a presidential mission of this kind;" the Commission's 361-page report having been produced in ten weeks of "night-and-day activity."[8]

The reason so few hours, proportionately, are spent on full commission meetings consists in the fact that the bulk of the research is done by the staffs. Further, as the commissions are sometimes divided into study areas, presided over by a portion of the commissioners who conduct their own efforts before reporting to the commission as a whole, the need for full commission meetings prior to the writing of the final report is lessened. Cooperation is also facilitated by correspondence and the fact that various reports and related materials are made available to all commissioners before, or during, full commission meetings for deliberation before any decisions are made.[9]

### "Taking a stand" and the desire for unanimity

The full commission meets for purposes of initiating its work, conducting hearings, and compiling its report. It is at the report stage, in particular, that problems may arise in connection with "the fact that commissioners must begin to take stands on matters of public policy."[10] In addition, mistrust may develop between the commissioners and the staff.[11] At this point, accommodation and compromise must take place or the commission may fragment beyond repair. Frequently, it is at this point that a competent chairman may become of value in calling forth more temperate rhetoric and positions from the various "sides" that may have developed around an issue. Associate Director Lloyd Ohlin reports that, on the Commission on Law Enforcement:

> The process of communication among Commission and staff members was designed to forestall the development of sharply conflicting positions and to achieve a compromise position wherever possible. The chairman showed considerable ingenuity and talent in his capacity to search out and negotiate compromise positions when serious conflicts developed. He was greatly assisted in this at both the Commission and staff levels by the executive and deputy directors of the Commission.[12]

An alternative strategy for avoiding intra-commission policy conflict was pursued by the Pornography Commission. The commission chose to defer all policy discussions until the very end of its work, the entire commission pursuing policy only during an intensive two-day session. Calm was maintained, but at the price of the commission's lacking a policy research theory to guide its work.[13] Consequently, an opportunity may have been lost to link research to policy more effectively, although the divisions within the commission would appear to have been largely irreconcilable.

Conflict on commissions may be restrained by a desire for unanimity growing out of the belief that a united front conveys more legitimacy than does a fragmented one. Martha Derthick feels this is the fundamental goal of the commission, as an organization; indeed, that it surpasses even the search for accuracy.[14] Ohlin maintains that the desire for unanimity on the Commission on Law Enforcement not only limited conflict but permitted maximum expression of the liberal sentiments of some commissioners and staff members, as well.[15] Frank Popper suggests that, since commissions operate by consensus, differences can nearly always be obscured.[16] Presidential Consultant John Roche goes further and suggests that unanimity is often the product of a lack of motivation to write dissents on the part of those in disagreement with majority findings.[17]

Cooperation may be facilitated further by a variation of a practice employed elsewhere in the conduct of government: deference to expertise. In debate, those with career interests in the area under discussion may be accorded the deference of their fellow commissioners.[18] This may also, it could be argued, increase the likelihood that commission findings in this area may be more acceptable to affected groups.

Finally, we must refer again to the phenomenon of commissioner growth, discussed in Chapter 3, as an aid to cooperation during full commission meetings. Violence Commission General Counsel James Campbell has discussed this in some detail:

> People subject their ideas to group scrutiny and discussion and people begin to understand *other* peoples' points of view. I think that individuals change and moderate their views in the course of this process; it's a tremendous education . . . the commissioners are intended to be persons who deliberate. They are not executives, to try and accomplish something; they're not set up to run a program or to "get from here to there." They're just supposed to think about problems and come up with ideas and recommendations. . . . They can move from those [constituency] ties or from where they are on a particular issue and come to another position based on a better understanding and a better appreciation of other peoples' points of view. It's really a process of education and I think that people's attitudes do change as a result of education. This is just a particularly intense form of education, directed to certain areas for these people.[19]

This process can be aided by privacy during commission meetings. The thoughts of Clarence Randall, chairman of the Commission on Foreign Economic Policy which made its report in 1954, offer interesting insights into the role of confidentiality:

> He [Randall] believed that in truly private discussion men would be honest and that, in being honest, they could not help but reach liberal conclusions on the nation's interest. He saw his problem not as one of political bargaining but one of group dynamics.[20]

Although not every chairman may seek liberal conclusions, the facilitation of free discussion may be a more widespread goal.

## Choosing an audience

A key decision commissions must make during the report-writing stage involves the question of at whom the report should be aimed. Who will be the primary audience or audiences for the commission's work? Of course, the report will go to the President and Congress. But this decision raises questions of strategies for implementation, basic commission purpose, and levels of technicality.

The Kerner Commission chose two basic groups as audiences for its message: the white middle class and American blacks. Former Senator Fred Harris, a member of the commission, explained the sentiment behind the choice of the first audience: "We wrote it [the report] in plain language. We aimed it at the American people. It was they, we felt, who must decide to act. We hoped they would be able to see through our eyes what we had seen."[21] With regard to the second audience, Lipsky and Olson report it was felt that "the country's black population . . . needed reassurance that American political institutions had not abandoned them."[22]

Commissioner Martha Derthick suggests that the Scranton Commission on Campus Unrest "tended to conceive of its own effectiveness as the ability to evoke action—that is, to get holders of power to do what it prescribed about campus unrest."[23] This strategy involved reaching the President through "a manifesto to the press and public."[24]

Staff reports, as well, may be written with audiences in mind. Jerome Skolnick, who led staff preparation of *The Politics of Protest* for the Eisenhower Commission on Violence, reports that the staff sought to reach three audiences:

> First, we were concerned with trying to persuade the commissioners of the validity of our findings and the validity of our analysis. They were our primary audience. Our second was the general public, an audience we had little confidence in being able to influence except, perhaps, through persuading the commissioners. Most reports have a limited readership—and *The Politics of Protest* isn't exactly *The Love Machine.* So our third audience was the academic community and the media representatives. In the long run, the university had to be our major audience, since the report is scholarly and the media treated with publication as news, quickly displaced by other stories.[25]

A point raised by these examples is the fact that although commissions are, for the most part, presidential creations they do not necessarily perceive themselves as speaking only to the President, nor do they see things only from his perspective. While it is possible this may decrease the likelihood of favorable presidential consideration of commission findings, it nonetheless suggests commissions enjoy considerable freedom of inquiry. James Campbell has discussed this difference in perspective:

> people on a study commission, and particularly one where the individuals are not saying "I hereby order that an extra billion dollars be spent on this," . . . are merely saying, to the President or somebody else, "You know, we think you really ought to consider seriously spending this. Now, we understand that maybe you're fighting a war in Southeast Asia and you can't do this. But, looking at it from the way *we* look at it, we think you ought to consider that." So, there's a kind of detachment about it which . . . enables the individual to step back a little bit from his environment that he comes from and be a little more objective about it.[26]

Commissions, then, run the risk of sacrificing implementation for the sake of objectivity.

## Questions of pressure and emphasis

Determining an audience is but one aspect of preparation of the written report. During the final stages of commission work participants move into "high gear" and lawyers' capabilities are called upon: "the ability to work all day and night, the capacity to absorb endless criticism without taking personal affront, and the ability to synthesize the sentiments of the commissioners, or to anticipate their sentiments regarding various issues."[27] Commissioners and staff members are involved in the last-minute gathering of information, meetings, writing, and editorial decision making.

At this stage there may be some communication with the White House regarding the direction the report is likely to take. David Ginsburg, Executive Director of the Kerner Commission, is said to have "discussed aspects of the *Report* with key members of the cabinet. In some cases the document was altered to accommodate their suggestions."[28] Also, with regard to the Kerner Commission, Harry McPherson reports:

> there were a lot of messages communicated, usually to the chairman and the executive director. . . . I know Joe Califano spent an awful lot of time with Kerner and with John Lindsay and with David Ginsburg . . . and I think he was passing a lot of word from Johnson. Johnson recognized, I think, (he didn't like it, but he recognized) that these things were going to be to a large extent independent of him and that they would make their own recommendations. But he didn't want crazy things said and he hoped that they would try to stop it.[29]

McPherson does not feel the commission's report was politically dictated.[30] Indeed, as will be discussed later, Johnson was more than a little displeased with the Kerner report.

Similar pressures may appear with regard to the staff. Again, in the case of the Kerner Commission, the staff developed last-minute fears of a conservative interpretation of the data. Leaks to the press led to commission denials. The final report's generally progressive bent put staff fears to rest but suggested that the staff's actions at a critical time may have helped the direction of the report.[31]

It is also possible, however, that such actions do not substantially affect results. Commissioners are subject to numerous cross-pressures and influences—from the commission staff, their constituencies, their preconceptions, the President, the data. As a result, the truth regarding commission results may be as James Campbell has said: "I think they're politically *influenced,* but I don't think they're dictated.

That's one of the reasons commissioners are not captives of their staffs."[32]

The final writing of the report involves obtaining agreement from commission members on exactly what, in light of the information gathered, is to be said. It involves, as well, decisions regarding tenor of language, specificity in making charges of responsibility for the situations under examination, and the appropriateness of relying on attention-getting phraseology. These decisions are important in that they may affect reception of the report by those in positions of authority and by the public. Although commissioners do enjoy considerable freedom of inquiry, they may find themselves in the position of "having to deal critically with the behavior of the political executives upon whom they are at least partially dependent for the implementation of their recommendations."[33]

Reports from the Kerner Commission experience indicate how a number of these kinds of questions may be resolved. The commission chose to use strong language, indicting "white racism," to ensure its being heard. This was perceived as being particularly effective since, as Tom Wicker wrote,

> just as it sometimes takes a hawk to settle a war—Eisenhower in Korea, deGaulle in Algeria—so did it take bona fide moderates to validate the case that had to be made. A commission made up of militants, or even influenced by them, could not conceivably have spoken with a voice so effective, so sure to be heard in white, moderate, responsible America.[34]

Yet, in order to not preclude the possibility of implementation of its recommendations, the commission avoided specific "fingerpointing" at culpable institutions. Such specificity might also have damaged commission unity. Thus, as Lipsky and Olson put it, "criticism of past performances were apparently avoided in the hope that future positive commitments might be forthcoming."[35]

The Kerner Commission's use of key phrases, such as "white racism," was seen as "sensational, assuring a maximum impact for the commission's labors."[36] Other commissions, however, felt that this strategy would ultimately sacrifice comprehensive consideration of their results. To avoid narrowly focused publicity and to ensure a maximum likelihood of implementation, the Commission on Law Enforcement went so far as to consciously avoid certain emotionally charged issues, e.g. marijuana use, capital punishment, wiretapping. "It was repeatedly stressed," writes Associate Director Lloyd Ohlin,

> that the entire work of the Commission would be lost if public attention at the time of publication of the report were focused on these emotional issues, with the conflicting opinions being expressed. Although all such loaded issues were discussed sometimes at great length and with great conviction, they were seen as basically unresolvable within the mandate of the Commission, and they were passed on for further discussion and ultimate resolution by other groups, such as Congress or state and local governments.[37]

The Violence Commission, writes Co-Director of Research James F. Short, "deliberately sought to avoid identification of the Commission position with catch phrases such as the 'white racism' label which so dominated the public image of the Kerner Commission."[38] The Commission on Population Growth did not skirt issues but "divided publication of its report into three sections . . . in order to prevent the resulting publicity from focusing exclusively on the abortion issues."[39] Derthick reports, however, that within the Commission on Campus Unrest "one argument against moderate, restrained language was that it would make the report seem a step backward from that of the Kerner Commission."[40] While Derthick perceives an organizational need for reliance on "crisis rhetoric,"[41] there would seem to be considerable variance in the determinations commissions make regarding language use.

Each commission must make its own judgments as to how it might best be heard, be considered, be implemented. The resultant decisions involve questions of what to emphasize, how specifically the report's key points should be made, and what kinds of words will most effectively convey what the commission has learned. These decisions are made within a context of cross-pressures which help shape the report but, to some degree, contribute to the maintenance of commission independence.

## Preparing the report

The actual writing of commission reports is, like so many other aspects of the commission process, a collective undertaking. Early drafts may be prepared by the staff for ultimate consideration and approval by the commissioners. Consultant reports may become the bases for chapters. Contrary to the common notion, the commissioners themselves may be substantially involved in both writing and editing. Much of the report of the Commission on Marijuana and Drug Abuse was written by the commissioners, including Chairman Shafer.[42] Milton Eisenhower reviewed and edited the report of the Violence Commission in its entirety and contributed original writing.[43]

The staff reports, field reports, consultant papers, and hearings testimony, together with the impressions the commissioners have received during the course of the commission's investigation, are combined for final distillation into a report. Draft sections are presented or read to the commissioners. In the case of the Shafer Commission on Marijuana, drafts were sent to authorities for examination and suggestions.[44]

Of course, objections arise at this point, as commissioners come to grips with the necessity of interpreting data and taking stands on policy. One observer suggests that it is at this stage that:

> swing members, the ones with open minds and without ideological preconceptions, assert themselves. They make worthwhile, influential suggestions about the drafts. Apparently vulnerable people like women and clergymen can pull a lot of weight here.[45]

The Kerner Commission deferred policy discussions until the final stages of its work. Executive Director David Ginsburg then read drafts of the commission report aloud to the commission:

> Only in this way, he felt, could he obtain the signatures of all the commissioners. Where obvious conflicts arose, the staff could try to resolve them. But when commissioners expressed only vague feelings of uneasiness they had to be specific if their complaints were to be accommodated. . . . Unable to mount specific criticisms, commissioners with doubts remaining signed the *Report*.[46]

A similar strategy was used, at one point, by a motivated group within the commission. It has been reported that Commissioner John V. Lindsay and his staff felt the language of the draft commission report was not sufficiently pointed. Consequently, a hastily prepared summary was presented to the commission by Lindsay along with an indication that, if it was not included, Lindsay might well release it independently. The commission, lacking an alternative document, accepted the summary. Although the summary did not alter the facts of the report, it did focus attention on the "white racism" concept and, in all likelihood, increased the visibility of the final report.[47]

Commissions, then, may pursue strategies designed to limit last-minute conflict, but motivated participants may influence the report even as it is being written. In some cases, no strategy is sufficient to quell implacable dissent and commissions are forced to issue their reports without the imprimatur of unanimity.

## Concurrence, dissent, and minority reports

Despite myriad and continuing efforts at avoiding disunity throughout the commission process, preparation of the final report requires that commissioners take a stand on the situation they have investigated. Although, as has been seen, many commissioners revise their views once they have been exposed to new facts, arguments, and perspectives, some commissioners feel they must supplement the final report with a statement of concurrence, with qualifications, or with a proclamation of outright dissent. The Katzenbach Commission on Law Enforcement acknowledged this reality when it stated:

> While the members of the Commission have considered carefully the entire report, this does not necessarily mean that there is complete agreement with every detail of each recommendation or statement. Except where otherwise noted, however, there is agreement with the substance of every important conclusion and recommendation. The nature of the general agreement and the extent of incidental disagreement are those to be expected when members of a Commission individually have given serious thought to a major and complex problem, have sought to achieve a joint resolution in furtherance of the Commission's task as a deliberative body.[48]

Some commissions, of course, are more successful in this regard than others. The Kerner Commission, for example, despite all the pressures, deadlines, and politicking experienced during its lifetime, produced a unanimous report without supplementary statements. The Eisenhower Commission on Violence made fully eighty-one recommendations, all but two of which were unanimously supported.

In fact, of the eight major commissions under study, only three—the Commission on Law Enforcement, the Commission on Population Growth, and the Pornography Commission—contained supplementary statements. In the case of the Commission on Population Growth, eleven of the twenty-four commissioners appended separate statements on various aspects of the questions of population growth and control. Three separate statements were attached to the report of the Commission on Law Enforcement, although they were designed not so much to criticize the commission's findings as they were to suggest that the commission could have pursued some questions further.

The archetype for commission dissent is found, of course, in the experience of the Commission on Obscenity and Pornography. As was discussed in Chapter 3, the Pornography Commission knew, long before it began writing its report, that there were those among the commission membership who would be satisfied with only one finding, chief among these individuals being Charles Keating. This expectation was not disappointed.

Because of the nature of its subject, the commission decided not to seek the kind of united front often sought by other commissions. As Chairman William Lockhart said, later:

> We deliberately did not seek to water down our recommendations in order to try to arrive at a consensus. It seemed to us that for the purpose of clarifying the issues it was better to let our divisions stand as it was.[49]

And stand they did. Keating, in his efforts at subverting the commission, disrupted commission procedure and leaked material to the press. The final report was supported by twelve of the eighteen commissioners; two other commissioners, although voting against the majority report, accepted the bulk of its findings.[50] Eight separate statements were attached to the report, two of which comprised the bulk of dissent. These latter two, written by Commissioners Hill and Link, and Commissioner Keating, took up fully 244 of the report's 700 pages (commercial edition). Keating's statement itself, including "exhibits," required 122 pages. Its prose must be read to be appreciated, but a few excerpts may serve to suggest its tenor:

> laws prohibiting obscenity and pornography have played an important role in the creativity and excellence of our system and our

society . . . Accordingly, it seems incredible to this writer that the majority . . . opts for a "Danish" solution to the problem of pornography; namely, to remove the controls—to repeal the law. The shocking and anarchistic recommendation of the majority is difficult to comprehend. . . . If courts are to merit the confidence of our citizens, it can no longer be pretended that four-letter-word substitutes for fecal matter and copulation are not obscene merely by veiling them with such hocus-pocus phrasing as "redeeming social value" and the like. . . . What is rotten in Denmark is already positively putrid in this country—and all this only in anticipation of the release of the soft-line Majority Report! . . . I can only comment that if the majority . . . has its way . . . we will witness complete moral anarchy in this country that will soon spread to the entire free world.[51]

Truly, the Keating dissent represents one of the more colorful documents ever released by the United States government. The Keating experience does suggest, however, the lengths to which commission dissent may be carried and the amount of disruption one determined commissioner may cause.

## Final compilation

A commission's findings are supplemented by recommendations. Commissions may be specific in their recommendations regarding agencies and institutions, policies and procedures. Other recommendations may be more general and call for changes in attitudes, directions, and priorities.

Staff, task force, and consultant reports may be included in the final report. In addition, appendices may supply information regarding research, methodology, and statistics related to the commission's findings. Also included may be legislative and executive documents concerning the commission.

The combined findings, recommendations, separate statements, staff and consultant reports, and appendices comprise the final report of the presidential commission.

## Releasing the report

Standard procedure for the release of a commission report involves a presentation of the report by the chairman and other commission members to the President at the White House. Presentations may also be made to the President of the Senate and the Speaker of the House of Representatives. Frequently, a press conference is held in conjunction with the presentation to the President, at which point the report is released to the public and the press (although the press may receive advance copies). All finished materials are submitted to the National Archives.

Beyond this "standard procedure," however, are questions of strategy, politics, and public relations. Commissions, beyond their search for information, are interested in being heard. Accordingly, although their resources are limited and their existence is subject to a limited time frame, commisions may seek methods which will maximize the attention their reports receive.

The timing of the release of a report may be particularly important. The top staff personnel of the Kerner Commission, for example, determined that an early release of the commission's final report (ahead of the scheduled deadline) was vital if it was to have any chance of helping avert new summer urban riots in 1968.[52] Further, release of the report during the beginning of the 1968 presidential campaign might have meant it could have been used against President Johnson by his political opponents (Johnson was, at this point, still considered a candidate for re-election), hardly a situation designed for rational consideration of the commission report.[53]

Different commissions devise different strategies for "being heard." The Katzenbach Commission on Law Enforcement set up, among others, a task force whose job it was to develop "strategies for implementation of Commission recommendations."[54] Aware of its own mortality and the fact that its recommendations had to be implemented by others, the commission sponsored conferences and awarded grants of $25,000 for the staffing of state planning committees. Over half the states developed such agencies and their representatives attended a conference in Washington, D.C., at which the President spoke.[55] "The involvement of so many practitioners in the Commission's study," Deputy Director Henry Ruth wrote later, "created a base of experts who understood and for the most part advocated the Commission's recommendations."[56] Further, funds were allocated for distribution of 100,000 copies of the commission's various reports to relevant agencies, officials, and groups, including all members of Congress and the state legislatures, police, correctional agencies and courts, members of concerned professional and academic groups, scholars and educators, governors, mayors, and city managers, and businessmen and community leaders.[57]

The Kerner Commission concerned itself with public relations and with maximizing its impact for some time, prior to release of its final report. Recommendations were discussed, as they developed, with executive branch departments. Regular contact was maintained with the presidential staff and a typescript copy of the report was sent to the White House as soon as it was available.[58] Lipsky and Olson conclude that, at least in the case of this commission, "Attempts had been made to tailor the report to presidential needs."[59] The Commission was equally diligent in the area of public relations. Executive Director Ginsburg briefed the three commercial television networks a week prior to release of the final report. Members of the black press, with whom meetings had been held during the commission's deliberations, were also briefed. Assistance was provided to the Public Broadcasting Laboratory of the National Educational Television network, which was preparing a documentary based on the commission's work. In the interest of rapid publication and distribution of the final report, paperback book publishers were considered. Bantam Books was chosen over two other publishers because of its experience with the report of the Warren Commission.[60]

Commissioner Martha Derthick reports that the Scranton Commission saw establishment of "credibility" as its primary public relations goal. During a period of low governmental credibility and, particularly, presidential credibility, the commission sought to demonstrate "openness to all points of view; independence, in principle of any outside influence, in practice of the administration specifically; and objectivity."[61] At the conclusion of its work, copies of the commission's reports on the Kent State and Jackson State killings were sent to relevant federal government officials. These were accompanied by a letter offering consultation by the Executive Director or other commission participants.[62]

The Eisenhower Commission adopted a strategy geared toward elongating the period during which it might normally have expected to receive attention. As each chapter of the commission's report was finished, as well as each task force report, it was released on its own to the press. On some twenty occasions commission releases received separate, page-one coverage in newspapers around the nation as well as on television news broadcasts. Coverage was particularly extensive in such prominent papers as *The New York Times* and *The Washington Post,* where summaries of commission texts ran to several thousand words.[63] Upon its completion, the final report was released in one volume and the commission's task force reports were released as separate volumes.

The Commission on Population Growth developed a new mode of reporting. In addition to producing a written report, the commission made a filmed report which was broadcast in November, 1972, by Public Broadcasting Service affiliate WGBH television in Boston. Following the film, which encapsulized the commission's major findings and recommendations, a discussion was held between six of the commissioners on one hand, and a group of organizational leaders and observers on the other, regarding some of the central issues raised by the commission.

The Commission on Marijuana and Drug Abuse also made use of television. Chairman Shafer and others participated in a live national broadcast during which they responded to telephone calls from viewers. The commission actually finished its work with a surplus of funds. In retrospect, Shafer has said he feels the money should have been used to print more copies of the final report for distribution to every library in the country.[64]

Because television is the predominant means of mass communication in the country, it would seem that the examples of the latter two commissions might be fruitfully followed by future commissions concerned with widespread social phenomena. In any event, it is clear that commissions pursue a variety of strategies to ensure that their message is "heard" and, it is hoped, that their recommendations might be implemented. In addition, commission public relations may serve an ancillary purpose in contributing to commissioners' and staffs' thinking of themselves as members of a coherent group.[65]

## Publication

Initially, commission reports are published by the U.S. Government Printing Office. Occasionally, a lack of sufficient funds may delay, for some time, printing of some commission work. Speaking six months after the commission's final report, Lloyd N. Cutler, Executive Director of the Commission on the Causes and Prevention of Violence, told a House subcommittee that three volumes of commission staff research on violent crime and a one-volume transcript of the commission's six days of hearings on the media had yet to be published because of a lack of funds. Cutler reported that efforts were being made to "beg" the money—about $35,000—from the Justice Department, which was seen as having an interest in the material's distribution.[66] These were, eventually, published.[67] Cutler's counterpart on the Douglas Commission on Urban Problems, Howard E. Shuman, offered a more startling example: "Some of our studies are still being printed, and a couple of them are going to come out, almost 2 years after we have disbanded."[68]

The Katzenbach Commission on Law Enforcement enjoyed a more successful experience. Its reports were sold by the Government Printing Office, and, by December 1967, over 180,000 copies had been purchased. Each of the commission's various reports was reprinted several times.[69]

Publication is not always left to governmental devices. No copyrights may be claimed on commission reports, and commercial publishers frequently release hard cover and paperback editions of major commission reports in cooperation with the commissions themselves. Sales and distribution of these editions have been extensive. The commercial paperback edition of the Warren Commission report was released, in a first printing of 700,000 copies, only eighty hours after the report's release by the President. "This establishes," the Bantam Books editors declared, "a new milestone in book publishing."[70] A group of 150 people, working in eight-hour shifts, around the clock, accomplished the printing of the report, which was then airlifted around the world. Hard cover editions of the report were prepared for the Book-of-the-Month Club, and the McGraw-Hill Company distributed hard cover editions to bookstores and libraries. A portion of the proceeds from the sale of the Bantam edition was donated to the John F. Kennedy Memorial Library.

The Kerner Commission supplied its final report in advance to Bantam Books. On the day the report was officially released, Bantam published its own edition. Lipsky and Olson report that the first commercial edition of 30,000 copies was sold out in three days and, between March and June of 1968, 1,600,000 copies were sold. The report went through 20 printings in the first four years following its release, with a monthly reorder rate of approximately 2,500 copies. By 1972, 1,900,000 paperback copies were in print.[71]

The Violence Commission saw four of its task force reports and two of its investigative reports, as well as its final report, published in one or more paperback editions. More than two million copies of the reports were printed.[72] And, as Co-Director of Research James F. Short has pointed out, these reports received a distribution largely unknown to most government documents, being "widely displayed in bookstores, airports, and other public places."[73]

The report of the Scranton Commission on Campus Unrest was published in five different editions by the Government Printing Office, the Commercial Clearing House, the *Chronicle of Higher Education,* Arno Press, and Avon Press.[74]

The Shafer Commission's first report sold 55,000 copies at $1.00 each and its final report sold 13,000 copies at $2.60.[75]

With the release of the final report, the work of the commission is essentially complete. The commission passes out of existence soon thereafter, and the report moves on to those who appointed the commission in the first place. The diagram that follows outlines the complete basic commission structure and procedure.

APPOINTMENTS   INVESTIGATION   REPORT

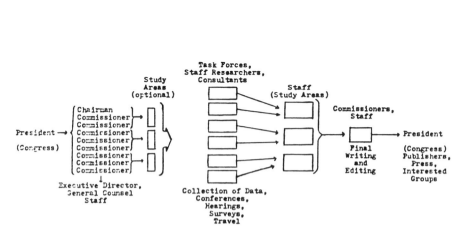

**BASIC COMMISSION STRUCTURE AND PROCEDURE**

# THE POLITICAL RESPONSE: THE PRESIDENT

> . . . the buck still stops with the President . . . Thus the President must take the commissions he appoints seriously. He must listen to what they say. He must treat them with respect and give them the courtesy of a responsive assessment of their proposals. To the extent he accepts these, he must set the wheels moving that translate suggestion into policy and policy into action.
>
> —Sen. Edward M. Kennedy[1]

The release of a report marks the conclusion of a commission as an entity. But the commission process continues. From this point the responses begin: from the President and the executive branch; Congress; the states; relevant groups and organizations; the press; the public; and, in some cases, from the commission itself. Responses may fall into two general categories: political, involving verbal, written, procedural, or legislative action by public figures and organizations; and social, involving a less definable process of general attitudinal change in society at large. This chapter will offer examples of presidential responses to the reports of presidential commissions and some of the factors which may shape them. Chapter 6 will examine some of the legislative and organizational responses and Chapter 7 will explore the concept of the social response to commissions.

## The Question of Expectations

Milton Eisenhower has said: "The minute a commission reports, even if it's 100 per cent right, you can't expect it to be done the next day."[2] While this may seem obvious, considerable disaffection may arise in the aftermath of commission investigations: When results are not forthcoming, the commission is blamed. It may be useful, in examining the responses of others to the work of commissions, to have in mind what some commission participants themselves have had to say with regard to responsibility for implementation.

In testimony before the Senate Judiciary Committee's Subcommittee on Administrative Practice and Procedure, William Lockhart, Chairman of the Commission on Obscenity and Pornography, made clear his understanding of the role of the commission in the area of implementation:

> This is not really the function or responsibility of the Commission which went out of existence on September 30, 1970, the day its report was issued. It is now the function of the press, the legislative bodies, and the interested public. They can ignore it, or forget it, or spurn it. Or they can study it, criticize it, test it, debate it, and give it whatever weight they find it deserves after careful study and debate.[3]

William Scranton, Chairman of the Commission on Campus Unrest, has stated a similar view: "It is clear to me . . . that a commission's function is not to make official policy, but rather to study a given problem in depth and to give specific advice."[4] James S. Campbell General Counsel to the Eisenhower Commission, has spoken at some length on the function of commissions and the question of what to expect from a commission report:

> the premise is that a national commission is a failure if it does not prompt swift executive and legislative action on its program of reforms. The correctness of this premise depends in turn upon the further assumption that the chief function of a commission is to make specific recommendations for immediate governmental implementation. No doubt this is the announced purpose of most commissions, but I would submit that the "recommendations function" is usually only a secondary and accidental part of the commission process. . . . the ad hoc national advisory commission is wholly without either legislative or executive authority: it can neither make laws nor assume any day-to-day operating responsibility in the areas of its concern. . . . [It] typically asserts its total independence of politics and leads a brief life of its own, often measuring

its success almost solely by the degree to which it is able in its final report to "tell it like it is."[5]

In short, one must not expect more from a commission than it has been empowered to give. American politics and the American culture perhaps foster a sense of immediacy, an expectation of instant results. Commercial television, technology generally, lavish campaign promises, and an emphasis on viewing many political situations as "crises," all may have contributed to a kind of psychology which leads to rejection of procedures or institutions which cannot meet expectations. Coupled with this may be a desire for simplicity in explanations; indeed, there may be a correlative relationship between the magnitude of a problem and an increasing desire for a simple solution. Commissions do not tend to fulfill this expectation, either, as James Q. Wilson acknowledged with regard to the report of the Katzenbach Commission: "[it] is not likely to be a best-seller. In this, it will be no different from the report of most other blue-ribbon commissions, and for the same reasons: it offers no convenient answers to the question of what we might do short of solving it."[6]

With some of these thoughts in mind, we may go on to an examination of the responses of those in a position to take action on the basis of commission reports.

## Conditioning Factors

In contrast with their solemn appointments of commissions, Presidents seldom welcome commission reports. The reports of most of the commissions under study were not, it is safe to say, eagerly awaited in the White House. Indeed, reactions to reports often range "from cool to indignant."[7] (President Jimmy Carter's ceremonial reception of the report of his Commission on Mental Health must have been a "first" in commission experience: As he received the bound report he kissed the commission's honorary chairperson—his wife.)[8]

The presidential response is conditioned by two broad categories of factors: the political environment and the presidential (that is, human) personality. These two factors may impinge upon the President and shape his response to commission reports. They may, at times, reinforce one another.

Doris Kearns Goodwin suggests that the "political circumstances" of an administration at the time it receives a report will largely affect the tenor of the response.[9] On the one hand, the President is faced with a report, made by a group essentially beyond his control, that recommends policy. This may put him in a political bind if he has already committed his resources in other policy areas and has little in reserve. On the other hand, Goodwin points out, it is possible that the recommendations of an outside group may give the President leverage with Congress in promoting new policy. In this sense, then, the nature of the presidential response to commission reports is seen as being related to his conception of his own political needs and the circumstances of the current political environment.[10] Political constraints, to be discussed below, seem to have been the larger factor in Lyndon Johnson's responses.

Considerations of personality may affect presidential reception of commission reports. In this case, the response is determined by whether the President is capable, intellectually or emotionally, of entertaining ideas and proposals other than his own. This seems to have been a primary factor in Richard Nixon's responses to commissions. No doubt, Nixon honestly disagreed with various commissions and their recommendations. But the nature of much Nixon action, and that of officials beholden to him, suggests something beyond this. Nixon, frequently, was simply not interested in contrary advice.[11]

In addition, there may be a very human resentment of giving credit to others. Lloyd Cutler, Executive Director of the Commission on the Causes and Prevention of Violence, has observed:

> to whatever extent an administration agrees with some of the things the Commission is saying it rarely wants to come out to the American people and say, "The so and so Commissison had a good idea. I am for it." It is the President who has to have the idea, and to whatever extent the commission does have an impact, it tends to be an anonymous one.[12]

Illustrative responses of both Presidents Johnson and Nixon will be examined below.

Aside from factors of the political environment and personality, there are other factors which condition presidential response. As a result of the Federal Advisory Committee Act (Public Law 92-463, signed by President Nixon October 6, 1972), the President is required to make a report to Congress with regard to all commission reports, within one year of their submission. Prior to this act, a period which includes the reports of all the commissions in this study (with the exception of the second Shafer Commission report), there was no requirement for a response to commissison reports despite the fact that millions of dollars and hundreds of hours were invested in commission activities. The temptations presented by this situation are obvious.

A report on commissions, prepared by the House Government Operations Committee, has suggested there may be a constitutional obligation ("to give to the Congress information of the state of the Union" and "to take care that the laws be faithfully executed," Constitution, Art. 2, Sec. 3) for the President to report, at least to Congress, regarding commission reports.[13] The responses of both the Johnson and Nixon administrations in this regard, however, indicated no perception of such an obligation.

Tepid receptions are not necessarily the rule. Bradley H. Patterson, Jr., Executive Director of the National Advisory Council on Economic Opportunity, has pointed out that, in the Eisenhower administration, reports "would have been placed on the Cabinet agenda for a full presentation by the chairman, and a thorough discussion."[14] Presidents since Eisenhower, however, have been increasingly loath to consult their Cabinets, relying instead on a growing body of White House advisers who are protected from congressional and public scrutiny. George Reedy's work on this subject, *The Twilight of the Presidency,* depicts presidential isolation and its potentially disastrous effects on the conduct of public business:

> There is built into the presidency a series of devices that tend to remove the occupant of the Oval Room from all of the forces which require most men to rub up against the hard facts of life on a daily basis. The life of the White House is the life of a court. It is a structure designed for one purpose and one purpose only—to serve the material needs and the desires of a single man. It is felt that this man is grappling with problems of such tremendous consequence that every effort must be made to relieve him of the irritations that vex the average citizen. . . . It is not that the people who compose the ménage are any worse than any other collection of human beings. It is rather that the White House is an ideal cloak for intrigue, pomposity and ambition.[15]

Lyndon Johnson had his in-house group of foreign policy advisers who played such an important part in United States involvement in Southeast Asia. Richard Nixon went even further to build what amounted to a separate State Department within the White House and an internal security group distinct from the F.B.I. The extent of presidential isolation and secrecy was clearly evidenced in the Watergate conspiracy.

William S. Scranton, Chairman of the Commission on Campus Unrest, has suggested the relevance of commissions to this particular phenomenon of the presidency:

> [Presidents] are becoming more and more insulated from thoughts and ideas from the outside, because of the fact that they have so much to do. And we demand of our President more than is demanded of the head of any other State or Nation in the world, and he does just automatically over the course of time become somewhat insulated from outside thoughts and people, and as the enormity of his task grows, it is harder for outside viewpoints and outside people to get to the President. And I think commissions can be very helpful in this respect. They normally are outside people and they normally give a somewhat different viewpoint than the ordinary viewpoint that comes to him. And I think they help to break through that insulation. And it is very direct and useful, too, in this day and age when the Presidents should have a great deal of thinking coming to them from all sides.[16]

During the Johnson and Nixon years a lack of required response, coupled with increasing presidential independence and isolation, left the question of presidential response to commission reports, to some degree, up to the whim of the incumbent.

## The Johnson Response

Lyndon Johnson's responses to commission reports were often shaped by what he perceived as political restraints. Particularly in the earlier stages of his administration, he was open to new ideas and did not reject reports out of an unwillingness to consider the thinking of others; as Doris Kearns Goodwin puts it: ''. . . I think he had a mind that, in fact, delighted in the possibility of some new solution."[17] Increasingly, however, the extent of Johnson's commitment of his and the nation's resources to the Vietnam War limited his ability to initiate costly programs. Vietnam became an "obsession"[18] with Johnson, and the hopes of the Great Society were curtailed. Special Counsel Harry McPherson recalls that in 1967 the unreleased report of the Commission on Rural Poverty was sent to the Bureau of the Budget for costing out. The estimated costs of the commission's recommended programs ranged from $21 billion to $42 billion. When told of this, Johnson's response was: "I don't want to *see* that thing. . . . *you* take it!" Presentation of the report was made to a presidential aide.[19] As the war bore down on him, Johnson felt "cramped" and "his mind closed up more on new ideas."[20]

As is no doubt the case with most presidents, Lyndon Johnson did not read commission reports cover-to-cover; rather, aides prepared briefs for him.[21]

The presidential response to the report of the Katzenbach Commission on Law Enforcement and the Administration of Justice was positive. In his memoirs, Johnson says that the effect of the report was "like a light cutting through the darkness" in terms of its revelation of the "full dimensions of the problem."[22] Johnson then suggested his understanding of the report's message and his own response:

> The solution, as the crime commission viewed it, was a program in which the federal government was authorized to contribute financial assistance and research techniques to stimulate reforms in areas where the need was outstanding. That principle became the heart of the Safe Streets Act, which I subsequently asked the Congress to enact.[23]

Although in somewhat modified form, Congress did enact Johnson's proposal.

The immediate presidential response to the report of the Kerner Commission, according to those around him at the time, was quite clear: "Johnson was furious."[24] It "sent Johnson right up the wall."[25] Publicly, the President withheld comment for a week, after which he "praised only the scope of the *Report* and the energy and dedication of the commissioners."[26] Vice President Humphrey disputed the commission's warning of a divided society and Housing and Urban Development Secretary Robert Weaver criticized the commission's recommendations as unrealistic.[27]

A closer look at the circumstances surrounding the President at the time, however, reveals some of the problems that may unavoidably arise between presidents and their commissions, for commissions do not see things from the same perspective as the President and, even if he so desired, the President may be politically unable to do what a commissison asks. In addition, the specific language of a report may be a source of difficulty.

A basic problem arising with anyone's giving advice to the President, as Richard Neustadt has pointed out,[28] is that no one sees things in quite the same way as the President himself. The Kerner Commission members "came up with what was right for them," as Doris Kearns Goodwin has said.[29] And, as Lyndon Johnson saw it, there was no way he could offer a substantive response. Johnson spoke in his memoirs of the impossibility of his situation:

> analysis reflected extremely close agreement between the Commission's proposals and the administration's program. The major difference lay in the scale of effort recommended. . . . That was the problem—money. . . . I would have been delighted to have had an appropriation of an additional $30 billion to solve the problems of our cities but I knew that was unrealistic. Setting such an unattainable goal could easily have produced a negative reaction that in turn might have endangered funds for the many invaluable programs we had fought so long to establish and were trying so hard to strengthen and expand.[30]

In perhaps his most revealing comment in this respect Johnson said:

> I will never understand how the commission expected me to get . . . Congress to turn 180 degrees overnight and appropriate an additional $30 billion for the same programs that it was demanding I cut by $6 billion. This would have required a miracle.[31]

These remarks suggest the possibility that open-minded fact-finding has a certain limitation of utility in immediate presidential policy making. The goals and environments of commissions and presidents are different and the recommendations of one will not necessarily be compatible with what is feasible for the other.

There were further political obstacles facing Johnson. The partisan atmosphere of 1968 also contributed to his reaction to the report:

The nearer we came to the Presidential primaries in the spring of 1968, the more partisanship grew and the more I feared that many Republicans would oppose the tax bill so they could campaign in the midst of galloping inflation and blame it on my "reckless spending and fiscal irresponsibility." This was the situation when I received the Kerner report . . . and made the difficult decision not to respond directly to the call for major new programs. With the tax bill hanging by such slender threads, I knew that any call for increased spending would give my opponents the excuse they sought to call me a reckless spender and kill the tax bill.[32]

And, as Marvin J. Weinbaum has written, there was an additional aspect to the problem of partisanship: "Administration endorsement of a report critical of the white middle class was doubtful strategy in an election year when George Wallace threatened to draw away resentful Democratic voters."[33]

Johnson said later that with so little likelihood of congressional receptivity to new programs, the Kerner report's chief value would be in its call for a new public will to meet the nation's needs.[34] The report, however, was made when Vietnam, rather than the American ghetto, was of prime concern to the country, as well as to the President. Less than one month after receiving the Kerner report, Lyndon Johnson announced he would not seek reelection and, in effect, "abdicated any possible future role in fostering the Kerner recommendations in Congress."[35]

As for the President's anger, this may have represented, in large part, a personal reaction to certain wording in the report and the extent to which this was focused upon in the press.[36] Two of the key phrases of the report are those which declare that "White racism is esentially responsible for the explosive mixture which has been accumulating in our cities since the end of World War II" and warn that "This is our basic conclusion: Our Nation is moving toward two societies, one black, one white—separate and unequal."[37] The force of this language may have been particularly discouraging and irritating to a president so committed to racial justice. The record suggests Johnson felt genuinely confused, hurt, and betrayed by the black urban riots. Doris Kearns reports his having asked: "How is it possible, after all we've accomplished? How could it be? Is the world topsy-turvy?"[38]

There is evidence the commission itself was concerned that Johnson might misinterpret its message. Vice Chairman John V. Lindsay has said that the commission's second worry, after achieving consensus, "was that LBJ would view the report as a criticism of him and his policies."[39] It would seem he did. Language, then, while offering a commission an instrument for drawing attention to its message, may put a president on the defensive. Political maneuverability or will, on the part of the President, may thereby be lost. In this case, Johnson would have been forced to admit that the Vietnam War had "cut into his hopes," and made it impossible for him to meet needs which he wanted to meet.[40] It may be that language which is perceived as an attack on the President or his policies, however cathartic it may be to critics, can only guarantee a negative response—or no response at all.

The experience of Lyndon Johnson and the Kerner Commission suggests that, even with a president potentially sympathetic to a commission's message, there remain obstacles of a magnitude sufficient to forestall a positive, substantive presidential response. The Johnson decision not to respond to the report of the Kerner Commission was shaped, in large measure, by the political environment: a Congress which was decidedly unreceptive to proposals for new spending; a partisan election year atmosphere; the focus of attention on the Vietnam War; and the decision by the President not to seek reelection. To these constraints were added the President's feelings of betrayal and frustration over the riots and the growing policy immobility that accompanied the Vietnam commitment, as well as his anger at the language of the report which received initial focus. The political factors mitigating against a presidential response can be formidable. In the case of the Kerner Commission they were largely responsible for precluding a substantive response from Lyndon Johnson. Personality factors also came into play, just as they would later and to a more significant extent in the case of Richard Nixon.

## The Nixon Response

A perhaps quantitative measure of the importance Richard Nixon attached to presidential commissions is provided by the memoirs of his presidency. In that volume of 1,120 pages, the number of pages devoted to discussion of commissions is 0.[41] This after-the-fact indicator is supported by an historical record which suggests Nixon's disagreements with commissions went far beyond simple differences over policy and entered the realm of an individual's unwillingness or inability to consider ideas beyond his own.

The first major commission to report to President Nixon (although appointed by President Johnson) was the National Commission on the Causes and Prevention of Violence. Chairman Milton Eisenhower has commented on the response to the report:

> When we delivered our report to him in December, 1969, he instructed his staff to study it closely and asked me to hold myseslf and my colleagues available for consultation with his staff on how our findings and recommendations could be put to best use.
>
> Unfortunately—and I do not think deliberately—nothing subsequently happened. . . . More importantly, there has never been any official administration response to our report as a whole . . .[42]

Dr. Eisenhower observed later: "I must confess that I am terribly disappointed that the one person in the United States who could be most influential has done essentially nothing."[43] As Commission General Counsel James Campbell said of the Nixon response: "There really *wasn't* any."[44] The product of a conglomeration of experts and facts was apparently shelved because it represented ideas the President had no intention of entertaining.

President Nixon took full advantage of the fact that the Commission on Obscenity and Pornography was appointed by his predecessor to make efforts to discredit it. The commission had not yet made its report when it began encountering abuse. With the report's release, the President unequivocally condemned the commission and its findings:

> I categorically reject its morally bankrupt conclusions and major recommendations. So long as I am in the White House, there will be no relaxation of the effort to control and eliminate smut from our national life.[45]

In making his criticism, Mr. Nixon made an unusual point of logic regarding the commission's findings:

> The Commission contends that the proliferation of filthy books and

plays has no lasting harmful effect on a man's character. If that were true, it must also be true that great books, great paintings and great plays have no ennobling effect on a man's conduct. Centuries of civilization and 10 minutes of common sense tell us otherwise.[46]

The Vice President made it clear that the Nixon administration had no interest in exploring the commission's report with an open mind. In commenting on the commission's tolerant approach to its subject, Mr. Agnew said that "As long as Richard Nixon is President, Main Street is not going to be turned into smut alley." In his inimitable fashion, Agnew blamed part of what he saw as an erosion of decency on "a political hedonism that permeates the philosophy of the radical liberals."[47]

Mr. Nixon would seem to have found some vindication of his position in the 1973 Supreme Court rulings on obscenity.[48] But the central point here is that the President seemingly had no intention of making his response flexible (indeed, his sole appointment to the commission indicated this, long before the report was made).

President Nixon's own first major commission to report was the Scranton Commission on Campus Unrest. The President's appointments to the commission seemed to indicate his desire for a fair and thorough investigation. The commission did not, however, give the President what he apparently expected when it called for moral leadership in a time of serious national division:

> We will not pretend that it is easy for a President to inspire a diverse people or to set the tone for a nation: it is not. Yet he must strive to do just that. Especially in this time of division, every American must find in the President's leadership some reflection of what he believes and respects. We therefore urge the President to reassert his administration's openness to all views, including the voices of student protest . . .[49]

Indeed, Martha Derthick has reported that the President initially thought the commission would "address perpetrators of violence."[50]

The Nixon response to the commission came in the form of a letter to Chairman William Scranton, eleven weeks after the commission had made its report. The President said he had referred some specific commission recommendations to Cabinet officials for review.[51] The bulk of his letter, however, was given over to arguments against the commission's findings and, particularly, its call for moral leadership: "Responsibility for disruption of a university campus," he wrote, "rests squarely on the shoulders of the disrupters—and those among their elders in the faculty and the larger community who encourage or condone disruption."[52] The President declared that "few domestic issues have consumed more of my attention, interest and concern while in office" than campus unrest, and he saw appointment of the commission as "but one measure of that concern."[53] Yet, he had almost nothing to say about the killings at Kent State University and Jackson State College, analyses of which had taken up fully half of the commission's report. Mr. Nixon's focus was largely on the question of responsibility and his own interpretation of the matter. In short, the President seemed either not to understand much of what the commission was saying, or else was unwilling to discuss it. In this connection, a comment made by Nixon's Chief-of-Staff, H. R. Haldeman, appears revealing. The commission's call for moral leadership could well have been perceived as a personal attack; Haldeman has said that the area of personal difficulties "was the area in which Richard Nixon was the least effective."[54]

The Vice President, in his role as "mouthpiece," termed the report "pablum for permissivists,"[55] and the behavior of the administration, especially as evidenced in the 1970 congressional campaign, indicated that little consideration would be given to the moral leadership thrust of the commission report.

Commissioner Martha Derthick has sought to explain away this kind of presidential response as being a natural result of commissions expecting too much of presidents and of placing too much responsibility on them.[56] This view was not shared by her fellow commissioners, however. James F. Ahern saw the situation differently:

> To be sure, the recommendations of the other Presidential Commissions have also been ignored and cast aside. Yet, however limited the impact of such earlier bodies as the Kerner and Eisenhower Commissions may have been, ours was the unique experience of seeing the Administration that had appointed us take aggressive initiatives in direct conflict with all of our key recommendations to it.
>
> Of course the President was under no obligation to agree with us on all issues. Many of the Commission's recommendations may be wrong and most are assuredly arguable. But to appoint such a

body with great solemnity and fanfare, and then to fly in the face of all its central recommendations suggests very strongly a cynical scheme to manipulate public opinion. At a minimum, it raises grave doubts about whether the President was even seriously concerned about identifying and alleviating the sources of campus unrest, suggesting rather that he sought only an expedient means of avoiding the rising pressure last spring.[57]

Chairman Scranton was, himself, conciliatory in his comments on the Nixon letter/response:

I deeply appreciate the fact that President Nixon has read and responded to our commission's report. I believe this is at least unusual and possibly unique in the annals of major Presidential commissions over the past several years.[58]

He said he felt the President agreed in "substance" with the commission's findings and that he had been invited to the White House to discuss the matter further.[59] Commissioner Joseph Rhodes, Jr. was much less impressed with the response. He declared that "The letter really doesn't say much about the substance of our report," and felt that Nixon's behavior during the 1970 elections was "diametrically the opposite of what we recommended in the report. The campaign was his basic statement on the report."[60] Rhodes later told a Senate subcommittee his impression of the response:

I depict it myself as a crudely cynical one and a very political one. There was no need to wait for 3 months for the quality of a letter that was sent to Governor Scranton. I don't think that was anything but an attempt to wait until the Commission's public visibility had passed.[61]

Other commissioners who offered immediate reactions to the President's letter were generally conciliatory.[62]

It would seem that presidential actions spoke louder than presidential words in the case of the response to the Scranton Commission.

A particular irony attached itself to former Governor Shafer's Commission on Marijuana and Drug Abuse. Fully ten months before the commission's interim report *The New Republic* pointed out, with reference to the Scranton Commission: "Unfortunately, Mr. Nixon has a habit of ignoring his own commissions, particularly those headed by Republican ex-governors of Pennsylvania, and has already stated that he'll ignore this one if it recommends legalizing marijuana."[63] Almost from the commision's inception, the President had announced what he would not consider, contrary to the most fundamental principle of the presidential commission, i.e. the gleaning of all facts and the presentation of recommendations for the best approach to a problem.

The commission's interim report on the effects of marijuana in American society found few friends in the administration, but Governor Shafer, questioned on NBC's "Meet the Press," dismissed the criticism and reiterated the basic commission role—regardless of the incumbent President's desires:

> MR. GRAHAM (*The New York Times*): There are members of the administration and a great many other people though who have said your recommendations are permissiveness gone wild. How do you answer this charge that you are opening up the door to another avenue in the society?

> MR. SHAFER: In a few words, that kind of an analysis is just a bunch of "turgent tosh." We are not getting permissive. What we are attempting to do is to face realistically a problem in our society, not just the pharmacological problem of marijuana, but the sociological problem.[64]

When the Commission delivered its final report, a year later, on the broader issue of drug abuse generally in the nation, the response was predictable. The immediate White House reaction was reported to be "frosty." Gerald Warren, the deputy press secretary, indicated that the President would make no comment. When Chairman Shafer formally presented the report to the President no photographs were allowed. Further, it was announced that the President would submit to Congress a plan for governmental reorganization which would combine a number of drug agencies into a new unit of the Justice Department, a step which was contrary to a commission recommendation.[65]

In retrospect, Governor Shafer is, like his colleague Governor Scranton, charitable toward Nixon. He feels the President's response to the commission was hampered by the events of Watergate, and he takes a stoic attitude toward the politics involved in presidential-commission relations. He has said that, while Milton Eisenhower had been quite distressed by the Nixon response to the Violence Commission, this was a result of Eisenhower's not having considered the politics of response. As a politician, Shafer says he was not surprised by the President's response to his commission; indeed, he expected it.[66]

Finally, the report of the Population Commission also found a reception of distinct silence. Commissioner Reverend Jesse Jackson leveled one of the harshest charges at presidential neglect on record, on a special Public Broadcasting Service broadcast: "This Commission is one of Mr. Nixon's 'bastard children' and he ought to come home to it."[67] (Neglect was not, of course, unique to Richard Nixon. Indeed, Howard Shuman, Executive Director of President Johnson's National Commission on Urban Problems, has suggested the flavor of association with an ignored commission in an article titled "Behind the Scenes—and Under the Rug;" "At times we felt like former Russian political figures, references to whom had been expunged from all public records."[68])

The President is in a unique position with regard to commissions and his response to their findings and recommendations can have a potentially positive or negative bearing on the process of implementation. There is a "credibility loan" which the President may give to a commission and the commission, in turn, can give a basis of authority to his actions if he chooses to consider its conclusions as a foundation for policy. Stewart Alsop, in commenting on the Scranton Commission, noted one way in which the commission's call for moral leadership might have been of assistance to the President in adapting to the times:

> President Nixon is not about to abandon his basic political strategy . . . He is not, in other words, going to have nice things to say about campus militants . . . But the President can, and sensible people must hope that he will, do something quite different. This is to use his political power to contain and control and canalize the flood tide toward the right, of which he is a part, just as Franklin Roosevelt contained and controlled the tide to the left, of which he was a part.[69]

Commissions can serve a definite purpose in this kind of capacity even if their actual recommendations are not implemented legislatively. But, of course, this requires that a president at least be receptive to the commission's possibilities. A commission's initial impact may be weakened by a president's withholding of his credibility loan. Mr. Nixon did nothing to assuage the controversy over the Pornography Commission; indeed, he contributed to it. The Scranton Commission was handpicked, yet the President in effect rejected its primary recommendations. He rejected and ignored other commissions. As has been suggested, his reactions implied an understanding of commission use fundamentally at variance with the stated purpose of analysis and recommendation.

Although President Nixon's responses to the commissions under study were predominantly negative, he was apparently capable of some positive interpretations of commission ideas. The National Advisory Commission on Selective Service, headed by former Assistant Attorney General Burke Marshall, was called "the cutting edge of draft reform;" both Presidents Johnson and Nixon were seen as having successfully proposed reforms to Congress.[70] The National Commission on Reform of Federal Criminal Laws, a Nixon commission, received favorable treatment. In ordering Attorney General John Mitchell to prepare and submit to Congress a comprehensive reform of the Criminal Code, the President said that the commission's final report provided "a useful framework for considering the issues involved in reforming penal law."[71] In addition, he asked that Mitchell study the commission report and work with congressional committees in preparing the reforms.

## Commission Overlap

An additional factor helping shape the presidential response is the phenomenon of commission overlap. By this is implied the situation wherein one president's appointed commission may survive his tenure and deliver its report to his successor. This was, in fact, the case with the Eisenhower Commission on Violence and the Commission on Obscenity and Pornography, both of which were appointed by Lyndon Johnson but reported to Richard Nixon. To a certain extent, this may be said to have been true of the Kerner Commission as well, since its report did not reach the Johnson Administration until essentially the same time as the President was deciding not to seek reelection.[72]

The extent to which this phenomenon may have contributed to the Nixon response to the Eisenhower and Lockhart Commissions is not hard to imagine. In the case of the Lockhart Commission on Pornography, Mr. Nixon made clear his feelings about the commission with his appointment of Charles Keating as commissioner, well before the final report was made. When the commission delivered its report, in September 1970, Mr. Nixon was presented with the difficulty of commission overlap; i.e. he had to respond to a commission which he had not (and probably *would not have*) appointed. His response has been discussed above but the more general point, here, is that this dilemma must be kept in mind when evaluating presidential responses to the commissions of previous administrations. The resultant response, if it comes at all, may represent a forced comment on an issue that the receiving President may never have been inclined to investigate in the first place. As *Newsweek* observed, with regard to the Commission on Obscenity and Pornography: "well-publicized leaks of the majority's laissez-faire recommendations had already prompted a politically sensitive White House to disown the entire project as the misbegotten child of the previous administration."[73] Milton Eisenhower, whose own commission experienced overlap, felt that "What he [Johnson] would have done would probably have been different from what Nixon has done."[74]

In addition, whether or not the President agrees with the report of an overlap commission, there may simply be an element of personal reluctance to offer laurels to a predecessor. Former Attorney General and commission chairman Nicholas Katzenbach has said, "one difficulty with commissions is that even if they are bipartisan in nature, they nonetheless are appointed by a particular President and his successor, whether he agrees or disagrees with the conclusions, is somewhat unlikely to pass too much credit to a former administration."[75] Overlap can be a factor which contributes to whether a commission's findings are even considered, much less acted upon.

Negative results of overlap may not be preordained, however. At least one recent commission (albeit, not a major social issue commission) sought to bridge the gap between changing administrations. The report of the President's Commission on Olympic Sports, which was released in January 1977, was submitted to both President Gerald

Ford and President-elect Jimmy Carter, a move which, on the face of it, would seem to have strategic merit.[76]

Further, an interesting hypothesis has been raised by James Campbell, General Counsel to the Eisenhower Commission and a student of the commission process. He suggests that the results of commission studies may be more likely to find their way into the thinking of *later* administrations simply because incumbent officials have too little time to assimilate the specifics of massive reports when they are released:

> the pace is so hectic at the policy making level in government that one is usually sort of drawing on intellectual capital that's already been built up in some prior experience. . . . In the case of the commission report, some big, fat commission report comes out in the middle of the time you're serving in government and you read the newspaper account of it—a couple of paragraphs. Maybe somebody brings you a copy and you skim a couple of paragraphs out of the introduction and that's about it. Whereas, somebody who's *not* in government at that point may read it carefully, digest it, and it becomes part of his intellectual equipment when he goes into government service.[77]

In the short run, then, substantive implementation is seen as a somewhat unrealistic expectation; in the long run, there is some likelihood of commission ideas finding their way into government.

This "delayed reaction" theory of commission overlap may have been reflected in Carl Marcy's observation regarding the report of the Research Committee on Social Trends, delivered to President Herbert Hoover. The report, he said, "more nearly suggests a New Deal primer than a 'scientific' guide for Mr. Hoover's social policies."[78] And Thomas Cronin has pointed out that the process of bringing policy to fruition may require as many as three or four presidencies.[79]

Application of these ideas to the commissions under study, however, would be impractical because of the disjointed, disrupted nature of American politics—and the presidency, in particular—throughout most of the decade following the late 1960s. The intrusions of Vietnam and Watergate, the resignations of both a president and a vice president, Gerald Ford's brief incumbency: All served to disrupt the conduct of public affairs and what otherwise might have been the orderly transitions from one administration to another. Whether or not later administrations will prove to have incorporated the ideas of the major social-issue commissions remains to be seen.

## The Cabinet

The President's personal response to a commission may be supplemented or complemented by Cabinet agencies. Responses may be positive or negative, verbal or procedural. Generally, the Cabinet response cannot be expected to vary significantly from that of the President. It may, however, be more specific.

The Department of Housing and Urban Development's response to Senator Paul Douglas' National Commission on Urban Problems exemplifies some of the negative options available to a Cabinet department. As Commission Executive Director Howard Shuman recalls:

> *The Large Poor Family—A Housing Gap,* which I coauthored with Walter Smart and Walter Rybeck was openly opposed by HUD because it indicated that virtually no housing was being built for the poor family with more than two children. Eighty percent or more of the need goes unmet. It also proved how difficult it was for us to get publications printed. Everything except the cover we typed out in this form, in photoready copy.
>
> All it needed was a cover. It took HUD 8 weeks to print it. Then they lost it for a week. That experience may indicate why very little housing for poor people is being built under their auspices. . . . The public has a right to the studies. The public paid for them. They should be issued and not merely stamped secret which is what HUD wanted us to do with a number of the critical ones.[80]

HUD was more cooperative with the Katzenbach Commission on Law Enforcement and the Administration of Justice. Along with the Office of Economic Opportunity, HUD was involved in an incentive program that "awarded grants to urban communities for experimental programs that adopt particular recommendations of the Commission."[81] This is one way a receptive executive or Cabinet officer can pursue the implementation process.

Senator Fred Harris, a member of the Kerner Commission, while expressing distress over a lack of comprehensive action in response to the commission, has noted that "The President did ask all agency and department heads to reexamine their programs in the light of the report."[82] Chairman Otto Kerner has elaborated:

> I think considerable progress has been made. . . . There was a specific direction to the FBI to develop crowd control, police planning, rumor controls, and things of this nature with area meetings throughout the entire United States to educate them as to what the problem is and how to overcome it.
>
> Also the Defense Department was requested to develop new training methods, both in the Army and the National Guard, recommending integration in the Services, their future integration in the Service, and for the development of new programs of crowd control. The National Guard and Army at that time had manuals but they were for control in enemy territory and not in the area of what we consider to be domestic problems.[83]

This may represent one way in which a president may induce a somewhat less visible response when the finds himself in an awkward position politically, as Lyndon Johnson did at the time of the release of the Kerner report. It must also be said, though, that these particular responses dealing with riot control would probably have met with far less resistance than might have proposals for new social programs.

Although it was essentially unreceptive to the Eisenhower Commission on Violence, the Nixon administration was persuaded, at one point, to act in concert with commission findings. In the fall of 1969, the Justice Department denied parade permits to antiwar groups for a silent march around the White House. This action, coming less than a year after the release of the commission's reports on *Rights in Conflict, Violence in America, The Politics of Protest,* and *Rights in Concord* stimulated considerable publicity focusing on the incongruity between the department's action and the commission's findings. The point was also raised in personal contact with the White House by a commission representative. As a result, the action of the Justice Department was reversed and the march took place without incident.[84]

The Commission on Obscenity and Pornography fared poorly with the Cabinet. In fact, Cabinet action was taken against it even before it had released its report. Originally, an illustrated edition of the commission's study had been envisioned. But questionable entrepreneurs abused their commercial publishing rights to the report by attempting to supplement it with illustrations not included or authorized by the commission. As a result, the Criminal Division of the Justice Department brought "a criminal prosecution in the Southern District of California based upon the interstate transportation of that publication and advertisements promoting its sale and distribution. . . . That prosecution was based upon a violation of the Federal obscenity statutes, 18 U.S.C. 1461, et seq."[85] The prosecution was successful and, although there was no specific prohibition against going ahead with publication of an illustrated report, the commercial edition of the report that finally emerged was devoid of illustration.

A footnote remains to the episode, however, and it is with great irony that one discovers that Title 18, Section 1461 of the United States Code, under which the illustrated report was suppressed, is precisely the first Federal Statute which the commission report recommends be repealed.[86]

The Scranton Commission, while receiving administration attacks in public, was not totally rejected on the Cabinet level. In commenting on the President's written reply to the commission report, Governor Scranton referred to then Health, Education and Welfare Secretary Elliot Richardson's "espousing this report."[87] Elaboration of a mixed Cabinet response was made in testimony by the Governor before Senator Kennedy's Judiciary Subcommittee on Administrative Practice and Procedure:

> [From the Scranton statement] In his letter to me of Dec. 10, [1970] President Nixon directed the Departments of Defense, Justice, Labor, and Health, Education, and Welfare to report to him on a continuing basis the actions they have taken to implement our recommendations. . . .
> Senator KENNEDY. How would you characterize the responses by the Departments in terms of the kind of urgency which you dwell upon in your report?
> Mr. SCRANTON. Well, first of all, I think I have characterized it in two ways already. One is, I am glad it was done. But the second is, that I don't think it is by any means fully responsive to our recommendations.
> You take, for example, the Justice Department. They refer only to the Kent State and the Jackson State affairs, which, of course,

are extremely important. But everyone of our many other recommendations concerning law enforcement have gone without response.[88]

With some passage of time, Governor Scranton has observed possitive action in the Department of Defense, beginning under then Secretary Melvin Laird:

> Secretary Laird not only adopted in principle all the suggestions we made about law enforcement on the part of the National Guard, but quietly held meetings around the country of National Guard leaders and they are developing re-training as well as working on a re-equipment process which, so far, has resulted in no National Guardsmen appearing on campus at all and no use of lethal weapons by the National Guard in instances of this sort. In short, . . . considerable changes in training and in equipment are occurring and all for the good.[89]

A harsh or silent presidential response, then, does not necessarily mean there will be no action taken at the Cabinet or agency level. The action may be contrary to the basic message of a commission, or it may be in conformance with it. Undoubtedly, the President sets the tone; but it is possible that an effectively presented and relevant commission report may have an effect on the thinking and policy direction of a receptive Cabinet official which may be quietly manifested in action.

The presidential response to presidential commissions is tempered by a number of factors. The political environment may not be conducive to the kinds of proposals commissions urge on presidents. The President may perceive his needs as being different from those of a commission. The presidential personality may not be receptive to new ideas and the opinions of others. The very language of commission reports may be a problem for the President. Commissions may overlap administrations, to their detriment. In addition, during the period under study there was no legislative requirement that the President respond to commissions reports.

Of course, the President may find it possible, convenient, or desirable to act substantively on commission recommendations. But the practical effect of all the above-mentioned considerations is that: 1) presidents may find it convenient to ignore or criticize commission reports; 2) even if they are favorably disposed toward a report, presidents may be unable to take action.

# 6

# THE POLITICAL RESPONSE: LEGISLATIVE AND ORGANIZATIONAL

Once a presidential commission has released its report, the President's response becomes the immediate focus of attention. Others may have responses of their own to offer, however. Congress, which in some cases has established the commissions, the states, public and private organizations, and the press have all reacted to commission reports. And, as is the case with the President, responses may be positive or negative, verbal or procedural. Finally, some groups may engage in follow-up activities, examining the fate of particular commission reports. This chapter will offer examples of the kinds of political responses to commissions that may be found beyond the presidency.

## Congress

The nature of the congressional response to commission reports depends, in large part, on the same kinds of factors as determine the presidential response: the partisan atmosphere, questions of political feasibility, receptivity to new thinking. In addition, commission reports may face numerous obstacles reflecting the institutional nature of Congress. Consequently, one must approach the subject of response with sober expectations, for commission proposals are perhaps no more likely to see implementation, on a grand scale, at the hands of Congress than are most other comprehensive reform packages.

Congressmen work in pursuit of certain identifiable goals. Richard F. Fenno, Jr. sees the three most basic as: re-election, influence within the parent body, and the making of good public policy.[1] David R. Mayhew sees re-election as the fundamental goal of the congressman and suggests that Congress is organized institutionally in such a way as to promote this goal.[2] He says that, "For the most part it makes sense for congressmen to follow conservative strategies," to traffic in particularized benefits, to respond to the organized, to claim as much credit as possible, to mobilize only when credit can be claimed, and to "make pleasing judgmental statements" rather than "make pleasing things happen."[3] Congressional structures are seen as facilitating these behaviors: the Capitol Hill office with its resources for electioneering and casework services; congressional committees, which provide platforms for position-taking, permit benefit provision, allow a division of labor, and assist in institutional maintenance; and parties, which do not prevent members from taking positions advantageous to their own interests.[4]

Commissions, as groups which pass out of existence as soon as they have articulated their "demands," which have no ongoing presence or resources for pressure, and which are more suited to making broad-ranging proposals than requests for particularized benefits, are not likely to be perceived by congressmen as instruments for the achievement of their goals. Although many commission recommendations are quite specific, they may at times lack the hard details required for the drafting and passage of legislation. In addition, commission recommendations may lack political "pizzazz," as Nicholas Katzenbach has put it, an attractiveness sufficient to turn people away from "the easy route" and on to the road to reform.[5] Advocating reform or new social initiatives involves political risks for congressmen, particularly when proposed reforms may alienate organized and active groups.[6] Milton Eisenhower, a veteran commission participant, has spoken of this constraint with regard to gun control, something his Commission on the Causes and Prevention of Violence recommended:

> I'll bet you anything if you could take a confidential poll of both the Senate and the House then ninety per cent would be in favor of gun control. But we don't get gun control for political reasons. And why? Because the most powerful single lobby in America is the National Rifle Association. . . . Unfortunately, in politics, it

seems not to be possible to free one's mind of preconceptions because you're always thinking of your own constituents.[7]

Perhaps the most significant thing that can be said of the congressional response to commission recommendations is that Congress is probably more likely to respond to recommendations for low-key procedural adjustments than it is to calls for social reorganization or bold initiatives in areas of extreme controversy. Examples of Congress' responses to a number of commissions will suggest what can be expected of the legislative branch.

Although some of the Warren Commissions's findings are still disputed, the commission did see some of its recommendations adopted. In the area of presidential protection, commission recommendations were enacted which called for: making an attack on the President a federal crime, improved coordination of FBI and Secret Service activities, an increase in the Secret Service budget, and improvement of preventive intelligence capabilities and liaison with local law enforcement agencies.[8] Some of these actions involved Congress. To be sure, some of them may have been controversial within certain contexts. But they were largely of a procedural nature and did not involve what could be perceived as radical reforms. The lesson here is that relatively low-visibility recommendations, focused on a specific problem, were successful. The area of concern was not of a highly partisan nature.

In the case of the Katzenbach Commission on Law Enforcement and the Administration of Justice, the congressional response was mixed. As Isidore Silver suggested, "Congressional opinion was not substantially influenced by the Report's breadth and humanity."[9] Indeed, Congress' passage of a repressive District of Columbia Crime Bill, four months after release of the commission's report, suggested disenchantment. The Juvenile Delinquency Prevention and Control Act was passed, however, embodying commission recommendations for federal funding of state innovative programs in the areas of prevention and rehabilitation.[10]

Perhaps most significantly, the commission participated in preparation of the proposed Omnibus Crime Control Act, passed in 1968 and known popularly as the Safe Streets Act. This act was intended to give the Justice Department authority to dispense funds directly to agencies carrying out changes such as those proposed by the commission. Conflict between the Johnson administration and Senator John McClellan, however, led to inclusion of authorization of electronic surveillance (which the administration had opposed) and modification of the proposed Justice Department role.[11] The act established a new Law Enforcement Assistance Administration, within the Justice Department, to provide "technical assistance and information to the states and local communities, to distribute block grants to the states for law enforcement purposes based on a population formula, to provide discretionary grants for research and demonstration, and to promote training of criminal justice personnel."[12] State planning agencies were established to receive the new funds. The potential for federal initiative was less than what had originally been envisioned. Yet, as Lloyd Ohlin has pointed out, "a whole new structure at federal, state and local levels now exists for channeling money directly to improvements in the criminal justice system and to programs of crime prevention and control."[13] The Katzenbach Commission saw some success with Congress, but the response was decidedly shaped by the vicissitudes of the congressional mood.

The experience of the Kerner Commission offers case-study lessons on the problems commission recommendations may face in Congress. Both Senator Edward Kennedy and former Senator and Commissioner Fred Harris have reported what they saw as residual effects of Kerner Commission recommendations in some congressional proposals and actions.[14] The political and institutional obstacles the commission faced in Congress, however, prevented any kind of comprehensive response. Lipsky and Olson have suggested that the commission's decision to present a report of wide scope was made at the expense of the kind of specificity that might have won it more congressional support.[15] Under any circumstances, the nature of Congress would have made a response difficult. In a wide-ranging analysis of the congressional environment into which the Kerner report was introduced, Marvin J. Weinbaum has pointed out institutional, political, and class-based obstacles. First, he writes, as an institution "more accustomed to stop-gap legislating, a departmentalization of effort, and incrementalism in policy," Congress could not be expected to provide a systematic handling of the commission's findings.[16] Indeed, Weinbaum reports, "By conservative estimate, at least ten committees of the 90th Congress could claim jurisdiction over legislation suggested by the *Kerner Report*."[17] Further, he suggests that safe-seat committee chairmen from the South and major northern cities had strong motives for avoiding identification with a commission that declared white racism responsible for urban racial problems. And he sees class-based motives for many congressmen's lack of support for commission recommendations: "The Commission's admonition that the crisis of the cities would intensify in the face of national inaction was viewed by some legislators as a form of blackmail against the middle-class white taxpayer. . . . The anti-inflationary mood that reached the Congress by 1968 armed many lawmakers with welcomed justification for deferring new programs for the poor and unemployed."[18]

Weinbaum sees further institutional impediments. For example, he describes the commission's recommendations as belonging to "a category of policy temperamentally disturbing for the Congress," inasmuch as its members "prefer legislation whose benefits are largely calculable . . . . programs for the underprivileged typically defy direct measurement."[19] Timing was a problem because the commission proposals came to a Congress whose legislative agenda was already set and which was eager to adjourn early, in time for elections. Finally, in an era in which Congress tended to defer to presidential initiative, "Lyndon Johnson's icy silence was decisive."[20]

The Kerner Commission experience suggests that the presentation of a comprehensive picture of social ills may not be of much use in the institutional and political setting of Congress. Considering the nature of the obstacles the Kerner Commission faced, however, as well as the nature of its fundamental message, it would seem unlikely that greater specificity in its recommendations would have markedly improved the prospects for implementation.

The National Commission on the Causes and Prevention of Violence, although ignored by President Nixon, has seen action taken in a number of areas it considered. Among its eighty-one recommendations were calls for lowering the voting age to eighteen, establishment of a guaranteed family income and guaranteed employment, development of a non-lethal weapon, and marijuana research. Some of these have remained alive in the realm of ideas and policy proposals, e.g. guarantees of family income floors and full employment. Others have seen enactment. In addition to the eighteen-year-old vote, the commission's recommendation of research on marijuana saw fruition in the Comprehensive Drug Abuse

Prevention and Control Act of 1970, in which Congress established the National Commission on Marijuana and Drug Abuse. Commissioner and Senator Philip A. Hart said later, "We would be frauds if we claimed the commission was solely responsible for the progress."[21] It may, however, have been a contributing factor.

The Commission on Obscenity and Pornography, as might be expected, offers examples of the extreme behavior which commissions may provoke. This commission's problems with Congress began even before it was officially established. For, although it was the commission's mandate to consider scientific evidence of the effects of obscenity, it was widely assumed that "such evidence would surely show that obscenity had ill effects."[22] In Public Law 90-100, Congress had directed the commission,

> after a thorough study which shall include a study of the causal relationship of such materials to antisocial behavior, to recommend advisable, appropriate, effective, and constitutional means to deal effectively with such traffic in obscenity and pornography.[23]

House Report 521,[24] the basis of Public Law 90-100, provided clear explanations of the commission's mandates. With regard to the commission's task of recommending legislative or other measures for regulation of pornography, it said:

> The power to legislate does not necessarily mean that the power ought always be exercised. Thus, it may be that after the final report of the Commission, Congress may determine that the illicit traffic in pornography is not an evil of sufficient magnitude to require legislative action. In that event, then Congress would serve the country well by not enacting any further legislation in this area.[25]

Someone should have told the commissioners what Congress really had in mind, but authority to appoint them was sent over to the President. Chairman Lockhart can perhaps be excused, then, for his understanding of the situation:

> Certainly Congress could never have intended a Commission made up of responsible citizens giving their time at the request of the Government to make recommendations inconsistent with its findings on the very questions that Congress asked the Commission to

investigate. . . . [Congress] was asking for the judgment of the Commission as to what kinds of legislative, administrative and other action were appropriate in the light of the Commission's findings . . . Congress would never have asked the Commission to study the effects of pornography if it had intended the Commission to propose tighter controls to regulate the pornography industry regardless what its findings on effects might be.[26]

Apparently, this was not quite the case. Precisely thirteen days after the commission submitted its report the Senate rejected it outright, 60-5, in what may have been one of the fastest and clearest responses ever to the report of a commission.[27] Comments rendered by Senator Strom Thurmond in a constitutent newsletter suggest, again, that some legislators were not looking for an open-minded study from the commission but, rather, confirmation of their own preconceptions. Thurmond's comments exemplify the extreme reactions which may greet commissions in Congress. The Senate vote, he said,

was created by the Commission's shocking perversion of its own mandate. The Commission's report amounted to nothing more than a license for filth. . . . Thus the Commission spent $1.7 million to say that the best way to get rid of the *illegal* traffic in pornography was to make it *legal*. . . . At the very moment when we have reached a crisis of permissiveness and pornography in our civilization, this Commission urged us to rush headlong into the mire which has swallowed up all the decadent and corrupt civilizations of history. . . . The people wanted solid proposals for stopping the trade in obscenity, and for coping with the crimes which are incited and inflamed by its spread.

This traffic has increased principally because the U.S. Supreme Court, in a series of decisions over recent years, has forced this filth upon the people. . . . But instead of offering recommendations to overcome this Court-induced menace, the Commission chose to encourage it. . . . Some may wonder how a report that is fundamentally evil in its basic assumptions could be produced with public funds.[28]

Whether or not Senator Thurmond's remarks were motivated by a perception of political advantage or by genuine conviction, it would seem there was almost no limit to the vitriol of the Pornography Commission's opponents.

Ironically, one Pornography Commission proposal did find expression in law. The commission favored legislative provision of protection for persons not wishing to receive unsolicited advertisements for obscene materials through the mail. Accordingly, in a progress report of July 1969, the commission's legal panel offered a draft statute which would provide such protection. Although utilizing somewhat different methods from those suggested by the commission, Congress' Postal Reorganization Act of 1970[29] established the recommended protection.[30] It is perhaps interesting to note that these events transpired *before* release of the commission's final report.

In the assessment of Commissioner Otto Larsen, the Commission on Obscenity and Pornography failed, in the sense that it was unable, "for the time being at least, to penetrate the policy realm with the principle that empirical research is relevant."[31] The problem, however, may have had at least as much to do with the power of emotions as with the potential power of facts. Commissioner Edward Greenwood has suggested that a national policy is more likely to evolve from step-by-step actions at the local level than from federal action, "particularly because of the strong emotional factors involved . . ."[32] Indeed, the lesson of the Commission on Obscenity and Pornography, vis-à-vis Congress, may be that the nature of certain subjects precludes the commission process' being a useful prelude to the legislative process. Further, it would seem that congressional appointment of commissions is no greater a guarantee of success than is presidential appointment.

Participants in later commissions have perceived manifestations of their work in legislation. Governor Raymond P. Shafer, Chairman of the Commission on Marijuana and Drug Abuse, feels that the Senate Judiciary Committee voted to decriminalize possession of small amounts of marijuana as a direct result of the commission's report.[33] Charles F. Westoff, Executive Director of the Commission on Population Growth and the American Future, says "The only law that I know was actually enacted which might be traced in some measure to the Commission report was the mid-decade census." Yet, he adds, "The Commission was only one of many stimuli in getting that off the ground . . ."[34]

The congressional response to the presidential commissions under study suggests that Congress may be more likely to act on low-key procedural proposals, that it is reluctant to embrace comprehensive proposals for social reform, and that the institutional structure of Congress complements and reinforces this latter tendency. There do exist concrete examples of legislation which has grown out of commission proposals, and some observers suggest qualifications on how we should view this aspect of the commission process. For example, Nicholas Katzenbach feels that while commission results are not always evident on the face of legislation, they nonetheless have an impact: "I do believe that often it is difficult to measure the impact of the commission's work, perhaps because it is not always given credit for legislative or policy impacts that in fact can be traced to it."[35] In addition, Frank Popper suggests that "if several commissions make similar recommendations, they may, over the long run, have a combined impact on public opinion far greater than any one of them may have had."[36] Finally, William Lockhart, Chairman of the Commission on Obscenity and Pornography, expresses what may be the most stoic attitude of all, in speaking of his commission: "I did not expect it to produce much in the way of legislative results for 10 to 15 years."[37] Any of these theories of response may be applicable in certain contexts. In many cases, though, the temptations may be greatest for Congress to do nothing at all.

## State and Local Responses

In some cases, state and local bodies have been more receptive to the reports of commissions than have those who appointed the commissions. The Katzenbach Commission seems to have been particularly sucessful, in this regard. This may have been attributable, at least in part, to its deliberately adopted strategy of including in its work those who would later be in a position to implement its recommendations. "From the outset," Chairman Katzenbach has said, "the Commission was very concerned that it should involve everyone, whatever his viewpoint, with expertise on the subject of law enforcement."[38] The commission proposed that the governors of all the states set up parallel commissions to work with the commission and help implement recommendations: "We wished to get people . . . thinking about our major recommendations."[39] A two-day conference was held at the University of Maryland; President Johnson attended. The commission set up a staff to work with the states. State planning agencies, stimulated by the commission, became "the conduit and planning agency for the distribution of block grants from LEAA."[40] In short, as Chairman Katzenbach said, "we realized that the implementation was going to be largely a matter for governments other than the Federal Government."[41]

The results of this strategy were mixed but contained encouraging elements. Commission Executive Director James Vorenberg has reported that, because the legislation establishing the Law Enforcement Assistance Administration ultimately left so much discretion to the states, much federal money was "wasted," some of it being spent on "military equipment for riot control."[42] There were, however, some successful developments in response to commission recommendations regarding police-community relations.[43] Hostility between police and youths, particularly blacks, was seen as having been reduced. This was all the more noteworthy because it occurred in a period during which Richard Nixon, as a presidential candidate, had "invited" the police and the public to blame crime on Supreme Court decisions which limited police behavior. Much progress was attributed to such cities as Oakland and New York, where police chiefs set decent treatment of citizens as a top priority and used it in considerations for promotions and assignments. Police departments established in-house legal offices for instructions on due process. Improved police training in community relations was cited by the Brandeis University Center for the Study of Violence as one factor in a five-year decline in disorders. The numbers of minority group police officers were increased and this was seen as having been of help, although the record was mixed. Vorenberg adds that, unfortunately, these developments did not correlate with a significant reduction in crime itself.[44] There were, also, successful responses to commission recommendations regarding the corrections system. Vorenberg cites progress in Massachusetts and California. In the latter, a work-furlough program was developed and subsidies were offered to counties which lowered the state prison population by putting more individuals on probation. In three years the number of prisoners declined from 28,000 to 21,000. As a result, it was possible to drop plans for new prisons and to close some existing prisons.[45] The Katzenbach Commission saw a tangible response to some of its recommendations. Because many of these required state and local implementation, it would seem likely that the commission's strategy of involving officials from these levels in its work can be said to have been successful.

The Kerner Commission found a positive response in some of the same areas as the Katzenbach Commission, perhaps owing to the latter body's having helped pave the way to acceptability for certain kinds of proposals. In the area of police acquisition of military-type equipment, the Kerner Commission put a halt to what had been an unintended response to the Katzenbach Commission (See above, page 136). According to Otto Kerner:

> a great deal has occurred at the state and local levels, and in industry. The attitude of police departments has been completely turned around. Right after the report was released, many of the police departments that had purchased arsenals of automatic weapons and armored vehicles, disposed of these items. Police departments set up human relations groups with local communities to better understand the problems and also to assist in their problems. Numerous communities set up local city halls in neighborhoods to provide a service to those people who are least able to know what to do and where to go to solve their problems.
>
> Expanded health facilities have aided those who need them most and there have been many local ordinances establishing freedom of residence.[46]

A further response to the commission was the establishment of state and local "Little Kerner Commissions" to do for them "what the *Report* had done for the nation."[47] Reports were made in Wisconsin, St. Louis, and Houston;[48] "from Boston to East Palo Alto," as Senator Fred Harris put it.[49] In addition, portions of the commission's report were used by police chiefs during seminars conducted by the Justice Department in Washington.[50]

Despite these examples, the state response was not all that it might have been. In a study of the response of the Illinois General Assembly, which "could legitimately be expected to respond, in some fashion, to the findings of the *Kerner Commission Report*,"[51] Kitsos and Pisciotte found barriers to implementation which may be indicative of obstacles in other states as well. Although Otto Kerner was governor of Illinois at the time of the commission's report, he soon departed to become a federal judge. Succeeding governors were distracted from consideration of the commission report. In effect, this helped foreclose the possibility of action in the state legislature since, as Kitsos and Pisciotte put it:

> The Illinois General Assembly does not act—it reacts. Historically, most far-reaching proposals have had their origin outside the legislature. Governors, executive agencies, and lobbying groups have been the main sources of ideas. But, since the release of the *Kerner Commission Report,* not one outside agency or group has come before the legislature with a broad program based on the Commission's findings. . . . No pressure group developed a program of specific pieces of legislation to which the state legislature could react.[52]

Examination of a variety of partisan, institutional, and interest group organizational problems leads Kitsos and Pisciotte to conclude: "The problem rests both in and out of the legislature."[53] Illinois had a particular tie to the commission yet was unable to respond due to a variety of obstacles. The presence of similar obstacles may have precluded substantive responses in other states as well.

The beleaguered Commission on Obscenity and Pornography actually saw some positive legislative steps taken, at the state level, in response to its report. Less than a year after release of the report, Chairman Lockhart observed:

> Even in this first period of State legislative sessions since the report came out quite a large number of them have introduced and considered bills which we drafted and are in our report, particularly those dealing with public displays and with control over sales to children.[54]

Display laws were passed in Arizona on May 10, 1971, and in New York state.[55] Hawaii adopted "essentially all the majority legislative recommendations, including the one concerning the rights of consenting adults."[56] It would appear that the theory of a step-by-step evolution of national policy in this area is being borne out (See above, page 135). As Chairman Lockhart said, with regard to passage of the Arizona law: "Others, I am sure, will follow."[57]

Raymond Shafer reports that fully sixteen states (among them, Maine, Texas, and Oregon) have changed laws regarding marijuana since the report of the Commission on Marijuana and Drug Abuse.[58]

The response to commissions at the state and local levels may, in some cases, exceed the response at the federal level. This may be because state and local officials have been included in the work of a commission; because a previous commission has possibly opened the way to consideration of similar ideas; or because of promotion by federal agencies. States and localities, of course, are as capable of paltry responses as are presidents and congresses. In some cases, however, long-range hopes for implementation of commission ideas, particularly in areas of social controversy, might more profitably be directed at the lower levels of government. Implementation at these levels may be slow and of a patchwork nature, but it may be more than can sometimes be expected at the national level.

## Institutional and Organizational Responses

Institutions, organizations, and interested groups may respond to the reports of commissions which they feel have relevance to their goals or work. The Kerner Commission, for example, stimulated consideration of its findings and, in some cases, action, on the part of interested groups. A number of organizations, such as the B'nai B'rith Women and the League of Women Voters, "adopted the report as their plan for action."[59] At its 1968 national convention, the Democratic Party declared: "We acknowledge with concern the findings of the report of the bipartisan National Advisory Commission on Civil Disorders and we commit ourselves to implement its recommendations."[60] Had Hubert Humphrey been victorious in that year's presidential election it is possible the commission might have been subject to implementation efforts at the federal level. This would have been aided by a U.S. withdrawal from Vietnam and group pressure designed to hold the Democratic Party to its pledge.

In addition, there was a response to the Kerner Commission from elements of the business community. Meetings of corporation executives were held in a number of cities to consider the meaning of the report for the business world.[61] The commission's call for the creation of jobs by the private sector found a response in the JOBS program of the National Alliance of Businessmen. One analysis of this response suggests the JOBS program "has had considerable success in mobilizing business firms to increase their training and hiring of Negroes and other disadvantaged youths."[62] Not everyone perceived the same potential in the report's overall message. Presidential Special Counsel Harry McPherson reports that, while Lyndon Johnson was angered by the report,

> so were a lot of labor people—including black labor people, like Bayard Rustin—who would a whole lot rather have seen just a simple call for the creation of jobs rather than a psychoanalysis of whites. Because what this bunch of upper class, mostly white, professionals are saying is that lower class whites are racist and that they're the reason why the cities are burning. That is *so destructive* of the unity that is needed in the working class to get anything done; it causes the whites to feel furious. . . . It was generally seen as a disaster; [a] well-meaning, and probably true, but not very politically astute report.[63]

Chairman Kerner's conclusion, however, was that "In industry there has been a greater opportunity for minorities than there was previously, and now there are minorities visible at top levels in the private community."[64]

The report of the Commission on the Causes and Prevention of Violence was endorsed by national organizations. The National Council on Crime and Delinquency and the Anti-Defamation League distributed, "under their imprimatur," copies of the commission's recommendations.[65] The report was adopted for use as well by the National Urban Coalition.[66]

Participants in the work of the Commission on Campus Unrest perceived a positive response to their efforts at the university level. Commissioner Joseph Rhodes, Jr. reported that the commission "had a very positive, soothing and effective impact on this climate of extreme tension and anxiety in the country through its open hearings and its many investigations.[67] Chairman Scranton has said:

> Actually, we are delighted with the reactions on the campuses by administrators, faculty and students and others, particularly with our suggestions concerning grievance procedures and working together to create a better communications system and specific arrangements in the event of problems or outbreaks.[68]

These results would seem particularly noteworthy in light of the Nixon administration's response to the commission and its hostile attitude toward protest demonstrations.

Finally, William Lockhart reports that "Increasing study and attention is being given the report [of the Commission on Obscenity and Pornography] as time goes on."[69] In May 1971, in Chicago, the Federal Judicial Conference of the 7th Circuit, made up of federal judges and lawyers who practice before them, "spent a full afternoon listening to and questioning a panel of experts representing various views concerning the Commission's findings and recommendations."[70] In addition, the American Baptist Convention devoted two workshops at its 1971 national convention to discussion of the commission's findings. Chairman Lockhart participated in both these events and in "a great many similar sessions since the report was released."[71]

The organizational and group responses to commission reports may reflect, as much as anything, sponsorship of views already held by the group in question. The cases of the Kerner and Lockhart Commissions, however, suggest that groups may open themselves up to consideration of ideas they might not otherwise have entertained. Further mention of group response will appear in the next chapter.

## The Media Response

Frequently, the print and electronic media have provided extensive coverage of commissions and their reports. Coverage of the Kerner Commission may have been unequaled, but other commissions have fared well. The Katzenbach Commission was the subject of an unprecedented ninety-minute broadcast of "Meet the Press," on which five members of the commission and its executive director appeared.[72] In addition, according to Deputy Director Henry S. Ruth, the commission was the subject of newspaper, television, and magazine coverage for fully five months, in 1967.[73]

Frank Popper has said that the Kerner Commission's report "clearly escaped White House control and found an audience of its own."[74] Lipsky and Olson have recounted the comprehensive nature of the media response to the report's release. The following passage suggests, by implication, the potential utility of scheduling weekend release dates for commission reports:

On Friday, virtually every newspaper in the country reported on the contents of the summary. The following day reporters went into the background of the commission, interviewing commissioners and other public figures. On Sunday, March 3, the release date for the full text, newspapers devoted pages and pages to the commission. The *Boston Globe*, for example, devoted 14 pages to the subject, despite the fact that it had given it a full 20 pages two days earlier. The three television networks and the National Educational Television network devoted at least eight hours of programming to Kerner Commission affairs. NBC interviewed mayors of six riot-affected cities, CBS interviewed [Commission Vice Chairman] Lindsay on "Face the Nation," while ABC interviewed [Chairman and Commissioners] Kerner, Harris and Wilkins on "Issues and Answers."

Monday's press was devoted to reporting statements made on these programs. Through the week, press and television coverage concentrated on the reactions of President Johnson, Vice-President Hubert Humphrey, presidential hopeful Richard Nixon and local political figures. Columnists speculated on the implications of the *Report*; editorials were generally favorable.[75]

Coverage as extensive as this cannot but have helped encourage interest in the commission around the country, as well as discussion and thought about its findings.

The Kerner report did more than stimulate stories, however; it stimulated action. The media themselves responded to the commission's recommendations to them; recommendations which have been called "without question the best formulated ones, the most constructive ones, and certainly the 'most important.' "[76] The commission harshly criticized the media for what it saw as insufficient and unrealistic depictions of American Blacks; "the communications media, ironically, have failed to communicate," the commission said.[77] The media undertook what one analyst has called "tremendous progress" in response to the commission's calls for improved performance:

Reports on ghetto living and poverty sprang up everywhere. . . . The summer of 1968 saw a spate of media treatments of black history, black culture, biography, art, fashions, etc., etc. The subjects appeared in special newspaper supplements, special TV productions, magazines galore, on radio, billboards, books. Black proliferated in the entertainment and commercial faces of tube and slickprint as well as in the news. . . . [The] young black journalist . . . is fast on the way, thanks in part to the *Kerner Report.*[78]

The media response to commissions can be of both strategic and substantive value. A well-timed commission report can command significant amounts of air time and print space, thereby spreading its message across the country to non-specialized audiences. In addition, commission recommendations may actually stimulate action within the media themselves.

## Follow-up Activities

Commissions are responded to, largely, while memories of their activities are still fresh. In some cases, however, follow-up activities may be undertaken to gauge the response to a commission's report, the degree of implementation of its recommendations, or to promote or "keep alive" a commission's message. These activities may be undertaken by the same institutions or groups that originally offered a response, or by new ones; they may involve members of the commission itself. Follow-up activities may come shortly after the commission has completed its work or as much as a decade later.

Although commissions generally go out of business the day they issue their reports, the utility of what Eisenhower Commission Executive Director Lloyd Cutler has called a "continuing presence"[79] has been recognized by more than one commission. This may be manifested in efforts to promote implementation of commission recommendations or, more generally, an understanding of the commission's work. The Katzenbach Commission, as has been seen, was concerned throughout its lifetime with implementation. Accordingly, it informally recommended that key members and staff meet at regular intervals, following release of its report, to assess the progress of implementation. The Justice Department declined to accept this recommendation, although Chairman Katzenbach later said "I believed at the time, and do in retrospect, that it was a wise one."[80]

Kerner Commission members seem to have been vigorous in their efforts to promote their report. Lipsky and Olson note that Otto Kerner, John Lindsay and other members of the commission offered testimony to congressional committees. Stephen Kurzman, a commission staff member, assisted a committee of liberal Republican Congressmen in preparing proposals based on the final report. Commissioners Brooke and Harris "interpreted" the report to the Senate. New York Mayor Lindsay used the report for identifying city priorities. Atlanta Police Chief Jenkins required all his officers to read the final report and write their reactions.[81] Commissioner and Senator Fred Harris wrote a follow-up article for a national circulation magazine, *LOOK*,[82] and "[i]n speeches, symposia, lectures and discussion groups, some staff members and commissioners continued to talk about the *Report* in the weeks, months and years to follow."[83] Indeed, Lindsay, who had unsuccessfully proposed establishment of a group to monitor implementation, offered annual statements of progress of his own.[84] In addition to having helped keep the commission's message alive, these activities offer a testament, of sorts, to the commission participants' commitment to what they felt they had learned.

Participants in even relatively low-visibility commissions may be provided numerous opportunities for follow-up activities after completion of their work. For example, in the first month after his work on President Nixon's commission on the usefulness of United States information-spreading efforts abroad, Milton Eisenhower received fully 108 speaking invitations.[85]

Following the report of the Pornography Commission, Executive Director W. Cody Wilson appeared on the ABC television network's "Dick Cavett Show" to defend the commission's findings and methods.[86] Chairman Lockhart, however, has discussed his conception of his own follow-up role:

> I have not considered it my role as former chairman to "sell" the Commission's report or its recommendations to any group. My role, as I view it, is to help people to understand the Commission's findings, to acquaint them with the kind of data that underlies these findings, and encourage them to study the report and reach their own conclusions.[87]

In this case, education is seen as the proper goal of follow-up activities; for, even had he wished otherwise, Lockhart did not expect legislative results in the short run (See above, page 135).

Groups and organizations may follow up on commission reports. An interesting harbinger of such efforts was provided some decades ago by the Citizens' Committee for the Hoover Report. This privately financed group was established following the 1949 report of the first Commission on the Organization of the Executive Branch of Government, chaired by Herbert Hoover. It continued its promotional activities throughout the existence of the second Hoover Commission, from 1953 to 1955. Following the report of the second commission, a book was released which outlined the commission's work and its relevance to the citizenry.[88]

Efforts were made to assess progress, or the lack thereof, made in response to the Kerner report. In 1969, the National Urban Coalition and Urban America, Inc. published *One Year Later,* which concluded that insufficient progress had been made.[89] In 1971, the Urban Coalition established a Commission on the Cities in the '70s, to examine progress in the cities. Significantly, the commission was co-chaired by former Kerner Commissioners John Lindsay and Fred Harris. The commission's report, *The State of the Cities,* was also pessimistic.[90] Credit has been given to another commission for follow-up on the Kerner group's work. According to one observer, the Kerner report "would be forgotten by now save that the permanent U.S. Commission on Civil Rights, under tough-talking Father Hesburgh, president of Notre Dame, keeps its message alive."[91]

Attempts were made to spread the message of the Eisenhower Commission on the Causes and Prevention of Violence. Initially, plans were made for the establishment of a national committee, composed of prominent individuals and chaired by "an eminent university president," to promote the commission's recommendations and follow up its analysis. The group, as was the case with those proposed for previous commissions, was not formed.[92] In 1970, at Johns Hopkins University, where Milton Eisenhower was President Emeritus, students prepared a series of twelve programs on violence, based on the commission's report. The series was presented on national public television and, later, on commercial television in a reduced, one-hour form.[93]

An indication of follow-up on activities of the Population Commission was the formation in 1971 of the Coalition for a National Population Policy, one of whose leaders, interestingly enough, was Milton Eisenhower. In commenting on the group, *The New York Times* noted that "Last March the President's Commission on Population Growth and the American Future issued a report that pointed strongly toward the goals that animate the new coalition."[94]

Congress has followed up the work of commissions through hearings and a particular piece of legislation. In August 1969, the Special Studies Subcommittee of the House Government Operations Committee began "a comprehensive review of advisory bodies within the Federal Government . . ."[95] In March and May of 1970, the committee held hearings to "ascertain the number and history, the adequacy of the guidelines for management and operation, the use and purpose, and the supervision and funding of Presidential advisory committees."[96] The scope of the hearings was broad and went beyond presidential commissions to include all forms of executive and interagency advisory committees, task forces, panels and other such groups. Following the hearings, the committee prepared and submitted to Congress a report entitled *The Role and Effectiveness of Federal Advisory Committees.*[97]

In April, 1972, the committee reported to the House H.R. 4383 which was passed on May 9. An amended version of the bill passed the Senate and the Federal Advisory Committee Act of 1972 (86 Stat. 770) was signed by the President on October 6.[98] Relevant portions of the law are reproduced below:

> SEC. 2 (b) . . .
> (4)standards and uniform procedures should govern the establishment, operation, administration, and duration of advisory committees;
> (5)the Congress and the public should be kept informed with respect to the number, purpose, membership, activities, and cost of advisory committees; . . .
> SEC. 5. (b) . . . Any such legislation [establishing a committee] shall—
> (1)contain a clearly defined purpose for the advisory committee;
> (2)require the membership of the advisory committee to be fairly balanced in terms of the points of view represented and the functions to be performed by the advisory committee;
> (3)contain appropriate provision to assure that the advice and recommendations of the advisory committee will not be inappropriately influenced by the appointing authority or by any special interest, but will instead be the result of the advisory committee's independent judgment;
> (4)contain provisions dealing with authorization of appropriations, the date for submission of reports (if any), the duration

of the advisory committee, and the publication of reports and other materials, . . .

(5)contain provisions which will assure that the advisory committee will have adequate staff (either supplied by an agency or employed by it), will be provided with adequate quarters, and will have funds available to meet its other necessary expenses.

(c) To the extent they are applicable, the guidelines set out in subsection (b) of this section shall be followed by the President, agency heads, or other Federal officials in creating an advisory committee.

RESPONSIBILITIES OF THE PRESIDENT

SEC. 6. (a) The President may delegate responsibility for evaluating and taking action, where appropriate, with respect to all public recommendations made to him by Presidential advisory committees.

(b) Within one year after a Presidential advisory committee has submitted a public report to the President, the President or his delegate shall make a report to the Congress stating either his proposals for action or his reasons for inaction, with respect to the recommendations contained in the public report.

(c) The President shall, not later than March 31 of each calendar year (after the year in which this Act is enacted), make an annual report to the Congress on the activities, status, and changes in the composition of advisory committees in existence during the preceding calendar year. . . .

RESPONSIBILITIES OF THE DIRECTOR, OFFICE OF MANAGEMENT AND BUDGET

SEC. 7. (a) The Director shall establish and maintain within the Office of Management and Budget a Committee Management Secretariat, which shall be responsible for all matters relating to advisory committees. . . .

(e) The Director shall include in budget recommendations a summary of the amounts he deems necessary for the expenses of advisory committees, including the expenses for publication of reports where appropriate. . . .

RESPONSIBILITIES OF LIBRARY OF CONGRESS

SEC. 13. . . . the Director shall provide for the filing with the Library of Congress of at least eight copies of each report made by every advisory committee and, where appropriate, background papers prepared by consultants. . . .[99]

The Federal Advisory Committee Act represents one of the most significant efforts ever made to follow up on the work of commissions. While it does not attempt to compel implementation of specific commission recommendations, it does strengthen certain vulnerable aspects of commission procedure (e.g. funding, publication) and seeks to lessen the likelihood of partisan abuse in terms of appointments and the temptation to ignore reports.[100] By its very existence, the act suggests that the historical question of the presidential right to appoint commissions (See Chapter 2) has finally been resolved. In the contemporary era, advisory bodies have become a fact of life, perhaps a necessity.

Two qualifications must be raised with regard to the act. First, it was not enacted in time to affect the reports of the major commissions studied herein (with the exception of the second report of the Commission on Marijuana and Drug Abuse, a commission which was repudiated by the President). Second, as is suggested by the exception just mentioned, any attempt at requiring responses will be limited by the commitment of the personalities involved. As Doris Kearns Goodwin has put it: "You can't require the *quality* of the response."[101] The requirement made by the Federal Advisory Committee Act is an improvement over past practice to the extent that *any* response is considered better than no response at all. It does not, however, require implementation of commission recommendations. Even if the President does offer a seemingly favorable response, there is no guarantee that he will act on his words.

In the Senate, extensive follow-up activities were undertaken by Senator Edward M. Kennedy's Subcommittee on Administrative Practice and Procedure, of the Judiciary Committee. In May, June, and July of 1971, the subcommittee conducted hearings of wide scope on the work and results of a number of presidential commissions.[102] Senator Kennedy stated the goal of the hearings at their opening session:

> The purpose of these hearings . . . is in essence to determine how future commissions can increase their success and reduce their failures. . . . We will want not only to assure ourselves that someone, somewhere in Government is following up on their reports, but also to seek their views as to the institutional, personal and coincidental barriers they faced, and how they can be avoided. We will try to develop the outlines of a statute or an Executive order which will guarantee at least that when a commission speaks, the

> Government listens, that after it listens, it thinks, that after it thinks,
> it responds, and that after it responds, it follows through.[103]

The subcommittee heard from, among others, the chairmen of five of the eight commissions under study. The chairmen were accompanied by members of the commissions' staffs and, in the case of the Scranton Commission, by fellow commissioners. The hearings represented one of the only comprehensive and public first-person records ever compiled of the activities of the commissions as perceived by their participants. And, as Senator Kennedy observed, "the hearings demonstrated that our inaction about so many problems is not for lack of good ideas."[104]

Finally, follow-up efforts may be made by the press. For example, during a two-month period in 1971, journalist Richard Strout devoted four of his weekly columns in *The New Republic* to presidential commissions, the problems they have examined, and the need for action based on their findings.[105] In 1978, the tenth anniversary of the Kerner Commission report, *The New York Times* initiated an extensive series entitled "Two Societies: America Since the Kerner Report." The series, which ran four days and was supplemented by later articles, engaged in analyses of the nation's progress and needs in the area of race. In conjunction with the series the *Times*, along with CBS News, conducted a poll seeking indications of changes, since 1968, in the attitude of white and black Americans toward race.[106]

Follow-up activities, then, may be undertaken by government, private groups and institutions, the press, and by commission members themselves. These efforts may involve promotion of commission recommendations, information regarding findings, and legislation. More than once, suggestions that commissions establish mechanisms by which they might offer periodic updates on the progress made in response to their work have been rejected. As a result, the kinds of efforts described above become more crucial to preservation of commission messages.

The political response to commission reports from those other than the President has been positive and negative, verbal and substantive. Congress may respond with legislation, but the temptations, both partisan and institutional, to ignore or reject the reports of controversial commissions are formidable and often persuasive. State and local governmental responses have, in some cases, been surprisingly enthusiastic; many commission recommendations have been adopted and put into practice at these levels. Organizations and interested groups have studied commission reports and the news media have offered coverage and exposure to reports, at times, extensively. Many of these parties, as well as commissioners themselves, have followed up commission reports with promotional and educational activities.

On the whole, it may be said that positive substantive results were at least as likely and sometimes *more* likely to have come from those other than the President and Congress. It has been seen that presidents and congressmen do not necessarily perceive championing of the kinds of social reform advocated by commissions as offering much in terms of their institutional and political needs. They are the most visible potential respondents to commission reports; consequently, they may perceive the greatest risks involved in responding. Officials and institutions on lower rungs of the political ladder may run risks in attempting reform as well. But they may be freer of pressures for comprehensive responses and, as a result, more able to pick and choose those recommendations upon which they most wish to act. In one case, implementation was aided by officials' having been brought in to participate in commission activities.

Beyond the political, substantive responses to the reports of presidential commissions are the social responses, the less measurable, but no less real, educational and attitudinal results. It is to this other aspect of the response to commissions that we must now turn.

# 7

# THE SOCIAL RESPONSE

Essentially, I guess, commissions provide part of the educational process that keeps evolutionary societies moving along toward the right goals while employing a reasonable set of priorities.

—Senator Philip A. Hart[1]

Significant numbers of commission participants agree: Presidential commissions are valuable simply for what they say. This kind of value defies the criteria of validity demanded by quantitative analysis. Nonetheless, it must be acknowledged that those who have participated in the process rather consistently argue this side of the question of commission utility. This chapter will explore this argument and the educational and attitudinal responses to commissions.

Previous chapters have examined the political responses to commissions, the legislative and procedural results. The record is mixed. The fact is, however, that commissions are not intended to bring about such results. Rather, they are expected to gather information and offer advice. As Carl Marcy pointed out, in 1945:

The effects of such reports are hard to estimate. The criterion of the successful opinion guiding commission is not whether legislation results; that is not the purpose. Success is measured by public awareness of the conclusions reached and stimulation which is traceable to the fact that the material was available.[2]

By these standards, commissions have largely been seen as successful. They have produced comprehensive collections of data on social phenomena—sometimes on an unprecedented scale—and stimulated further research. They have helped demythologize certain subjects. They have provided factual bases for the legitimization of policy. It is likely they have helped change the political climate, the attitudinal atmosphere in which social change occurs. Commission success is thus seen in terms of education and awareness. Senator Philip Hart, a member of the Eisenhower Commission, has offered some perspective on the criteria for success:

> Certainly, I am disappointed that many of our recommendations have not been acted upon but I would be even more agitated if commissions had the power to immediately enact every idea they come up with. If we content ourselves to think of commissions as educational forces, then I think we can conclude that the Violence Commission did a fairly good job.[3]

According to many persons in positions to know, commissions have been successful as "educational forces."

## Academic Awareness

Commission reports have enjoyed widespread utility in the academic context. They have been used as textbooks. They have provided vehicles by which scholarly views receive popular audiences. They have stimulated new research and actually created new areas of study.

Some commission reports have come to be regarded as standard works in their fields. Nicholas Katzenbach sees his commission's report as having become, "after all, the principal source today of information about crime and about the administration of police forces, the court system, and the penal system."[4] The commission's emphasis on local law enforcement as a coherent unified system has been adopted by states, cities, and counties. A commission flow chart has become "standard in police, criminal law, and criminology texts."[5] "Clearly," Frank Popper has said of these accomplishments, "the educational aspect of presidential commissions should not be underrated."[6] The Kerner report is said to have become "the standard work in schools and universities, police-community relations courses and the human resources departments of many state and local governments."[7] James Short, Co-Director of Research for the Eisenhower Commission, maintains that "the Commission's work has become a part of critical scholarly discourse."[8] Raymond Shafer says that his commission's report has become the "bible" in the drug work field and has been discussed in Europe as well.[9]

Reports have been used as texts. The Kerner report's use has been mentioned. The reports of the Eisenhower Commission have been adopted as texts at both the college and high school levels.[10] In addition, Executive Director Charles F. Westoff feels the Population Commission has been "very successful" in the area of education. The video edition of the commission's final report has been widely circulated in high schools.[11]

Commissions are limited in the extent to which they can generate new research. Their lifetimes, funds, compositions and mandates may all be limitations to "exploring or advocating radically new approaches to problems."[12] They can, however, pull together the state of existing knowledge in their fields; something which may not have been done, previously. In doing so, a commission may increase the potential influence of scholarly work:

> True creativity will necessarily be offered by a commission in only a few areas; its boldness and integrity is reflected primarily in its willingness to accept the existing ideas of progressive scholars and administrators who have been unable to influence or affect the existing system to any great degree.[13]

And, despite the limitations, commissions *have* stimulated original research. The Katzenbach Commission conducted the first national survey of unreported crime, and its compilation of data on the subject of law enforcement was comprehensive. Surveys were initiated which examined: promising new procedures in 2,200 police departments; police-community relations across the country; corrections; and juvenile courts. Information was collected on all manner of police practices and procedures, delinquency prevention and narcotics programs, court procedures, and organized crime.[14]

It has been suggested that the Eisenhower Commission, through its work, created an entirely new field of research. This was discussed in an exchange between the commission's Executive Director, Lloyd Cutler, and Representative John Monagan:

MR. MONAGAN. This must be one of the most extensive examples of participation on the part of numbers of people that has ever been carried on through the Government.

MR. CUTLER. Yes. I think that is right, Mr. Chairman. You might even say as our director of research did, Dr. Marvin Wolfgang, that we created a new field of scholarship that had not existed before. Scholars divided into criminologists, sociologists, psychiatrists, historians, law professors, but few of them had written anything from the vantage point of violence. How does a society become violent? What are the factors that lead it to violence? And we did create a literature in that field, which has become so important to all of us, that did not exist before.[15]

The Pornography Commission, Chairman Lockhart has said, "found books and magazines full of opinions with very little factual information. So we had to start almost from scratch to develop a research program . . ."[16] Development of data was part of the congressional mandate to the commission. The commission's research program, examining the effects of exposure to sexually explicit materials, involved:

(1) surveys employing national probability samples of adults and young persons; (2) quasi-experimental studies of selected populations; (3) controlled experimental studies; and (4) studies of rates and incidence of sex offenses and illegitimacy at the national level.[17]

The most ambitious project was a national face-to-face survey of 2,486 adults and 769 youths between the ages of 15 and 20.[18] Chairman Lockhart has assessed the importance of the commission's research:

The development of this extensive body of information about pornography, summarized in the Commission Report but backstopped by nine volumes of research reports, for the first time in history provides a solid basis for informed policy making in this most difficult area. This I believe to have been the most significant function assigned to the Commission by Congress, and our most valuable achievement.[19]

Commissions may stimulate new research beyond their own. This may not necessarily be supportive of commission findings. In one case, for example, Kerner Commission data were recalculated, leading to a conclusion that black rioters were among the least advantaged and not, as the commission had held, among the newly socialized, better-off groups.[20]

From an academic standpoint, then, commissions have seen success. Their reports are used as texts and some have come to be considered standard works in their fields. They have pulled together the current state of knowledge in their fields and sometimes generated significant new knowledge. They have stimulated new research.

## Social Awareness

Beyond the purely academic context, commissions have affected the social climate. They have helped to redefine issues, increase awareness, demythologize certain points, legitimize ideas, and inspire. They have been a part of attitudinal change, contributing to shifts in what is socially and politically acceptable.

### Public education

Although there are obstacles to citizen awareness of presidential commissions, such awareness does exist. Many commissions have found their way into the public spotlight and have become part of the language of certain subjects. Obstacles, naturally enough, grow out of the fact that commissions receive publicity of limited duration. Journalist Kenneth Crawford once pointed out, regarding media coverage of commission reports, that "Casual newspaper readers and television viewers will know only what these media have emphasized."[21] Martin Mayer has spoken of "the daily deception inherent in the fact that news has no memory."[22] In addition, prior to passage of the Federal Advisory Committee Act, even the government maintained no inventory of all existing government commissions.[23] Many commissions do receive considerable publicity, however, and the news may indeed "have a memory," as was the case with *The New York Times'* follow-up efforts on the Kerner Commission (See above, page 149).

The public, official as well as private, has been aware of commission reports. This has been demonstrated in a variety of ways and attested to by commission participants and observers, alike. It appears highly likely that commissions have contributed to a growth in public awareness. This is the public education function of commissions in a democratic society. The significance of this function is fundamental, as James Campbell has pointed out with regard to the consequences of maintaining an uninformed public:

> The result, of course, is that official actions which may have the most serious sorts of long-term political consequences are effectively freed from the restraints normally imposed by the democratic process on significant governmental activity.[24]

The existence and nature of "education-by-commission" may be seen in a number of ways. First, sheer numbers suggest the potential audience for some commission reports. By 1972, the report of the Kerner Commission had sold nearly two million copies.[25] Over two million copies of various Eisenhower Commission reports were printed.[26] Clearly, such figures would represent a significant readership for *any* book. The fact that these were government documents seems particularly noteworthy and suggests the utility of commissions as a medium of public education.

Commissions affect attitudes and help set the terms of reference for subjects. Nicholas Katzenbach has spoken of what he sees as his commission's success in this regard and of how this affects long-term prospects:

> I know for a fact that the relevant pieces of the study and the staff studies have been thoroughly read by the professionals in the area and generally highly regarded. When they make recommendations to their local government they may or may not refer to the commission's findings, but they are influential in their own thinking.[27]
>
> Despite difficulties and disappointments, the Commission report has had considerable impact, and will have greater impact, almost in spite of everything. I say this because I think the philosophy of the report . . . has been accepted now, almost without question. . . . Furthermore, it will have much effect in the future, for the very simple reason that the Commission Report is deeply embedded in every teaching and training program throughout the United States. . . . It is difficult to change the views of those who have been working on the job; it is much easier to change the views of those who are

young and entering into a new profession. And so I think the Commission Report, perhaps on its merits, perhaps by default of there being any other study of comparable scope, will have great influence in the future.[28]

The Kerner Commission is widely credited with having become, despite the President's silence, "the touchstone for discussions of race relations."[29] As one scholar put it, "the conclusions of the 'Kerner Commission' about 'White Racism' changed the focus of discourse about the causes of black unrest in America . . . . these shifts in orientation generated new pressures for action and altered the evaluation context of subsequent policy deliberations."[30] Commissioner and Senator Fred Harris has added: "No witness before any congressional committee dealing with a related subject was able to avoid reference to it. . . . The report . . . forces America to make conscious choices. We can no longer claim the luxury of unawareness."[31] The commission is seen as having been responsible for establishing new terms for the consideration of questions of race. The fact that American attitudes subsequently *did* change will be discussed in a later section.

Nicholas Katzenbach credits the Eisenhower Commission on Violence with "having had a considerable impact in this country." Despite a lack of "concrete" results, he says, "I do think they helped to change the climate."[32] And *The New York Times'* Clive Barnes offered a prediction as to the future of the Pornography Commission's report, suggesting it would be "very likely to become the yardstick of contemporary community standards in such matters."[33]

A commission may come to have a certain legitimacy of its own, to the extent that its report comes to be seen as an authoritative statement. Martha Derthick, a member of the Scranton Commission, reports that at one point a group of students met privately with the commission to urge that it investigate shootings which had occurred in Lawrence, Kansas. The example of the Kerner Commission was raised in support of the students' argument; it had "told it like it was," and the Scranton Commission was expected to do likewise.[34] Significantly, Chairman Scranton later remarked: "I think a great many young people have been helped by what we did because a lot of them, both personally and in groups, told us, as they put it, 'for the first time somebody listened to their side of the story.' "[35] In this case, awareness and acceptance of one commission's work were brought to bear on a subsequent commission's work.

Increased awareness is manifested in other examples. It is reflected in the comments of Lyndon Johnson upon receiving the report of the Katzenbach Commission:

> the effect was like a knife cutting through darkness. Reading the report, I felt for the first time that I could grasp the full dimensions of the problem. It was a more massive and profound problem than any of us had visualized.[36]

Similarly, when asked about the educational value of his commission, Raymond Shafer has remarked, "I got educated, too."[37] As was suggested in Chapter 6, various groups and organizations have taken cognizance of commission reports and, in some cases, have made use of them in educational work. A number of national groups adopted the Kerner Commission report as their "plan for action" and the Eisenhower Commission's report was similarly espoused.[38] In addition, the report of the Scranton Commission was received positively by the American Council on Education, the American Association of University Professors, and the Carnegie Commission on Higher Education.[39] The responses of these various groups reflect not only an organizational awareness of commission work but a potential for spreading awareness among group members, as well.

An unscientific, yet interesting and colorful indicator of public awareness is provided by readers' letters to national publications in response to news of commission reports. Excerpts from letters regarding the Kerner Commission, the Pornography Commission, and the Scranton Commission are reproduced below:

*Kerner Commission*
With wholehearted gratitude for the honesty finally given us as Americans, I applaud the Kerner report. We white Americans, are responsible for the civil discord in our country today. A solution has been presented to us. Let's not allow the report to be conveniently forgotten while ostensibly it is studied in depth by a committee. Any semblance of democracy which is left is slowly draining away. We are responsible for pulling the plug or securing it.

* * *

With no intention of disputing the soundness of the report's recommendations, I do take exception to the conclusion that white
racism is the essential cause of the urban riots. White racism has
always existed in America, and to a greater degree in previous
periods of our history than today. The true cause lies in the rising
expectations of Negroes. Now that they have been given a taste of
the rights they deserve, they want the rest that they see others
enjoying.

\* \* \*

The cities' salvation lies, not in further Federal coddling of an in-
dolent and lawless minority, but in the full and swift exercise of
the police, judicial and penal powers of the state and Federal governments. Let's be done with this corrosive national guilt complex
of which the riot commission's report is the latest psychotic symp-
tom, and demand that adherence to the law apply to all regardless
of race, color or creed.[40]

\* \* \*

Sir: I note the faults found and the remedies offered, including your
estimate of possibly "hundreds of billions of dollars." In no public
utterance or published news item have I read one important ingre-
dient: What are the responsibilities of the Negro community?[41]

*Pornography Commission*
To the Editor:
    I must register my dismay at the naivete of some statements made
by President Nixon in his repudiation of the report . . . I would
prefer to leave the choice of what is valuable and what is obscene
to individuals, rather than to Mr. Nixon or any government. I am
confident that Shakespeare will survive and that "I am Curious"
and its ilk will be forgotten. But in any case the result will stem
from free choice rather than from legislation.[42]

\* \* \*

Sir: . . . no one will even look at their findings. No one even thanks
them for what was a tough job. Those who criticize them have no
professional standing in the field they speak of. It is little wonder
that the younger generation has to blow up buildings to get some

of these people, who have minds like concrete—all mixed up and set solid—to listen. Most people over 30 were born with an open mind, and that was the last instant they had one.

* * *

Sir: I as a taxpayer demand that every cent this commission squandered in formulating its fraudulent report be returned to the U.S. Treasury. And that the twelve who view pornography positively be made to eat their report, page by page, before the nation's TV cameras.[43]

*Scranton Commission*
Govenor Scranton and his committee have done an admirable job of getting to the heart of the matter regarding our young people's unrest. Their report is a courageously honest piece of work and hands a challenge to each of us—young and old alike.

Surely the Administration will not dodge this one? Surely it will soon make some constructive comment indicating that it does understand? That it will show some leadership?

* * *

The commission tells it like it is when it calls the actions of the Jackson, Miss., police "an unreasonable, unjustified overreaction." . . . If the Jackson State murders had been committed in the U.S.S.R., Americans would be screaming about the injustice and inflexibility of the Soviet system. But it happened—and we hear no cries of injustice and anguish.

Utmost hypocrisy.[44]

Letters do not represent a statistically significant sampling of public opinion.[45] They do, however, suggest that commission reports *are* thought about by some numbers of citizens and that the depth of feeling they may tap or inspire *is* significant.

## Demythologizing and the lowering of emotions

A particular aspect of the process by which commissions contribute to public awareness consists in efforts to put popularly held misconceptions to rest and lower the emotional content of certain controversial issues. In some cases this may be unrealistic or simply beyond the realm of possibility. Some successes have been registered, however.

The Warren Commission sought to determine whether the assassination of President Kennedy was the result of a conspiracy, foreign or domestic, involving more individuals than Lee Harvey Oswald. Speculation about such a conspiracy was, at the time, widespread.[46] The commission's report found no evidence of any conspiracy.[47] Speculation and theorizing about the events have continued ever since (and despite) the report's findings, however, contributing to appointment of a House Select Committee on Assassinations in the late 1970s. The committee concluded that Kennedy was "probably" the victim of a conspiracy, but this "was greeted with some of the same kind of skepticism that the commission report encountered."[48] For many people, the Warren Commission did not settle the question of conspiracy. To some degree this may have been an impossible goal, for, as one writer observed, following the work of the House Committee: "The questions will go on, perhaps in ratio to the intensity of public distrust in leaders and institutions."[49]

The Katzenbach Commission conducted its investigation in a period when "crime in the streets" was a volatile partisan issue. In particular, the Republican presidential campaign of 1964 implied that the Johnson administration was undermining respect for law and order.[50] As a result, the commission saw as one of its goals the replacement of partisan rhetoric with facts:

> It was our sincere hope that with a comprehensive study and comprehensive recommendations on the problem we could eliminate it as a political issue, or at least compel responsible discussion in political campaigns at every level of office.[51]

It cannot be said that the commission was successful in this respect with regard to the Republican "law and order" campaign of 1968, but it is noteworthy that it perceived such a goal as relevant to its work.

During the urban riots of 1967, popular wisdom held that the disorders were fomented and coordinated as the result of some sort of conspiracy of individuals or organizations. Theories of this nature could be found not only among the citizenry, but in government as well. For example, Senator John McClellan's Permanent Subcommittee on Investigations conducted hearings which focused on the possibility of conspiracies, despite the fact that the Kerner Commission had already begun its work.[52] Upon completion of its study, the commission stated flatly that it had "found no evidence that all or any of the disorders or the incidents that led to them were planned or directed by any organization or group—international, national, or local."[53] This finding helped demythologize discussions of riot causation and was seen, as Senator Edward Kennedy later put it, as "one of the fundamental services that the Commission provided."[54] In addition, this type of commission function may be useful in preparing the way for acceptance of new ideas and policies (See below).

The Eisenhower Commission's Walker Report on the violence at the 1968 Democratic National Convention in Chicago "made credible to millions of Americans, for the first time," the charges of "police brutality" that had so often been made by Blacks and dissidents.[55] A majority of citizens did feel that the demonstrators in Chicago "got what they deserved," but as James Campbell has observed, "at least it could no longer be denied that they and others like them had in fact gotten it."[56]

William Lockhart's perception of the response to the Pornography Commission encouraged him to believe that "large numbers of Americans are willing and ready to study the problems of pornography without closing their minds to the available data."[57] He felt that, in the long run, legislators would do likewise.[58] The commission was seen as providing facts for those who wish to consider them. In this sense, a commission may reinforce the inclinations and efforts of those who do not wish to give in to preconceptions.

The Commission on Marijuana and Drug Abuse saw the deflation of myth and the lowering of emotion as important aspects of what it sought to accomplish. These points were emphasized in the letter of transmittal to the President and Congress that accompanied the Commission's first-year report:

> This Report . . . is an all-inclusive effort to present the facts as they are known today, to demythologize the controversy surrounding marihuana, and to place in proper perspective one of the most emotional and explosive issues of our time. We on the Commission sincerely hope it will play a significant role in bringing uniformity and rationality to our marihuana laws, both Federal and State, and that it will create a healthy climate for further discussion, for further

research and for a continuing advance in the development of a public social policy beneficial to all our citizens.[59]

Commissioner and Senator Harold E. Hughes reflected the same idea in an interview following release of the report: "I think as a result of this report that rather than creating an intensity of controversy, it is going to create an intensity of education."[60] Following release of the commission's second report, this process was still perceived as a chief commission function. One writer called the report:

> a long, conscious attempt to deflate some of the hysteria and, gently, [it] exposes what it perceives as the hypocrisy that Americans have invested in the "drug problem." . . . the commission's most lasting contribution may not be its formal recommendations but rather its low-key, nondramatic analysis of "drug abuse"—a term that it says ought to be stricken from the official vocabulary of the government.[61]

A year later, Chairman Raymond Shafer said he felt the wide dissemination of the report had helped "lower the emotionalism" about the subject.[62] This commission saw demystification as a basic goal of its work.

Finally, in both the televised and written versions of its report, the Commission on Population Growth challenged the axiom "bigger is better." In the opening words of its printed report, the commission confronted what it called "the population growth ethic":

> In the brief history of this nation, we have always assumed that progress and "the good life" are connected with population growth. In fact, population growth has frequently been regarded as a measure of our progress. If that were ever the case, it is not now. . . . One of the basic themes underlying our analysis and policy recommendations is the substitution of quality for quantity . . .[63]

The commission, running counter to a popular assumption, declared that its immediate goal was "to encourage the American people to make population choices, both in the individual family and society at large, on the basis of greater rationality rather than tradition or custom, ignorance or chance."[64]

## Legitimization of ideas

In a function which may be related to demythology, commissions may legitimize new ideas or policy proposals. Commissions, as prestigious national bodies, may lend acceptability to ideas which would be rejected if offered by individuals. They can, simply by their existence, lend legitimacy to discussion of their subjects. Their existence suggests official governmental concern about a given subject. Even though commissions' findings may be rejected by those who appointed the commissions, the findings stand as legitimate statements against which subsequent actions may be measured.

This commission function is revealed in a number of ways. In one sense, commissions can absorb adverse reactions to new ideas, without harm, to a degree elected officials probably would not choose. By the time public officials offer similar ideas, however, the proposals may no longer appear threatening.[65] In addition, commissions may make previously articulated ideas appear "more respectable, plausible, and thinkable."[66] This may include reinforcement of the findings and recommendations of previous commissions.[67] Further, commissions may impart a legitimacy which individuals cannot. Jerome Skolnick has written:

> Commission reports, whatever their analytical strictures, defects or omissions, come to have a special standing within the *political* community. If a social scientist or a journalist gathers "facts" concerning a particular institution, and these facts are presented in such a way as to offer a harshly critical appraisal of that social institution, the gathering and the analysis of such facts may be called "muckraking." But if the same or a similar set of facts is found by a commission, it may be seen as a series of startling and respectable social findings.[68]

Perhaps the best known example of the legitimization function was the Kerner Commission's indictment of white racism and its warning that America was "moving toward two societies, one black, one white—separate and unequal."[69] Although prejudice and discrimination had been decried before, and calls for racial justice had been heard, the Kerner report added a new dimension to public awareness of these issues. On the tenth anniversary of the report's release *The New York Times* editorialized:

the commission's words were heard nationally. They were words that had not been spoken before by so official, public—and white—a body.

It had been one thing for Northerners to denounce brutal Southern racism. It was quite another for a distinguished national body to say, "There is blame for all of us, Northerners as well; and there is a national responsibility for us all to act on."[70]

The Kerner Commission was part of the process whereby black claims on American society were legitimized. It made a dissident view the orthodox view. It dispelled the riot conspiracy myth; declared attitudinal, institutional, and socioeconomic factors to have been the fundamental causes of the riots; and "became a legitimizing instrument for diverse public-policy proposals."[71] Black scholar Mack H. Jones has summarized this function of the commission:

What it did was to reduce to eloquent and provocative language what many of us had known and been saying all the time. Thus, the only real value in having the Commission restate these concerns was to give legitimacy to them by enshrouding them with the imprimatur of the National Government.[72]

Indeed, this may be among the most important potential functions of presidential social issue commissions. For, although they cannot enact *anything,* commissions can alter the political climate by giving national-level recognition and credence to claims, interpretations, or proposals previously thought to be outside the mainstream.

## Inspiration

Beyond their collection of facts and proffering of recommendations, commissions may seek to inspire. This is evident from examination of the wording of report texts. Although nothing specifically directs commissions to call on the nation, the commissions' in-depth study of the issues and their desire to be heard may bring forth prose which goes beyond scholarly discourse. Commissioner Fred Harris has written of this aspect of the Kerner Commission report:

What did the Kerner report accomplish? Very little, and then again, a lot. It sought to call forth the best in America, to tap the great reservoir of goodness in our people. It set our sights a little higher. It made action easier to imagine and undertake.[73]

Indeed, the commission had prefaced its recommendations for national action with its "basic conclusion: the need is not so much for the Government to design new programs as it is for the Nation to generate new will."[74] And President Johnson later identified this call as "the key to the report . . . The Kerner report went part way in helping to create this 'public will.' "[75]

Inspirational language was not confined to the Kerner Commission. Examples from the Kerner, Eisenhower, and Scranton commissions should suggest the nature and tone of the efforts to inspire:

*Kerner Commission*
The alternative is not blind repression or capitulation to lawlessness. It is the realization of common opportunities for all within a single society.

This alternative will require a commitment to national action—compassionate, massive, and sustained, backed by the resources of the most powerful and the richest nation on this earth. From every American it will require new attitudes, new understanding, and, above all, new will. . . . Violence and destruction must be ended—in the streets of the ghetto and in the lives of people.[76]

*Eisenhower Commission*
Some ordinary citizens feel they can do nothing to influence the direction and the destiny of their nation. But more and more Americans are proving this to be a myth. A growing number of our citizens have found they need not stand idle while our cities rot, people live in fear, householders build individual fortresses, and human and financial resources flow to less urgent endeavors. A new generation of Americans is emerging, with the energy and the talent and the determination to fulfill the promise of the nation. . . . The greatness and durability of most civilizations has been finally determined by how they have responded to . . . challenges from within. Ours will be no exception.[77]

*Scranton Commission*
Despite the differences among us, powerful values and sympathies unite us. The very motto of our nation calls for both unity and diversity: from many, one. Out of our divisions, we must now recreate understanding and respect for those different from ourselves.

Violence must end.

Understanding must be renewed.

All Americans must come to see each other not as symbols or stereotypes but as human beings.

Reconciliation must begin.

We share the impatience of those who call for change. We believe there is still time and opportunity to achieve change. We believe we can still fulfill our shared national commitment to peace, justice, decency, equality, and the celebration of human life.

We must start. All of us.[78]

Commissions seek not only to inform but to inspire the citizenry to *do something* with their information. Through the combined effects of factual presentation, myth dissolution, legitimization of ideas, and inspiration, commissions seek to educate the public and alter the attitudinal landscape.

## The Kerner Case: Changing Attitudes

The Kerner Commission offers a test case for measuring whether commission-sponsored social goals were achieved in the aftermath of a commission's report.

The Kerner Commission was part of the process whereby the concepts and realities of racial justice were altered in America. It conducted its investigation, and drew its unexpected conclusions, in a period of protest, violence, and change. The civil rights movement, led by Dr. Martin Luther King, Jr., had achieved great publicity, the endorsements of political leaders, and significant legislative successes such as the Civil Rights Act of 1964 and the Voting Rights Act of 1965. The Kerner Commission contributed to the process of change, as an agency of the federal government, by declaring white society to be responsible for black dissatisfaction and by providing what has been called the "touchstone for race relations."[79]

The Kerner Commission's fulfillment of the various potential commission roles has been discussed, above. In sales, the Kerner report qualifies as a best-seller. It has been used as a text and it established new standards for discussions of questions of race. It demystified the question of the origin of urban riots and it legitimized the charge of white responsibility for the ghetto. It called for changes in policy and attitudes sufficient to "make good the promises of American democracy to all citizens."[80]

Measurable change has come. And, although the promise of the Kerner Commission has by no means been fully met, there exist factual indicators of the significant progress which has been made. Change is clearly identifiable in the attitudes of the American public, both black and white; in shifts in the socio-economic and political positions of blacks; and in the rhetoric of public officials. "In a sense," one writer has said, the civil rights movement "is the victim of its own success. . . ."

> Not long ago, the victims of racial discrimination could turn for aid only to organized civil rights groups. Now, Government has become a major advocate for minorities. . . . Blatant acts of racism and violence have all but vanished, and so have their conspicuous advocates . . .[81]

This was echoed by Andrew Young's observation that issues which were once items for protest "are now an agenda for action."[82] There is no evidence to suggest that the Kerner Commission was solely or even primarily responsible for all the change which has come. If nothing else, however, the commission was one element, highly visible and prestigious, in the definition of the problem, the identification of requisite reform, and the inspiration thereto. It is not unreasonable to assume that it shares some measure of responsibility for the change which has come about in accordance with its entreaties.

During the commission's investigation, Otto Kerner stated: "My concern all the time about this commission has been that at the conclusion our greatest problem is going to be to educate the white, rather than the Negro," and Commissioner Charles Thornton said, "the attitudinal problem is perhaps the biggest problem. And the government can't force that to change."[83] As has been seen, the conclusions and language of the commission's report sought to reorient white perceptions. One observer has suggested the commission was aided in this effort by the fact that its report followed, by a month, the assassination of Martin Luther King, Jr.; a period in which there was already "a great deal of white soul-searching."[84]

White attitudes on the subject of race have changed since the time when the Kerner report was released. In the decade following the report Whites became more tolerant of the ideas of black progress, black neighbors, and even a black president. In fact, most Whites felt Blacks had achieved significant gains. Opinion polling at the end of the decade revealed noteworthy and surprising changes in White attitudes regarding Black freedom to choose a place of residence—without concomitant "white flight."[85] White support was recorded for the Supreme Court's Bakke decision[86] which struck down quotas but permitted race to be considered as a factor in professional school admissions.[87] Increased contacts between Whites and Blacks were revealed, in both on-the-job and social situations and this was characterized as "pleasant and easy." As a result, negative White stereotypes of Blacks declined.[88] Whites accepted, by a vast majority, the idea of a qualified black presidential candidacy.[89] Overall, the White perception was that Blacks had made, "a lot of progress" in destroying discrimination.[90] It was felt that "there are indeed new attitudes about race relations and new understanding among whites . . . They feel that blacks are making good progress and they seem to find little real urgency in the black situation."[91]

The polls also examined the Black perspective. By the late 1970s, Blacks perceived "more sensitive and tolerant attitudes on race" on the part of Whites.[92] Many Blacks felt Whites did not care too much about them, or their situation, one way or the other.[93] In other words, the prejudice of 1968 had become the complacency or indifference of 1978. Ironically, Blacks did not see a general lowering of prejudice as having alleviated difficulties in attaining jobs, promotions, and housing. Many Blacks felt there had not been much progress in fighting discrimination and that government was not committed to full equality—although Whites felt it *was* committed.[94] Blacks did not feel great hostility toward Whites. Rather, among urban Blacks, "a sense of neglect, resignation, and perhaps futility" seemed to prevail.[95]

In material terms, figures indicated that the gap between the earnings of Whites and Blacks, for both men and women, had narrowed significantly. Blacks were found to be receiving wage increases which were similar to those of comparably educated Whites and it was found that Blacks were not being relegated to "dead-end jobs." Improved black education, rather than government pressure, was seen as being primarily responsible for wage improvements.[96]

Politically, while Blacks were found to be voting in fewer numbers than Whites, greater numbers of Blacks were holding public office, from municipal officials, mayors, and state legislators, to members of Congress.[97] In 1984, Jesse Jackson's campaign for the Democratic presidential nomination was widely perceived as a symbolic victory in the legitimization of the Black role in American politics.

One of the most remarkable indications of progress has been the emergence of a "bright, educated, optimistic and independent" black middle class.[98] Indeed, as one writer put it, "one of the most striking developments in American society in the last decade has been the abandonment of the ghetto by millions of upwardly mobile blacks."[99] The Kerner Commission despaired of the black middle class opening "an escape hatch from the ghetto"[100] but, in fact:

> the new black middle class, led by a segment of upwardly mobile young professionals, has opened a double-door exit from the ghetto. These blacks are moving away from the old neighborhoods, the ghettos, slums, and even the projects, into the fashionable rental and condominium developments, integrated neighborhoods, chic sections of big cities, and even the suburbs.[101]

Ten years after the Kerner report, an "American black middle/professional class is flourishing and swelling . . . carving a distinct identity for itself"; a group whose members "glide throughout society."[102] The new members of the black middle class are described as products of the 1960s, many of whom were participants in the civil rights/black power movements and who were "quick to rush through the doors those movements opened to them."[103] Their socio-economic position reflects progress in income and education, black college enrollment having risen 275 percent between 1966 and 1976.[104] Interestingly, despite the black discouragement registered in some polls, a Gallup poll found feelings of satisfaction and optimism among Blacks, who saw themselves as being likely to improve their status in the future.[105]

Overall, the emergence of the black middle class has made it "increasingly difficult today to define a 'black community.' "[106] For, although the Kerner Commission warned of the nation's becoming two separate societies, black and white, and although significant differences remain, "In fact, the division *between the classes of American blacks* is now a much more confounding and talked-about problem. Put simply, blacks who've made it, who have it, are saying today that they have more in common than ever before with their white counterparts—and sometimes more in common with them than with their black street brothers."[107] This helps explain, to some degree, the range of perspectives and opinions Blacks have offered in response to questions about their socio-economic positions and the climate of tolerance. For many Blacks things have not changed much, while for many others they have. And the differences between these two groups of Blacks have become significant.

The reality of the racial issue has changed to the point where racism and racial differences are no longer universally being discussed as the independent variables which explain poverty among Blacks.[108] For, although the trend in 1968 was seen to be toward two societies differentiated unequally by race, by 1978 change had occurred to the point where "Today, it's probably more accurate to say that America is divided into two classes, one comfortable and one not."[109]

A final, and perhaps the most remarkable, aspect of the change in the racial situation is reflected in the evolution of politicians' rhetoric. In few areas is the contrast between an era of segregation and an era of integration more sharply exemplified. In 1978, for example, South Carolina Republican Senator Strom Thurmond, a long-time stalwart in the resistance to integration, made a considerable effort to win black support in his campaign for re-election.[110] In 1976, the Democratic Party platform called for the birthday of Martin Luther King, Jr. to be designated a national holiday. In 1979, President Jimmy Carter, himself a symbol of changed attitudes in the South, publicly called on Congress to declare the holiday. Carter's comment came in a speech given on the anniversary of Martin Luther King, Jr.'s birthday, in which he promised his administration would remain true to the slain civil rights leader's goals.[111] The holiday was eventually recognized and celebrated, for the first time, in 1986.

Nowhere was a change in rhetoric more evident than in the state of Alabama in 1979. As his gubernatorial term drew to a close, George C. Wallace, perhaps the nation's most prominent incarnate symbol of the segregationist viewpoint, offered thoughts on Blacks that once might have been unimaginable. Wallace conceded that Alabama was better off without segregation and said that racial killings in Alabama, during his three terms as governor, "broke my heart."[112] Then, in words which might seem unbelievable to those who have ever heard him speak, Wallace elaborated on his motives in resisting integration and his personal feelings about Blacks:

"I was not an enemy of blacks in those days . . . I was the enemy of the Federal Government, big government. It's very unfortunate that it involved race when we raised those issues. . . . I was never saying anything that reflected on black people, and I'm sorry it was taken that way. . . . The first people I saw when I opened my eyes when I came into the world and could see were black people. I've lived among them all my life. Some of my finest friends—" he paused in embarrassment at the cliché. "You laugh when you make that statement, you know. I wouldn't know how to live where there were not black people. The country would be strange to me."[113]

Finally, Wallace spoke of segregation: "It's good that it's been changed. It's good that the civil rights bill has passed. It hasn't been the evil that we thought in attacking property rights. That's what we were against it for."[114] The skeptic may, understandably, interpret Wallace's remarks as a ploy to win favorable treatment in history books. Even if this were the case, however, it would only tend to confirm the fact that the atmosphere has changed; otherwise, even a Wallace with ulterior motives would have no incentive to offer such sentiments. There remains, of course, the possibility that Wallace meant what he said.

Final confirmation of the change in Alabama is offered by the contrast of Governor George Wallace's first inaugural address, on January 14, 1963, and governor Forrest H. James, Jr.'s first inaugural address on January 15, 1979. Excerpts from these two addresses are reproduced below:

*Wallace*
This nation was never meant to be a unit of one, but a unit of the many . . . and so it was meant to be in our racial lives . . . . if we amalgamate into the one unit as advocated by the Communist philosopher, then the enrichment of our lives, the freedom for our development is gone forever. We become, therefore, a mongrel unit of one under a single all-powerful government. And we stand for everything, and we stand for nothing . . . Today I have stood where Jefferson Davis stood, and took an oath to my people. It is very appropriate then that from this Cradle of the Confederacy, this very heart of the great Anglo-Saxon Southland, today we sound the drum for freedom . . . In the name of the greatest people that have ever trod this earth, I draw the line in the dust and toss the gauntlet before the feet of tyranny. And, I say, segregation now! Segregation tomorrow! Segregation forever!

*James*
On this beautiful day, the birthday of Martin Luther King, Jr., I claim
for all Alabamians a new beginning, free from racism and discrimination. Let us bury forever the negative prejudices of the past. The
same standards of justice, responsibility and reward are for one and
all. I stand on this commitment without equivocation. So be it. We
can be confident in the richness of our heritage. Our heroes are
many—if only we are not too arrogant to remember—too proud to
see. . . . I believe if Robert E. Lee and Martin Luther King Jr. were
here today, their cry to us—their prayer to God—would call for the
politics of unselfishness—a people together—determined to climb
the highest plateau of greatness . . . we have a new beginning. It
is time.[115]

Governor James, as a former businessman, reported that he did not
delve into politics for many years and that the Kerner report, itself,
had no impact on his racial attitudes. He said he did not "feel far
ahead of my time," on the issue of race, nor that his inaugural
comments were "especially noteworthy." Rather, James said, "The
race issue has kept our state divided for many years and has hampered
our progress and growth. I felt it was time we said publicly and
unequivocally that we in Alabama should put racial bias aside and
work for the common good."[116] Whether or not the governor felt
"ahead of his time," his comments stood in bold contrast to those
of his predecessor (in 1963) and reflected significant change in the
nature of acceptable public rhetoric and policy.

The Kerner Commission warned that the United States was "moving toward two societies, one black, one white—separate and unequal . . . Discrimination and segregation have long permeated much
of American life; they now threaten the future of every American."[117]
Having defined what it perceived as the problem, however, the commission raised the possibility of a solution:

This deepening racial division is not inevitable. The movement
apart can be reversed. Choice is still possible. Our principal task
is to define that choice and press for a national resolution. . . . The
alternative [to the present course] . . . is the realization of common
opportunities for all within a single society.

This alternative will require a commitment to national
action—compassionate, massive, and sustained, backed by the resources of the most powerful and the richest nation on this earth.

> From every American it will require new attitudes, new understanding, and, above all, new will . . . . this Nation will deserve neither safety nor progress unless it can demonstrate the wisdom and the will to undertake decisive action against the root causes of racial disorder. . . . The most important step toward domestic peace is an act of will; this country can do for its people what it chooses to do.[118]

An argument may be made that sufficient material commitment to black progress has not been made by the federal government or, for that matter, in the minds of every private citizen. Yet, the fact is that significant changes called for by the commission *have* been accomplished, most notably in the decline of racism as a prevalent and socially acceptable attitude among Whites. Moreover, the material, educational, and political position of Blacks has seen improvement to the point where class has become a more identifiable distinction among people than race. To a significant degree, the race problem of the 1960s has become the economic problem of the 1970s and 1980s—a problem which affects Blacks in disproportionate numbers. Progress has been reflected as increasing numbers of Blacks have entered the middle class—the mainstream of American life and culture—and begun to take on the attitudes and values of that culture. This is the kind of integrated reality the Kerner Commission alluded to when it referred to "Americans who are also Negroes."[119]

The issue of race has changed. The black urban riots of the 1960s have not been repeated, whites have become generally more tolerant, and the black material condition is improving, albeit slowly. Lyndon Johnson, Martin Luther King, Jr. and the civil rights movement, the Civil Rights and Voting Rights Acts, and the American people all contributed to change. The Kerner Commission as a visible, national body which called for these changes and specifically identified white attitudes as the chief barrier to them, would seem entitled to share the credit for having brought them about.

## Awareness in a democracy: a summary

Commissions, as investigative bodies, offer findings of fact and make recommendations for action. It is often hoped that legislative or procedural reform will follow the issuance of a commission report. Commissions, however, have no power or responsibility in these latter respects. The first function of the social-issue commissions is to educate not only the President and Congress but the citizenry and relevant groups as well. They seek to provide awareness, in perhaps the most acceptable manner a democracy recognizes: through persuasion based on facts. Many commissions have been successful by the educational standard. To be sure, many of those in a position to know—commission participants themselves—argue that the value of commissions must be seen in their performance of the educational function. William Scranton has spoken, at length, on this subject:

> even if there is little or no response from government, that fact does not necessarily mean that a commission has done its work in vain. One of the effects of some commissions—and here I think particularly of the Kerner and Eisenhower Commissions—has sometimes been to educate and mobilize, if not the President and Congress, then at least private citizens and people in positions of responsibility in the private sector. Who, for example, can doubt the large and still growing impact upon private individuals in their daily lives, businesses, universities, and other institutions, of the message of the Kerner Commission, which has been an inspiration and a call to conscience for millions of Americans. *Anyone who sought to measure the importance of that report only in terms of how the President and Congress responded to it*—though of course their response, or lack of response, also was important—*would have missed its full value and impact.* Anyone who sought to measure its impact after six or nine or twelve months would have been similarly deceived. Leadership of the sort that commissions provide takes effect not in days or months but rather over years. One may wish that change were a more rapid process in this nation, but it is not; and we may take it as an indication of the enduring importance of commissions that their impact is measured in the long run, for that means that their impact can be deep, broad, and lasting.[120]

Indeed, with respect to the enduring value of commission findings, Senator Edward Kennedy has said:

> The Kerner Commission report will forever be the definitive work on the anatomy of riots and rioters, and one of its findings alone ["two societies"] will make it live on . . . That statement was true on March 1, 1968, and a year later, and 2 years later, and 3 years later. And until it is no longer true, we will have to read and reread the Kerner report.[121]

Commissions can act as a social conscience and they do so with some legitimacy. They say things, from an official platform, which others either cannot or will not say. As Gary T. Marx said of the Kerner report: "in some important ways this is a document with a difference . . . . it suggests that a society can condemn itself."[122] And Jerome Skolnick, a scholar who endured a difficult relationship with the Commission on the Causes and Prevention of Violence, has written:

> Despite the increasing tendency among radicals and intellectuals to challenge the usefulness and integrity of commission reports, they do tend to create an interest over and above that of similar work by individual scholars . . . . whatever facts are gathered and presented to the public, they are in the public domain . . . . to the extent that a commission of inquiry develops facts, it necessarily has done something of social value. Its interpretations can be challenged. How those facts and how those interpretations will be met and used depends upon the integrity and ability of the intellectual community.[123]

Commissions deal in awareness; in jogging peoples' consciences and preconceptions just as those of the commissioners had been jogged during their investigiations. Milton Eisenhower has summarized this aspect of the commission function in one sentence: "I have the feeling if all the people of the United States could have been members of this commission, we would have had action."[124] Eisenhower has elaborated:

> Perhaps the most important value of Commissioneering as a tool for solving social problems in a democracy is the remarkable consensus they reflect among thoughtful citizens of all political persuasions, from all cultural groupings and from all walks of life, when they study a phenomenon such as social violence in sufficient depth to obtain an adequate perspective. If only we could assign the entire population one by one to serve on Presidential commissions, perhaps we could achieve as a nation the consensus for change at which the members of all recent Presidential commissions have arrived![125]

Thus, as Senator Philip Hart said, commissions are "part of the educational process that keeps evolutionary societies moving . . ."[126]

The social-issue commissions have fostered consensus in the midst of their own diversity, progressive advocacy in the midst of the moderate inclinations of their members. The major social issue commissions have raised strong calls for reform based on their in-depth exposure to the facts and complexities of their subjects of inquiry. These calls have come regardless of the partisan or constituency backgrounds commissioners have brought with them and regardless of what presidents or congresses might otherwise have wished to hear. As Milton Eisenhower has said: ". . . this is what happens to the human mind when you free yourself of your preconceptions and work together over a long period of time, basing your judgment on facts as they develop."[127] And Lipsky and Olson have written: "disagreements over the nature of the recommendations are less significant than the commissioners' agreement on the necessity for radical departures from existing public policy."[128]

The social-issue commissions are successful, then, because nonpartisan in-depth analysis is "valuable in itself."[129] They offer what frequently become standard works in their fields; they stimulate research; they challenge preconceptions, demythologize, and lower emotions; they give legitimacy to ideas; they help alter attitudes; they inspire; they create awareness in a social milieu which values awareness as an instrument of growth. "So," as Milton Eisenhower has concluded, "a lot of educational work goes on; and in time it will have results."[130]

# 8

# CONCLUSIONS

At the outset of this book Pornography Commissioner Charles Keating was quoted as saying: "So-called Presidential commissions do not work. They never will. Such commissions, in my opinion, are not a valid part of the American political system."[1] At this point, some conclusions may be drawn as to the validity of this opinion.

## Accomplishments

Throughout this study, presidential advisory commissions have been defined as investigatory bodies, generally without statutory bases, which within a defined purview are directed to seek out all relevant information, sift it, piece it together, arrive at conclusions and, on the basis of their conclusions, make recommendations for legislative and/or social action. By this standard, commissions must be counted successful.

In the 1960s and early 1970s, presidential commissions were a primary governmental tool by which the President and Congress sought information and direction with regard to some of the most complex and awesome problems the nation has ever faced. Violence in many forms, racism, crime, drug use in all sectors of society, pornography, overpopulation, and the many questions these implied (e.g. permissiveness, conspiracies, national policy orientations and priorities), confronted the United States with questions about proper directions for the nation, a need for answers and, one might suggest with little risk, a considerable amount of fear. For a variety of reasons, commissions became a highly visible tool chosen to seek answers.

Commissions are appointed for a number of purposes. First, simply by their existence, commissions symbolize the highest level of cognizance and concern over a stituation. Commissions communicate that the President (or Congress) is aware of a situation and will begin a process of directing his and the nation's attention to it. This implies a search for facts and answers and a willingness to give the disaffected members of society a "fair hearing." This may involve not only a genuine desire for information on the part of an individual President but also fulfillment of a societal expectation of a presidential response to nearly any significant situation. In short, commissions represent the fact that the President is at least doing *something*.

Second, commissions may be appointed as part of the presidential (or congressional) policy process. They may be intended to: develop factual bases upon which policy may be constructed; educate, generally; legitimize already-considered proposals; represent an executive response to a particular group's request.

Third, commissions may be used as a tool for surmounting the pathologies of organizational complexity: for avoiding duplication of effort and circumventing bureaucratic obstacles. Commissions have made rapid, relatively efficient, comprehensive analyses of major problems. They have brought together resources, skills, and information on a scale difficult for single agencies or the private sector to match.

Fourth, commission appointments permit delay. They may provide a "cooling off" period during which tensions may be reduced. The evidence does not support the criticism that commissions are appointed out of some cynical desire to avoid a more substantive response.

Commissions have been most successful in the area of their primary task: education. Commissions have compiled bodies of data, frequently on an unprecedented scale, and placed it at the disposal of the President, Congress, state and local governments, interested groups and organizations, and the public in general. Commission reports are frequently considered standard works in their respective fields and have been adopted for use in schools, organizational projects, and government programs at all levels. Beyond this, they have affected the attitudinal atmosphere of society. They have helped demythologize subjects such as the conspiracy theory of riot origins and the assumption that increasing population growth is necessarily advantageous. Commissions have helped lower the emotional content of certain issues, such as marijuana use. They have legitimized interpretations of social phenomena previously unaccepted by society at large; the most profound example of legitimization was the Kerner Commission's identification of white attitudes as the cause of racial unrest. Commissions have often altered the terms in which issues are discussed and, although they have by no means either reached or convinced everyone of their findings, they have spread awareness to all levels of society, a not undesirable function in a democracy.

Commissions have seen some of their proposals enacted as legislation. The Commission on Law Enforcement and the Administration of Justice is generally credited with having prompted passage of the Safe Streets Act of 1968. Even the Pornography Commission saw its recommended postal regulation enacted. At the state level, there was a significant response to the Katzenbach Commission, and there were responses in line with the recommendations of the Pornography Commission and the Commission on Marijuana and Drug Abuse, as well.

Other responses to commissions have come from governmental agencies, at all levels, interested groups which have endorsed and disseminated commission reports, institutions, the news media, and congressional committees.

## Difficulties

Commissions have experienced certain difficulties during the course of their work and in response to their reports. These have included presidential (and, in one case, congressional) rejections, a lack of much identifiable legislation following their reports, appropriations and time limitations, and, in one celebrated case, a partisan attempt at commission sabotage. Many of these difficulties underlie criticisms of commissions, although the evidence suggests many criticisms are unwarranted and based on unfounded expectations regarding the role of commissions.

Probably the most important obstacles the social-issue commissions have faced have been presidents. This judgment must be most squarely made against Richard Nixon. In dealing with commissions appointed by Lyndon Johnson but reporting to Nixon, as well as with his own, President Nixon exhibited neglect, attempts at manipulation with regard to findings, partisan abuse of reports and an impression, generally, that commissions which did not return findings complimentary to, or compatible with, the incumbent administration's views should be condemned. Lyndon Johnson, as well, was capable of rejecting commission findings, yet he appears to have been far more genuine in the desire for understanding, which prompted many of his commission appointments.

The likelihood of a positive presidential response may be affected by the partisan environment and the President's perception of his political needs, the presidential personality, and, during the period under study, the fact that there was no requirement that the President respond. All these factors make it clear that criticism of commissions for a lack of presidential response is largely unfounded. The responsibility for presidential action, or for a lack thereof, lies with the President. As for a commission, its responsibility is to inform and advise. It has no legal power to force presidential acceptance of its advice; nor would there appear any utility in a commission's parroting presidential views in the hope of winning presidential approval. As a House Government Operations Committee report put it: "It is not in the public interest to fund advisory groups which act to support, without justification, the actions of public officials."[2] Indeed, it hardly seems unreasonable to say, with Senator Edward M. Kennedy, that "one may wish to see a commission's proposals implemented or one may oppose them on the merits, but it is hard to defend their simply being ignored."[3]

Beyond the question of presidential response, there is the lack of substantial legislative response. The institutional structure of Congress was seen to be largely responsible for this. Commissions present comprehensive reform packages to an institution which disperses jurisdiction, works incrementally, and is reluctant to embrace sweeping reforms. Further, the partisan climate may be resistant to new initiatives and there may be more electoral risks for congressmen than potential payoffs for advocacy of commission proposals. It was suggested that commission recommendations may not be sufficiently detailed for use as legislation. Overall, however, the temptations to either ignore or (as in the case of the Pornography Commission) reject a commission report may be most persuasive.

Legislation might appear to be a key indicator of commission failure or success, but this conclusion is based on a weak premise. Commissions, in fact, have no authority to legislate or do anything beyond conducting investigations and offering their best advice. Their only power, such as it is, resides in the persuasiveness of their words, their facts, and arguments. Even though these be offered in the most stirring and rationally based terms, Congress will respond from its own frame of reference, which may or may not be receptive to sweeping proposals at any given time. In short, commissions cannot reasonably be blamed if Congress does not care to take their advice.

The fact that many observers look to "the charade of the legislative box score," as Cronin has called it, as "the measure of policy success,"[4] reflects as much on the theoretical outlooks of the observers as on anything else. The elder Oliver Wendell Holmes once said that Americans are a people who want results they can see, feel, and touch. Yet, commissions have been given no authority to produce such results; that is the responsibility of others. As James Campbell has put it:

> The idea the commissions are not very valuable, I think, is the product of expecting more out of commissions than one can reasonably expect. . . . There is no one-to-one relationship between what a commission does and some Executive action or legislative proposal. . . . It seems to me the critics are so simple-minded about this. The process by which public policy is made is so complicated, and there are so many things that go into it.[5]

The projection on to commissions of the social scientific Weltanschauung of quantifiable standards of validity may not be appropriate. To criticize commissions for not doing what they were never intended to do is perhaps more revealing of the motives of the critics than of the functions of commissions.

One factor which may have affected the nature of both presidential and congressional responses was the "superheated" environments, as Harry McPherson has phrased it,[6] in which the social-issue commissions were appointed. Most of the social-issue commissions were established in periods of controversy and tension. This may have affected the tone of commission findings as well as the likelihood of a reasoned response from those in high positions. Facts may be of secondary importance in discussions of highly charged issues. James

Q. Wilson has suggested that, with subjects such as violence and obscenity, it is unlikely that "considerations of utility or disutility can be governing. These are moral issues, and ultimately all judgments . . . will have to rest on political and philosophical considerations."[7] Commissions, indeed, confront significant barriers of emotion, preconception, and prejudice. The fact that they have shown themselves able to penetrate such barriers is a measure of their success as educational vehicles. Commissions have seen greater success, in this regard, at other levels than the presidential and congressional. One does not conclude from a rejection of advice, however, that there should be no provision of advice.

Commissions may be—and have been—a step in the process of reform; they cannot be the vehicles of reform, nor does it further our understanding to evaluate them as if they were. Henry Ruth has written, from his experience with the Katzenbach Commission:

> A commission can serve only as a catalyst to national reform. Many other factors in society dominate the extent of the catalytic influence. It is doubtful if anyone can truly assess the effect of a commission's work in such a broad field as crime and crime control. No matter what the state of readiness for reform in the practitioners' world of criminal justice, they can move forward only if public opinion and elected officials permit them to do so."[8]

Implementation—action—depends on leadership.[9] Commissions provide factual bases for action, they inspire, and they contribute to attitudinal change. An active presidential or congressional response, however, depends on the President and Congress. The "problem" of commissions, then, is more accurately understood as a larger problem: a lack of willingness on the part of nationally elected officials to consider factually based analyses of social phenomena and calls for reform. Perhaps a commission should study this situation and suggest improvements.

Finally, with regard to procedural difficulties the commissions experienced, the Federal Advisory Committee Act has closed significant gaps in terms of appropriations and publication. It even attempts to limit the partisan temptation in commissioner appointments. The time pressures under which commissions work would seem likely to continue.

## The Maximum Response and the Minimum

What factors or conditions, then, are likely to bring the maximum and minimum possible responses to commission reports by the President, Congress, and the public at large? Interestingly, a chief factor associated with response seems to be the "superheated" nature of commission subjects of inquiry. All of the eight major social-issue commissions dealt with subjects of considerable controversy and emotional content. This can be seen as having both encouraged and discouraged responses from various audiences, for the very spark of controversiality which gains a public audience for a commission may, as well, lose it a congressional or presidential audience.

Controversial subject matter puts commission activities and reports in the public eye, a necessity if a public response is to be generated. Publicity, it has been seen, attends the release of commission reports. Commissions themselves may adopt strategies designed to increase their visibility and guarantee the widest possible distribution of their reports. Promotional activities and follow-up efforts can be employed. Relevant publics may be included, at some point, in the work of a commission. The language of commission reports may be specifically intended to be easily understood and to inspire. Any of these strategies may help increase the likelihood of a maximum response from the public in general as well as from concerned groups. Whether or not the response is favorable depends on the legitimacy of the commission, the persuasiveness of its arguments, the force of its language, and perhaps the possibility that social attitudes are already evolving in the direction of a commission's recommendations. Of course, the response might be greater if reports received the open endorsements of President and Congress. The fact that these have not been generally forthcoming, however, does not seem to have prevented noticeable public responses.

The minimum potential for public response may attend the reports of low-visibility commissions concerned primarily with subjects of limited interest, which the public, in all probability, does not know exist.

Controversiality may be a key, as well, to the congressional response. It has been seen, as in the case of the Senate's response to the report of the Pornography Commission, that a political "hot potato" can inspire a rapid rejection by those who may perceive risk in its embrace. Overall, Congress' response to the reports of the high-visibility social-issue commissions was meager. This reflected that body's institutional and political disinclination to champion the commisions' sweeping calls for reform. In addition, since commissions pass out of existence upon delivery of their reports, they have no direct organizational means of pressing their demands on Congress in any systematic or sustained way. This can leave them at a disadvantage in terms of legislative results.

On the other hand, it was seen that low-key procedural changes, based on commission recommendations, have occasionally been enacted. In at least one case—the Safe Streets Act—a major piece of legislation reflected a commission's work. The presentation of narrowly drawn, relatively non-threatening proposals may yield the maximum congressional response. Yet, this implies more of a specifically legislative function than advisory commissions generally perform. In general, Congress has little incentive to respond substantively to high-visibility commission reports. The controversial and comprehensive nature of many commission recommendations may lead most often to reluctance or rejection. To all this may be added the Federal Advisory Committee Act, which carries no legal requirement that Congress respond to commission reports.

The presidential response reflects factors largely beyond the power of commissions to control: the partisan environment, the presidential personality, and presidential priorities. Commissions, as presidential children, seem rather consistently to disappoint their parents. Highly visible commission findings which imply presidential blame or recommendations which call for policies the President finds repugnant—even though these be the commission's honest conclusions—are likely to be rejected. In addition, the political climate at the time a commission report happens to be made, and the degree to which presidential resources have already been committed in other areas, can make a substantive presidential response nearly impossible, even if the President agrees with commission findings. Finally, any commission's claim to legitimacy is at least partially defined in terms of its establishing independence from the body which appointed it. To some degree, then, the likelihood of a positive presidential response is thereby reduced since, in all probability, it will see things somewhat differently from the President.

Probably three basic factors can contribute to, although by no means guarantee, favorable consideration by the President: a) an absence of direct, abusive criticism of the President by a commission; b) a willingness, on the part of the President, to at least consider ideas which he did not develop himself; c) a receptive partisan environment. At the very least, a commission can consult with relevant officials in an administration and seek to tailor recommendations to their needs as much as possible. Certain reforms, at the Cabinet level, may follow commission recommendations. The pressures working against the showing of any presidential response at all, however (the Federal Advisory Committee Act notwithstanding), are formidable indeed. Perhaps the only strategy for a commission to adopt ultimately, and thereby win a presidential embrace, would involve a sacrifice of its integrity as an independent body and the espousal of presidentially inspired findings. It goes without saying, of course, that this would involve a sacrifice, as well, of any pretense at genuine utility. It is to the commissions' credit that they have avoided such a sacrifice.

Responses to commissions can be significantly affected by the degree of controversiality of commission subjects. Responses reflect the perceived needs of the various audiences which receive the reports. Those at high levels who perceive an electoral risk (congressmen) or a personal stake (presidents) in the issue may choose a hands-off policy. They are not likely to demonstrate overt acceptance of commission reports; indeed, they may demonstrate the opposite. Those at other levels (the public, various groups and organizations, and even states) may be stimulated to respond, in one form or another, to high-visibility commissions of which they have become aware through publicity, report distribution, or the organizational use of reports. Commissions, indeed, may perceive the public as their primary audience and they may speak in terms designed more to reach that audience than Congress or even the President.

## Reform

Commissions have demonstrated the ability to conduct reasonably thorough and efficient investigations. There are some aspects of the overall commission process, however, which might benefit from adjustment.

Perhaps the most significant weakness in the commission process, prior to passage of the Federal Advisory Committee Act, was the lack of a required presidential (or congressional, for that matter) response to commission reports. The Advisory Committee Act now requires, among many other things, submission of a presidential response to Congress within one year of a commission's report. Senator Edward Kennedy has suggested that the requirement for the presidential response be more specific. Accordingly, the President would "designate one Cabinet member as the responsible implementation official for each commission." Within one month, this official would publicly report his plans for implementation. A more detailed public response would be made six months later by the executive branch, and after a year the commission itself would reconvene to hear and question the implementation official. At the end of a second year, a final implementation report would be made, analyzing progress made and future goals.[10] A requirement such as this would seem useful insofar as it necessitates greater executive branch attention being given to commission reports which, after all, the executive requested in the first place. In addition, this provision for an "extended response" might serve the purpose of buying time during which the political environment might become more conducive to a positive presidential response; the inhibiting circumstances of *one* year might have changed by the *next* year. Further, the extended response would keep commission issues, findings, and responses in the public eye far longer than might otherwise be the case. Finally, such a provision might lessen the vagaries of commission overlap. The requirement of an extended response might have made it far more difficult for President Nixon to avoid responding to those Johnson commissions which reported to him.

A serious omission in the Advisory Committee Act is that, while it requires a presidential response, it does not apply the same standard to Congress. The need for such a requirement for Congress would seem clear. For, as was seen in the experience of the Pornography Commission, Congress (being no more virtuous than the President in this respect) will not hesitate to play fast and loose with a commission report. William Scranton has urged that a congressional response be made, perhaps by the committees concerned with a commission's subject matter. This would, Scranton suggests, "deter thoughtless or uninformed first-reactions by public officials."[11] David

Ginsburg, Executive Director of the Kerner Commission, has advocated the establishment of a Joint Senate-House Committee on Commission Oversight which would "serve as a preliminary forum for review and as a legislative routing agency." According to Ginsburg's plan, commission members could appear before this joint committee thirty days after release of the commission report, to present their recommendations and supporting evidence "and thus put the report on the table before the legislature."[12] Some sort of required congressional response would seem logical, useful, and wholly justifiable.

Of course, the final aspect of the issue of requiring a response was made clear by Doris Kearns Goodwin's comment that one cannot require the *quality* of the response.[13] Ideally, we might hope that an administration would "require itself, as an act of self-discipline, to respond," as James Campbell has put it.[14] This has not happened and, even though the President must now make some sort of reply to commissions, there remains no guarantee that it will be based on reasoned reflection. Campus Unrest Commissioner James F. Ahern has said:

> Only if the President and the Congress feel obliged to regard national Commissions with the same significance when they submit their reports as when they are appointed are Commissions likely to be of substantial value. What is required, I believe, is a willingness on the part of present and future Presidents and Congressional leaders to commit themselves to a serious appraisal of the recommendations of the Commissions they appoint.[15]

The quality of the response, the commitment to "a serious appraisal," is something which cannot be legislated; it is dependent upon the quality of those in positions of leadership.

A useful addition to the commission process might be a provision for the reconvening of commissions some time after they have made their reports. As Otto Kerner observed, ". . . we give greatest attention to that problem which is foremost at the time. . . . This is human nature."[16] It is easy, then, for commission reports and the issues with which they deal to fade from immediate public view. This can make it easier for those in positions of authority to avoid making a substantive response. Some sort of institutionalized follow-up could be useful, not only in publicizing commission findings, but in providing commissioners' reactions to responses to reports.[17] In order to establish this "continuing presence,"[18] commissions might be reconvened once or twice, at six- or twelve-month intervals, following release of their reports. This would help round out the commission process and put public officials on notice that a public assessment of their response will be forthcoming. An alternative measure, suggested by William Lockhart, would involve provision for a "small high-level staff" which would continue working for six months after a commission's report had been released. This staff would be "charged with responsibility to distribute, publicize, and interpret the Commission's Report . . ." As Lockhart sees it

> The cost of such a key force to insure distribution and understanding of the report . . . would be a worth-while investment in most cases and might make the difference between shelving the report and giving it serious and careful study.[19]

Whatever the means, there would seem merit in the establishment of some "continuing presence." The utility of this idea may have been included in the resolution calling for the Commission on Domestic and International Hunger and Malnutrition, in 1977: the commission was directed to "assist the President and the Congress in implementing its recommendations."[20] Commission reports represent the expenditure of taxpayers' money and the collective (sometimes exhaustive) efforts of many people to provide information on serious issues. Institutionalized follow-up procedures would seem a logical addition to the commission process.

Future commission efforts to improve the likelihood of response might include a strategy used by the Commission on Campus Unrest. As William Scranton described it,

> we concluded that we would address each of our recommendations to the individual or group with the ability to put them into effect, and that our report would in effect present each individual or group with an agenda for immediate action.[21]

This, combined with perhaps greater specificity (with an eye to legislation), might put the tasks more squarely and unavoidably before those who are responsible for action.

Ultimately, the kinds of proposals outlined so far reflect the fact that people do not always want to accept advice—even if it is sound and even if it has been asked for. This is reality and there is no way to resolve the frustrations it raises, short of either determining that presidents cannot request advice in a large-scale fashion or making presidential acceptance of commission recommendations mandatory, thus transforming commissions from advisory bodies into policy making bodies. Unless some sort of mandatory action is taken, presidents (and congresses) will continue to take the advice they wish to take.

Other suggestions that have been made concerning the commission process are worth consideration. The Population Commission, for example, recommended that future commissions include "substantial representation" of minorities, youth, women, the poor, and members of Congress, and that commission staffs include "significant numbers" of minorities, youth, and women. The commission cited its "racial and ethnic diversity" as a source of confidence underlying its recommendations.[22] Diversity is not new to commissions, but the Population Commission may have experienced it more than most. Greater diversity of membership would seem worth consideration on general principles and in the interest of possibly increasing the legitimacy of commission findings and recommendations. The evidence suggests, though, that an increase in diversity is not necessary to ensure a broad-ranging investigation.

Congress and President alike might keep in mind Representative Bertram Podell's advice to "apply strict birth-control regulation" to commissions.[23] Successive commissions carry the potential for being perceived as *excessive* commissions. If, indeed, "the marketplace is overflooded," as John P. Roche has put it, then "when the reports come out it's 'just another commission.' "[24] Commission appointments should be made judiciously or commissions may lose the ad hoc spontaneity and special attention they have enjoyed. On the other hand, it may be argued that strong commission messages on vital social issues will be required, again and again, until meaningful reform is undertaken. It goes without saying, of course, that neither President nor Congress should appoint commissions whose results they have from the start no intention of considering; this only contributes to a decline in government credibility in general.

Finally, everyone concerned might benefit from some reform in expectations vis-à-vis commissions. Scholars and journalists serve no educational purpose by glibly dismissing commissions as either handpicked puppets of the President or as useless because they do not produce much legislation. On the first point, the evidence does not support the notion that commissions are "doing the President's bidding," unable to make independent inquiries. In the case of the second point, the simple answer is the correct one: Commissions are not intended to legislate; responsibility for accepting or rejecting advice lies with others. More useful analyses of presidential commissions might be produced if these basic realities were kept in mind, if commissions were evaluated on the bases of their considerable information-gathering skills and the remarkable consensus they reflect, and if the fingers of "guilt"—such as it is—were pointed in more appropriate directions.

## Are Commissions Radical?

It is interesting to note that commissions have been seen and criticized as being either unrealistically radical or inherently conservative. From the left, commissions have received tongue-lashings for being instruments by which the status quo insidiously siphons off the legitimate anger of the downtrodden. Commissions are derided as being incapable of conducting sufficiently radical analyses of the evils of the American system or of offering appropriately revolutionary recommendations. Commissions are perceived as creations and prisoners of interest-group liberalism, contributing more to system maintenance than to the advancement of the aggrieved.[25]

Conversely, commissions may be perceived as having "gone too far." In other words, the degree of commission boldness depends on one's perspective. Lipsky and Olson's pluralist sop was something else entirely to Harry McPherson, who remarked, regarding the Kerner report, "What was produced, of course, went *way* beyond anything anybody'd ever imagined."[26] Similarly, political scientist Norton E. Long has commented on the "revolutionary" nature of the Kerner recommendations, which were "probably beyond the power of American society as presently constituted" to implement.[27] The label "revolutionary" was applied, as well, to the report of the Pornography Commission.[28]

As was suggested, above, the explanation for this discrepancy of viewpoints is that observers bring different perceptions to their evaluations of commissions. To those who represent, and depend upon, the social system as it is—that is, the majority—commission findings may be genuinely progressive, even revolutionary. To those who are outside the system and/or perceive it as the fundamental problem, no argument short of abolition will be entirely satisfactory. Riot commissions, and those which examine other forms of violence, may describe methods for the maintenance of order—just as they have been asked to do. There is nothing necessarily insidious in this, however. It may be an interesting theoretical exercise to see the justification for protest and violence, but there are generally very few citizens who would support such advocacy. And, any national leader who did not conceive his duties as including the maintenance of public order and safety would likely be adjudged essentially irresponsible. Many people do not see violence as a legitimate method of social adjustment.[29] A desire to protect public safety, however, does not have to imply some deep pro-systemic bias, intellectual timidity, or inhospitality to proposals for change. To the extent that commissions make it easier for those in positions of authority to better prevent and control outbreaks of violence on the part of those with grievances, commissions do contribute to maintenance of the status quo. The other side of this coin is the fact that, while commissions seek containment of violence, they rather consistently end up advocating the positions of the aggrieved parties. (Indeed, the Kerner Commission came close to excusing the black urban riots of the 1960s.) It is perhaps easy, after the fact, to claim that commissions should have said things more strongly. In the context of their own day, however, the conclusions and recommendations of many social-issue commissions have been as strong as—or stronger than—anything being said by any other legitimate bodies of government. To criticize them for not having gone further is, to quote a writer in a different context, "a little like criticizing Babe Ruth for not hitting 70 home runs in 1927 instead of 60."[30]

The radical critique of commissions is based on an ideological stance. It defines commissions as an instrument by which the social system avoids a substantive response to what are seen as legitimate grievances. This function is looked upon unfavorably. The difficulty with this interpretation of the invalidity of commissions, however, is that it probably would not survive application to a different set of circumstances. For, as Jerome Corsi has said of those holding this theory, "One wonders what position they would take regarding a commission established to investigate violence from the right."[31] From the radical point of view, commissions might quite suddenly be perceived as legitimate.

The interpretation of commissions as radical or conservative depends largely upon one's own ideological perspective. For most citizens—leaders included—commissions are likely to seem quite progressive and, possibly, revolutionary.


## Conclusion: The Place of Commissions

Commissions have become a tool by which President and Congress seek information and advice. They collect facts on a grand scale, sometimes in an unprecedented manner, and render the considered opinions of their members regarding the subject at hand and what should be done about it. Beyond this, responsibility moves to others. Commissions can compel only through their words.

Commissions suggest to us the possibilities and limits of education as an instrument of policy in a democracy. What was said of a state-level advisory committee in New York is also true of commissions: They perform "a valuable service by posing clearly for productive debate the alternative to present policy."[32] Perhaps uniquely among institutions of government, they show a capacity for receptivity to new ideas which is reflected in the truly remarkable consensus many commissions have demonstrated on ideas their members would never have previously agreed upon or supported. Commissions reflect their eras and some of the most volatile, unavoidable issues extant. Clive Barnes' comment on the Pornography Commission report may be applied to the other social issue commissions: "As much as any other public document it represents the United States of America, 1970. Read it. You may love it or hate it, accept it or challenge it, but you shouldn't ignore it."[33] The commissions have played a part in raising awareness, setting new terms of debate, and bringing about changes in attitude. They have influenced legislation and administrative practice. Yet, often, they have been used as political footballs by elected officials, reminding us, again, of the short-run limits of education.

In the end, commissions may inform and advise. And, although it is not overtly part of their mandate, they may seek to lead. That they are able to do these things in spite of the obstacles they face—time and financial constraints, an absence of guaranteed support from anyone—is a measure of their success. That their reports are often unanimous in their progressive findings and recommendations is perhaps even more noteworthy.

The commissions tell us what many of us know but do not wish to hear; they make it official. They tell us what must be done and that the next move is ours. Edward Kennedy has said, of commissions:

> They tell us that all we lack is the courage, and the will, the sense of purpose and the spark of leadership. They warn us, too, that if we fail to act, our problems worsen rather than disappear. So, when we look . . . at our response to the best advice our country can muster, we are really looking at our national commitment to progress, our determination not only to face, but to face up to, the future. And if our leadership refuses to meet both the challenge and the opportunity in this advice, the task will be one for all the people, to rise as a Nation and say, "We can. We shall. We must."[34]

Kenneth Crawford's reflections, with reference to the Scranton Commission, may hold the key to the place of presidential commissions in society's efforts to deal with its most truculent problems:

> So the nine-man commission . . . has brought in a split decision. The students are right to protest but wrong to throw epithets and bombs. Authority is right to contain violence but wrong to shoot people in the process. Excesses on both sides must be restrained. Nobody is all right or all wrong. Perhaps a formal statement of the obvious will do some good.[35]

One may hope so.

# NOTES

# Notes

## Chapter 1

[1]U.S., Congress, Senate, Committee on the Judiciary, *Presidential Commissions, Hearings,* before the Subcommittee on Administrative Practice and Procedure of the Committee on the Judiciary, 92d Cong., 1st sess., 1971, p. 1.

[2]Commissioner Charles H. Keating in a dissenting opinion, in the *Report of the Commission on Obscenity and Pornography* (New York: Bantam Books, 1970), p. 583.

[3]Senate, *Presidential Commissions,* p. 3.

[4]U.S., Congress, House, Committee on Government Operations, *Presidential Advisory Committees (Part 2), Hearings,* before a subcommittee of the Committee on Government Operations, 91st Cong., 2d sess., 1970, p. 117.

[5]The works dealing strictly with presidential commissions include: Carl Marcy, *Presidential Commissions* (New York: King's Crown Press, 1945, reprinted in New York by Da Capo Press, 1973); Frank Popper, *The President's Commissions* (Millwood, N.Y.: Kraus Reprint Co., 1975 for the Twentieth Century Fund, 1970); Philip Meranto, ed., *The Kerner Report Revisited* (Urbana, Ill.: Institute of Government and Public Affairs, University of Illinois, 1970); Thomas R. Wolanin, *Presidential Advisory Commissions, Truman to Nixon* (Madison: University of Wisconsin Press, 1975); Mirra Komarovsky, ed., *Sociology and Public Policy: The Case of Presidential Commissions* (New York: Elsevier, 1975).

Works related to specific commissions include: Neil MacNeil and Howard W. Metz, *The Hoover Report, 1953-1955: What It Means To You As Citizen and Taxpayer* (New York: Macmillan Co., 1956); Mark Lane, *Rush to Judgment* (New York: Holt, Rinehart and Winston, 1966); Edward Jay Epstein, *Inquest: The Warren Commission and the Establishment of Truth* (New York: The Viking Press, 1966); David W. Belin, *November 22, 1963: You Are the Jury* (New York: Quadrangle, 1973).

Works which include discussion of presidential commissions are: Anthony Platt, ed., *The Politics of Riot Commissions, 1917-1970* (New York: Collier Books, 1971), and Michael Lipsky and David J. Olson, *Commission Politics: The Processing of Racial Crisis in America* (New Brunswick, N.J.: Transaction Books, 1977).

[6]See: James Q. Wilson, "A Reader's Guide to the Crime Commission Reports," *The Public Interest,* 9 (Fall, 1967), pp. 64-82; Henry S. Ruth, Jr., "To Dust Shall Ye Return?" *Notre Dame Lawyer,* LXIII, No. 6 (1968), pp. 811-833; Michael Lipsky and David J. Olson, "Riot Commission Politics," *Trans-action,* VI (July/August, 1969), pp. 9-21; Jerome H. Skolnick, "Violence Commission Violence," *Transaction,* Vol. 7, No. 12, October, 1970, pp. 32-38; Andrew Kopkind, "White On Black: The Riot Commission and the Rhetoric of Reform," and Alan Silver, "Official Interpretations of Racial Riots," both in David Boesel and Peter H. Rossi, eds., *Cities Under Siege: An Anatomy of the Ghetto Riots, 1964-1968* (New York: Basic Books,

1971); George T. Sulzner, "The Policy Process and the Uses of National Governmental Study Commissions," *Western Political Quarterly,* XXIV (September, 1971), pp. 438-448; James Q. Wilson, "Violence, Pornography, and Social Science," *The Public Interest,* 22 Winter, 1971; Lloyd N. Cutler, "Thomas Jefferson, Won't You Please Come Home," Annals of the American Academy of Political and Social Science, Vol. 391 (September, 1970), pp. 168-176; James S. Campbell, "The Usefulness of Commission Studies of Collective Violence," reprinted in U.S., Congress, Senate, Committee on the Judiciary, *Presidential Commissions, Hearings,* before the Subcommittee on Administrative Practice and Procedure of the Committee on the Judiciary, United States Senate, 92d Cong., 1st sess., 1971, pp. 115-121; Martha Derthick, "On Commissionship—Presidential Variety," Brookings Reprint No. 245 (Washington, D.C.: Brookings Institution, 1972).

# Chapter 2

[1]Quoted in Carl Marcy, *Presidential Commissions* (New York: King's Crown Press, 1945, reprinted in New York by Da Capo Press, 1973), p. 109.

[2]Richard B. Morris, ed., *Encyclopedia of American History* (New York: Harper and Brothers, 1953), p. 126.

[3]Marcy, *Presidential Commissions,* p. 109.

[4]Elizabeth B. Drew, "On Giving Oneself a Hotfoot: Government by Commission," *The Atlantic,* May, 1968, p. 45.

[5]Marcy, *Presidential Commissions,* p. 109.

[6]*Ibid.,* p. 8.

[7]Appendix to *Congressional Globe,* p. 370, 27th Cong., 2d sess., April 30, 1842.

[8]*New York Herald Tribune,* April 16, 1931, p. 1, quoted in Henry S. Ruth, "To Dust Shall Ye Return?," *Notre Dame Lawyer,* XLIII, No. 6 (1968), 811.

[9]Quoted in Marcy, *Presidential Commissions,* p. 8.

[10]Act of August 26, 1842, 31 U.S.C. 672, 5 Stat. 533.

[11]Theodore Roosevelt, *State Papers as Governor and President, 1899-1909.* in *The Works of Theodore Roosevelt, National Edition,* XV (New York: Charles Scribner's Sons, 1926), p. 162.

[12]Theodore Roosevelt, *An Autobiography,* in *The Works of Theodore Roosevelt, National Edition,* XX (New York: Charles Scribner's Sons, 1926), p. 386.

[13]Roosevelt, *State Papers,* p. 162.

[14]*Ibid.,* P. 193.

[15]*Ibid.,* p. 446.

[16]Roosevelt, *Autobiography,* p. 399.

[17]*Ibid.,* p. 400. For an interesting discussion of the relationship between acts and the political settings in which they take place, see Ch. 5, "Political Settings as Symbolism," in Murray Edelman, *The Symbolic Uses of Politics* (Urbana, Ill.: University of Illinois Press, 1964).

[18]Emmet John Hughes, *The Living Presidency* (New York: Coward, McCann and Geoghegan, Inc., 1973), p. 91.

[19]Roosevelt, *Autobiography,* p. 400.

[20]*Ibid.,* p. 401.

[21]*Ibid.*

[22]*Ibid.,* p. 408.

[23]*Ibid.*

[24]Useful discussions of this issue will be found in Marcy, *Presidential Commissions,* pp. 17-21, and Thomas R. Wolanin, *Presidential Advisory Commissions, Truman to Nixon* (Madison: University of Wisconsin Press, 1975), pp. 65-72.

[25]Roosevelt, Autobiography, p. 407.

[26]Quoted in Arthur Schlesinger, Jr., *Violence: America in the Sixties* (New York: Signet, 1968), p. 33.

[27]Quoted in *Ibid.*, p. 92.

[28]*Ibid.*, p. ix.

[29]Michael Harrington, *Socialism* (New York: Saturday Review Press, 1972), p. 369.

[30]TRB from Washington (Richard Strout), "Tick, Tick, Tick," *The New Republic,* May 29, 1971.

[31]James M. Gavin and Arthur T. Hadley, *Crisis Now* (New York: Vintage, 1968), p. 9.

[32]U.S., Congress, House, Committee on Government Operations, *The Role and Effectiveness of Federal Advisory Committees,* Forty-third Report by the Committee on Government Operations, 91st Cong., 2d sess., 1970, p. 5.

[33]U.S., Congress, Senate, Committee on the Judiciary, *Presidential Commissions, Hearings,* before the Subcommittee on Administrative Practice and Procedure of the Committee on the Judiciary, 92d Cong., 1st sess., 1971, p. 220.

[34]George E. Reedy, "A Symbol Is Worth More than a Thousand Words," *TV Guide,* December 31, 1977, p. 3.

[35]*Report of the Warren Commission on the Assassination of President Kennedy* (New York: Bantam Books, 1964), p. 4.

[36]Alan Silver, "Official Interpretations of Racial Riots," in *Cities Under Siege: An Anatomy of the Ghetto Riots 1964-1968,* ed. by David Boesel and Peter H. Rossi (New York: Basic Books, 1971), p. 266.

[37]Martha Derthick, "On Commissionship—Presidential Variety," Brookings Reprint No. 245 (Washington, D.C.: Brookings Institution, 1972), p. 630.

[38]*Ibid.* For an extended discussion of exaggerated expectations and the presidency, see Thomas E. Cronin, *The State of the Presidency* (Boston: Little, Brown, 1975).

[39]Drew, "Government by Commission," p. 46.

[40]Harry C. McPherson, Jr. private interview in Washington, D.C., February, 1978.

[41]Doris Kearns Goodwin, private interview by telephone, December, 1978.

[42]Gary T. Marx, "A Document with a Difference," review of the *Report of the National Advisory Commission on Civil Disorders,* in *Trans-action,* V (September, 1968), p. 58.

[43]Governor Raymond P. Shafer, private interview by telephone, October, 1977.

[44]Professor John P. Roche, private interview at the Fletcher School of Law and Diplomacy, Medford, Massachusetts, October, 1977.

[45]Lloyd E. Ohlin, "Report On the President's Commission On Law Enforcement and Administration Of Justice," in *Sociology and Public Policy: The Case of Presidential Commissions,* ed. by Mirra Komarovsky (New York: Elsevier, 1975), p. 95.

[46]George T. Sulzner, "The Policy Process and the Uses of National Governmental Study Commissions," *Western Political Quarterly,* XXIV (September, 1971), 443.

[47]McPherson, private interview.

[48]Roche, private interview.

[49]McPherson, private interview.

[50]*Ibid.*

[51]Derthick, "On Commissionship," p. 630.

[52]Sulzner, "The Policy Process," p. 446.

[53]Derthick, "On Commissionship," pp. 630-31.

[54]H. Res. 784, S. Res. 271, 95th Cong., 1st sess., 1977.

[55]For a complete narrative of Chapin's lobbying efforts and the Congressional response, see Dave Marsh, "Singing For the World's Supper," *Rolling Stone,* April 6, 1978, pp. 32-37.

[56]An example is provided by Otto N. Larsen with regard to the Commission on Obscenity and Pornography in his "The Commission on Obscenity and Pornography: Form, Function, and Failure," in Komarovsky, ed., *Sociology and Public Policy,* especially pp. 10-13.

[57]*Warren Commission,* p. 5.

[58]*Ibid.*

[59]Marcy, *Presidential Commissions,* p. 97.

[60]Harold L. Wilensky, *Organizational Intelligence* (New York: Basic Books, 1967), pp. 165, 171-72.

[61]Marcy, *Presidential Commissions,* p. 101; see also, on this point, p. 24.

[62]See Sulzner, "The Policy Process."

[63]For a discussion of incrementalism, see David Braybrooke and Charles E. Lindblom, *A Strategy of Decision* (New York: The Free Press, 1963).

[64]Sulzner, "The Policy Process," pp. 447-48, 442.

[65]McPherson, private interview.

[66]See Sulzner, "The Policy Process," p. 447.

[67]Roche, private interview.

[68]Sulzner, "The Policy Process," p. 447.

[69]See Ruth, "To Dust Shall Ye Return?," especially p. 811, and Drew, "Government by Commission," pp. 45-49.

[70]McPherson, private interview.

[71]Roche, private interview. See also, on this point, Doris Kearns, *Lyndon Johnson and the American Dream* (New York: Harper and Row, 1976), pp. 304-307.

[72]James S. Campbell, private interview in Washington, D.C., August, 1977.

[73]Ohlin, "Report On the President's Commission," in Komarovsky, ed., *Sociology and Public Policy,* p. 95.

[74]On these points, see James David Barber, *The Presidential Character: Predicting Performance in the White House* (Englewood Cliffs, N.J.: Prentice-Hall, 1972), particularly ch. 3; also, Kearns, *Lyndon Johnson,* especially ch. 8.

[75]Goodwin, private interview.

[76]Appendix I (Executive Order 11130, November 30, 1963) to *Warren Commission,* p. 447.

[77]Appendix II to *Warren Commission,* p. 448.

[78]James Reston, "The Warren Commission Report—The Servant of History," in *Warren Commission,* p. xxxix.

[79]*Warren Commission,* p. 41.

[80]See Mark Lane, *Rush to Judgment* (New York: Holt, Rinehart and Winston, 1966); Edward Jay Epstein, *Inquest: The Warren Commission and the Establishment of Truth* (New York: The Viking Press, 1966); Josiah Thompson, *Six Seconds in Dallas: A Micro-Study of the Kennedy Assassination* (New York: Bernard Geis Associates, 1967).

[81]*The Challenge of Crime in a Free Society: A Report of the President's Commission on Law Enforcement and the Administration of Justice* (New York: Avon Books, 1968), p. 5.

[82]Isidore Silver, Introduction to *Commission on Law Enforcement,* p. 18.

[83]*Ibid.*

[84]*Commission on Law Enforcement,* p. 37.

[85]*Ibid.,* pp. 39-40.

[86]Appendix C to *Report of the National Advisory Commission on Civil Disorders* (Washington, D.C.: U.S. Government Printing Office, 1968), p. 297.

[87]Appendix B to *Commission on Civil Disorders,* p. 296.

[88]*Ibid.*

[89]*Ibid.,* pp. 296-97.

[90]*Commission on Civil Disorders,* pp. 1, 16.

[91]Appendix 2 to *To Establish Justice, To Insure Domestic Tranquility: The Final Report of the National Commission on the Causes and Prevention of Violence* (New York: Bantam Books, 1970), p. 237.

[92]*Ibid.,* p. 241.

[93]*Ibid.*

[94]*Commission on Obscenity and Pornography,* p. 1.

[95]*Ibid.*

[96]*Ibid.*

[97]Larsen, "The Commission on Obscenity and Pornography," in Komarovksy, ed., *Sociology and Public Policy,* p. 9.

[98]Clive Barnes, Special Introduction to *Commission on Obscenity and Pornography*, p. xvii.

[99]*The Report of the President's Commission on Campus Unrest* (New York: Discus Books, 1971), p. 535.

[100]*Ibid.*, pp. 1, 5, 6.

[101]*Ibid.*, pp. 2, 8-9.

[102]*Ibid.*, p. 289.

[103]*Ibid.*, p. 462.

[104]*Population and The American Future: The Report of the Commission on Population Growth and the American Future* (New York: Signet, 1972), p. xv.

[105]*Ibid.*

[106]Roe v. Wade, 410 U.S. 113, 93 S.C. 705, 35 Lawyers' Edition, 2d, 147.

[107]*Marijuana: A Signal of Misunderstanding, The Report of the National Commission on Marijuana and Drug Abuse* (New York: Signet, 1972), p. 1.

[108]Shafer, private interview.

[109]Summary from Warren Weaver, Jr., "U.S. Drug Study Stresses Treatment, Not Penalties," *The New York Times*, March 23, 1973, pp. 1, 19.

# Chapter 3

[1]The figures in this paragraph are from MacNeil and Metz, *The Hoover Report*, p. 9.

[2]*Commission on Population Growth*, pp. 358-59.

[3]Jerome H. Skolnick, "Violence Commission Violence," *Trans-action*, October, 1970, p. 32.

[4]James F. Short, Jr., "The National Commission on the Causes and Prevention of Violence: Reflections on the Contributions of Sociology and Sociologists," in Komarovsky, ed., *Sociology and Public Policy*, p. 70.

[5]Larsen, "The Commission on Obscenity and Pornography," in Komarovsky, ed., *Sociology and Public Policy*, p. 19.

[6]Roche, private interview.

[7]See Andrew Kopkind, "White on Black: The Riot Commission and the Rhetoric of Reform," in Boesel and Rossi, eds., *Cities Under Siege*, pp. 228-29.

[8]Larsen, "The Commission on Obscenity and Pornography," in Komarovsky, ed., *Sociology and Public Policy*, p. 18.

[9]Popper, *The President's Commissions*, p. 16.

[10]*Ibid.* For a critical analysis of commissions from a pluralist standpoint, see Anthony Platt, ed., *The Politics of Riot Commissions, 1917-1970* (New York: Collier Books, 1971), pp. 19-20.

[11]Derthick, "On Commissionship," p. 631.

[12]*Ibid.*

[13]See Ohlin, "Report On the President's Commission," in Komarovsky, ed., *Sociology and Public Policy*, pp. 96, 97.

[14]Drew, "Government by Commission," p. 48.

[15]Roche, private interview.

[16]*Commission on Campus Unrest*, pp. 8-10.

[17]Lyndon Baines Johnson, *The Vantage Point—Perspectives of the Presidency, 1963-1969* (New York: Popular Library, 1971), p. 26.

[18]Milton S. Eisenhower, private interview at the Johns Hopkins University, Baltimore, Maryland, February, 1973.

[19]Howard E. Shuman in House, *Presidential Advisory Committees (Part 2)*, p. 152.

[20]House, *Presidential Advisory Committees (Part 2)*, p. 118.

[21]Larsen, "The Commission on Obscenity and Pornography," in Komarovsky, ed., *Sociology and Public Policy*, pp. 24-25.

[22]"Man Who Gave Name to Report Faced Scandal," *The New York Times*, February 26, 1978, p. 28.

[23]Kopkind, "White on Black," in Boesel and Rossi, eds., *Cities Under Siege*, p. 253.

[24]Johnson, *The Vantage Point*, pp. 26-27.

[25]Eisenhower, private interview.

[26]House, *Presidential Advisory Committttees (Part 2)*, p. 142. Much of the material on the Douglas Commission, which follows, is derived from Howard Shuman, "Behind the Scenes—And Under the Rug," *The Washington Monthly*, July, 1969, reprinted in House, *Presidential Advisory Committees (Part 2)*, pp. 143-49.

[27]Shuman, "Behind the Scenes," reprinted in House, *Presidential Adivisory Committees (Part 2)*, p. 145.

[28]*Ibid.*

[29]*Ibid.*, p. 149.

[30]U.S., Congress, House, Committee on Government Operations, *Advisory Committees, Hearing*, before a subcommittee of the Committee on Government Operations, House of Representatives, on H.R. 4383, 92d Cong., 1st sess., 1971, p. 60.

[31]U.S., Congress, House, Committee on Government Operations, *Presidential Advisory Committees, Hearings*, before a subcommittee of the Committee on Government Operations, House of Representatives, 91st Cong., 2d sess., 1970, p. 36.

[32]House, *Role and Effectiveness*, p. 16.

[33]See Kopkind, "White on Black," in Boesel and Rossi, eds., *Cities Under Siege*, pp. 254, 237.

[34]*Ibid.*, p. 229.

[35]Lipsky and Olson, "Riot Commission Politics," p. 16.

[36]*Commission on Obscenity and Pornography*, p. 585.

[37]William Lockhart reports that he considered this a temporary appointment. Indeed, members of the Commission later elected him Chairman by unanimous vote. Senate, *Presidential Commissions*, p. 26.

[38]*Commission on Obscenity and Pornography*, pp. 585-87.

[39]Larsen, "The Commission on Obscenity and Pornography," in Komarovsky, ed., *Sociology and Public Policy*, pp. 20-21.

[40]Senate, *Presidential Commissions*, p. 44.

[41]Larsen, "The Commission on Obscenity and Pornography," in Komarovsky, ed., *Sociology and Public Policy*, p. 19.

[42]Marcy, *Presidential Commissions*, p. 25.

[43]Charles H. Keating, Jr., "The Report That Shocked the Nation," *The Reader's Digest*, January, 1971, p. 38.

[44]*The Los Angeles Times*, March 25, 1970, quoted in Larsen, "The Commission on Obscenity and Pornography," in Komarovsky, ed., *Sociology and Public Policy*, p. 20.

[45]Senate, *Presidential Commissions*, pp. 74, 76-77.

[46]*Ibid.* Unless otherwise indicated, the events described in this paragraph are from *Ibid.*, pp. 74-84.

[47]See the Commission meeting minutes and the remarkable series of correspondence between Chairman Lockhart and Commissioner Keating, in *Ibid.*, pp. 71-84.

[48]*Ibid.*, p. 69.

[49]*Ibid.*, p. 34.

[50]Popper, *The President's Commissions*, p. 24.

[51]*Ibid.*, p. 22.

[52]Michael Lipsky and David J. Olson, *Commission Politics: The Processing of Racial Crisis in America* (New Brunswick, N.J.: Transaction Books, 1977), p. 169.

[53]On the latter point, see Ohlin, "Report On the President's Commission," in Komarovsky, ed., *Sociology and Public Policy*, p. 97.

[54]See Charles F. Westoff, "The Commission on Population Growth and the American Future: It's Origins, Operation, and Aftermath," p. 48, and Short, "The National Commission on the

Causes and Prevention of Violence," p. 62, both in Komarovsky, ed., *Sociology and Public Policy.*

[55]Drew, "Government by Commission," p. 48. See also, charges of intra-staff conflict in Kopkind, "White on Black," in Boesel and Rossi, eds., *Cities Under Siege,* p. 251.

[56]Lipsky and Olson, "Riot Commission Politics," p. 14.

[57]Eisenhower, private interview.

[58]*The Wall Street Journal,* July 9, 1968, quoted in Popper, *The President's Commissions,* p. 25.

[59]Kopkind, "White on Black," in Boesel and Rossi, eds., *Cities Under Siege,* pp. 234-35.

[60]Lipsky and Olson, "Riot Commission Politics," p. 11.

[61]*Ibid.*

[62]Short, "The National Commission on the Causes and Prevention of Violence," in Komarovsky, ed., *Sociology and Public Policy,* p. 77.

[63]Ohlin, "Report On the President's Commission," in Komarovsky, ed., *Sociology and Public Policy,* p. 110.

[64]Campbell, private interview.

[65]Short, "The National Commission on the Causes and Prevention of Violence," in Komarovsky, ed., *Sociology and Public Policy,* p. 79.

[66]A useful discussion of the beginning of the Kerner Commission's investigation will be found in Lipsky and Olson, *Commission Politics,* pp. 163-65, 170-72; see also, Larsen, "The Commission on Obscenity and Pornography," in Komarovsky, ed., *Sociology and Public Policy,* p. 27.

[67]Short, "The National Commission on the Causes and Prevention of Violence," in Komarovsky, ed., *Sociology and Public Policy,* p. 66.

[68]Campbell, private interview.

[69]*Commission on Obscenity and Pornography,* p. 2.

[70]*Commission on Law Enforcement,* p. 687.

[71]Ohlin, "Report On the President's Commission," in Komarovsky, ed., *Sociology and Public Policy,* p. 99.

[72]*Ibid.,* p. 102.

[73]House, *Presidential Advisory Committees (Part 2),* p. 127.

[74]Campbell, private interview.

[75]*Ibid.*

[76]Shafer, private interview.

[77]Reported by Roche, private interview.

[78]Popper, *The President's Commissions,* p. 28.

[79]Derthick, "On Commissionship," p. 627.

[80]Lipsky and Olson, *Commission Politics,* p. 223.

[81]Derthick, "On Commissionship," pp. 624-25.

[82]See Short, "The National Commission on the Causes and Prevention of Violence," in Komarovsky, ed., *Sociology and Public Policy,* pp. 66-67.

[83]See *Ibid.,* p. 72; also Campbell, private interview.

[84]Popper, *The President's Commissions,* p. 29.

[85]Information in this paragraph, on the Warren Commission investigation, is from *Warren Commission,* pp. 7, 8.

[86]Campbell, private interview.

[87]*Ibid.*

[88]Ohlin, "Report On the President's Commission," in Komarovsky, ed., *Sociology and Public Policy,* p. 102.

[89]*Ibid.,* p. 107.

[90]*Ibid.,* p. 102; also Lipsky and Olson, *Commission Politics,* p. 124.

[91]Lloyd Ohlin reports that, during research, the Commission on Law Enforcement observed police brutality and corruption which could not be reported because of a commitment of

confidentiality to informants. See Ohlin, "Report On the President's Commission," in Komarovsky, ed., *Sociology and Public Policy*, p. 103.

[92]Lipsky and Olson, *Commission Politics*, p. 178.

[93]*Ibid.*, pp. 176-81.

[94]Abraham H. Miller, Louis H. Bolce, and Mark R. Halligan, "The New Urban Blacks," *Ethnicity* 3 (1976), pp. 338-67.

[95]Roche, private interview.

[96]McPherson, private interview.

[97]Campbell, private interview.

[98]Lipsky and Olson, *Commission Politics*, p. 182.

[99]Short, "The National Commission on the Causes and Prevention of Violence," in Komarovsky, ed., *Sociology and Public Policy*, p. 74.

[100]Larsen, "The Commission on Obscenity and Pornography," in Komarovsky, ed., *Sociology and Public Policy*, p. 10.

[101]Lipsky and Olson, *Commission Politics*, p. 172.

[102]The information in this paragraph is from *Rights In Conflict: A Report Submitted by Daniel Walker, Director of the Chicago Study Team, to the National Commission on the Causes and Prevention of Violence* (New York: Bantam Books, 1968), pp. x-xiv.

[103]Kopkind, "White on Black," in Boesel and Rossi, eds., *Cities Under Siege*, p. 237.

[104]Popper, *The President's Commissions*, p. 26.

[105]See Short, "The National Commission on the Causes and Prevention of Violence," in Komarovsky, ed., *Sociology and Public Policy*, p. 83.

[106]*The Politics of Protest: A Report Submitted by Jerome H. Skolnick, Director, Task Force on Violent Aspects of Protest and Confrontation of the National Commission on the Causes and Prevention of Violence* (New York: Ballantine Books, 1969).

[107]For an extended discussion of this episode, see Lipsky and Olson, *Commission Politics*, pp. 183-88.

[108]The quotation and the information in this paragraph are from Larsen, "The Commission on Obscenity and Pornography," in Komarovsky, ed., *Sociology and Public Policy*, pp. 32-33.

[109]Ohlin, "Report On the President's Commission," in Komarovsky, ed., *Sociology and Public Policy*, pp. 101-102.

[110]Quoted in House, *Presidential Advisory Committees (Part 2)*, p. 138.

[111]Lipsky and Olson, *Commission Politics*, p. 173.

[112]Information in this paragraph is from *Commission on Civil Disorders*, p. 320.

[113]Lipsky and Olson, *Commission Politics*, pp. 217, 218.

[114]Ohlin, "Report On the President's Commission," in Komarovsky, ed., *Sociology and Public Policy*, p. 102.

[115]Skolnick, "Violence Commission Violence," p. 36.

[116]Derthick, "On Commissionship," p. 627.

[117]*Warren Commission*, pp. 8-9.

[118]*Commission on Civil Disorders*, p. 319.

[119]Lipsky and Olson, *Commission Politics*, p. 219.

[120]*Commission on Obscenity and Pornography*, p. 3.

[121]*Ibid.*

[122]*Ibid.*

[123]*Ibid.*

[124]Larsen, "The Commission on Obscenity and Pornography," in Komarovsky, ed., *Sociology and Public Policy*, p. 36.

[125]*Commission on the Causes and Prevention of Violence*, p. xxiii.

[126]*Ibid.*

[127]Campbell, private interview.

[128]Popper, *The President's Commissions*, p. 37.

[129]House, *Presidential Advisory Committees (Part 2)*, pp. 137, 139.

[130]Skolnick, "Violence Commission Violence," p. 36.

[131]Lipsky and Olson, *Commission Politics,* p. 219.

[132]Skolnick, "Violence Commission Violence," pp. 37-38.

[133]*Ibid.,* p. 36.

[134]See Larsen, "The Commission on Obscenity and Pornography," in Komarovsky, ed., *Sociology and Public Policy,* pp. 36-37.

[135]Concept from Lipsky and Olson, "Riot Commission Politics," p. 16.

[136]Derthick, "On Commissionship," pp. 627, 626.

[137]Information in this paragraph is from Ohlin, "Report On the President's Commission," in Komarovsky, ed., *Sociology and Public Policy,* p. 100.

[138]Information in this paragraph is from Lipsky and Olson, *Commission Politics,* p. 129.

[139]Campbell, private interview.

[140]Eisenhower, private interview.

[141]Shafer, private interview.

[142]Ohlin, "Report On the President's Commission," in Komarovsky, ed., *Sociology and Public Policy,* pp. 110-11.

[143]Derthick, "On Commissionship," pp. 628-29; also pp. 624, 632-33.

[144]Amitai Etzioni, "Why Task-Force Studies Go Wrong," *The Wall Street Journal,* July 9, 1968, p. 18, quoted in Sulzner, "The Policy Process," p. 444.

[145]Lipsky and Olson, "Riot Commission Politics," p. 17; the Lipsky and Olson discussion involves, primarily, competition among state and local riot commissions, rather than presidential commissions.

[146]Lipsky and Olson, *Commission Politics,* p. 122.

[147]Senate, *Presidential Commissions,* p. 12.

[148]Kopkind, "White on Black," in Boesel and Rossi, eds., *Cities Under Siege,* p. 251.

[149]Senate, *Presidential Commisions,* p. 195.

[150]House, *Presidential Advisory Committees (Part 2),* p. 128.

# Chapter 4

[1]Quoted in Kopkind, "White on Black," in Boesel and Rossi, eds., *Cities Under Siege,* p. 226.

[2]Appendix B to *Commission on Civil Disorders,* pp. 296-97.

[3]Popper, *The President's Commissions,* pp. 38-39.

[4]*Ibid.,* p. 39.

[5]*Ibid.*

[6]*Commission on Law Enforcement,* p. 689.

[7]*Commission on Civil Disorders,* p. 320.

[8]*The Christian Science Monitor,* December 7, 1970, p. 3.

[9]See, for example, *Commission on Law Enforcement,* p. 689, and *Commission on Civil Disorders,* p. 320.

[10]Lipsky and Olson, "Riot Commission Politics," p. 14.

[11]Popper, *The President's Commissions,* p. 31.

[12]Ohlin, "Report On the President's Commission," in Komarovsky, ed., *Sociology and Public Policy,* p. 105.

[13]Larsen, "The Commission on Obscenity and Pornography," in Komarovsky, ed., *Sociology and Public Policy,* pp. 22-23.

[14]Derthick, "On Commissionship," p. 629.

[15]Ohlin, "Report On the President's Commission," in Komarovsky, ed., *Sociology and Public Policy,* p. 106.

[16]Popper, *The President's Commissions,* p. 33.

[17]Roche, private interview.

[18]Lipsky and Olson, *Commission Politics*, p. 130.

[19]Campbell, private interview.

[20]Raymond A. Bauer, Ithiel de Sola Pool, Lewis Anthony Dexter, *American Business and Public Policy*, 2d ed., (Chicago: Aldine Publishing Co., 1972), p. 44.

[21]Sen. Fred R. Harris, "Mission Unaccomplished," *LOOK*, March 18, 1969, p. 72.

[22]Lipsky and Olson, *Commission Politics*, p. 130.

[23]Derthick, "On Commissionship," p. 625.

[24]*Ibid.*, p. 626.

[25]Skolnick, "Violence Commission Violence," p. 35.

[26]Campbell, private interview.

[27]Lipsky and Olson, "Riot Commission Politics," p. 12.

[28]Lipsky and Olson, *Commission Politics*, p. 125.

[29]McPherson, private interview.

[30]*Ibid.*

[31]Lipsky and Olson, "Riot Commission Politics," p. 16.

[32]Campbell, private interview.

[33]Lipsky and Olson, "Riot Commission Politics," p. 20.

[34]Tom Wicker, Introduction to *Commission on Civil Disorders*, p. v.

[35]Lipsky and Olson, "Riot Commission Politics," p. 17.

[36]*Ibid.*

[37]Ohlin, "Report On the President's Commission," in Komarovsky, ed., *Sociology and Public Policy*, p. 106.

[38]Short, "The National Commission on the Causes and Prevention of Violence," in Komarovsky, ed., *Sociology and Public Policy*, p. 87.

[39]Paul F. Lazarsfeld and Martin Jaeckel, "The Uses of Sociology by Presidential Commissions," in Komarovsky, ed., *Sociology and Public Policy*, p. 130.

[40]Derthick, "On Commissionship," p. 628.

[41]*Ibid.*; also, see p. 626.

[42]Shafer, private interview.

[43]House, *Presidential Advisory Committees (Part 2)*, p. 118.

[44]Shafer, private interview.

[45]Reported in Popper, *The President's Commissions*, p. 32.

[46]Lipsky and Olson, *Commission Politics*, pp. 224-25.

[47]See Lipsky and Olson, "Riot Commission Politics,' p. 13, and *Commission Politics*, pp. 132-33.

[48]*Commission on Law Enforcement*, p. 689.

[49]Senate, *Presidential Commissions*, p. 88.

[50]*Commission on Obscenity and Pornography*, p. x.

[51]*Ibid.*, pp. 579, 580, 605, 613-14.

[52]See Appendix K to *Commission on Civil Disorders*, p. 319; also Kopkind, "White on Black," in Boesel and Rossi, eds., *Cities Under Siege*, p. 235.

[53]Kopkind, "White on Black," in Boesel and Rossi, eds., *Cities Under Siege*, p. 235.

[54]Ohlin, "Report On the President's Commission," in Komarovsky, ed., *Sociology and Public Policy*, p. 97.

[55]*Ibid.*, p. 112.

[56]Ruth, "To Dust Shall Ye Return?," p. 830.

[57]See *Ibid.*, p. 831, and Ohlin, "Report On the President's Commission," in Komarovsky, ed., *Sociology and Public Policy*, p. 112.

[58]Lipsky and Olson, *Commission Politics*, p. 131.

[59]*Ibid.*

[60]Details on public relations are from *Ibid.*, p. 132.

[61]Derthick, "On Commissionship," p. 626.

[62]Senate, *Presidential Commissions*, p. 185.

[63]House, *Presidential Advisory Committees (Part 2)*, p. 116.

⁶⁴Shafer, private interview.

⁶⁵Popper, *The President's Commissions,* p. 36.

⁶⁶House, *Presidential Advisory Committees (Part 2),* p. 115.

⁶⁷Senate, *Presidential Commissions,* p. 104.

⁶⁸House, *Presidential Advisory Committees (Part 2),* p. 143.

⁶⁹Ruth, "To Dust Shall Ye Return?," p. 831.

⁷⁰*Warren Commission,* p. ii; the information in this paragraph is from pp. i, ii of the commercial Bantam Books edition.

⁷¹Lipsky and Olson, *Commission Politics,* p. 135.

⁷²Senate, *Presidential Commissions,* p. 104.

⁷³Short, "The National Commission on the Causes and Prevention of Violence," in Komarovsky, ed., *Sociology and Public Policy,* p. 89.

⁷⁴Senate, *Presidential Commissions,* p. 184.

⁷⁵"Follow-Up on the News: Marijuana Report," *The New York Times,* March 31, 1974, p. 33.

# Chapter 5

¹Senate, *Presidential Commissions,* p. 180.

²Eisenhower, private interview.

³Senate, *Presidential Commissions,* p. 86.

⁴*Ibid.,* p. 186.

⁵*Ibid.,* p. 116.

⁶James Q. Wilson, "A Reader's Guide to the Crime Commission Reports," *The Public Interest,* 9 (1967), p. 64.

⁷Ernest Holsendolph, "Five-Day-a-Week Postal Deliveries And Increased Subsidies Proposed," *The New York Times,* April 19, 1977, p. 64.

⁸April 27, 1978.

⁹Doris Kearns Goodwin, private interview by telephone, December, 1978.

¹⁰*Ibid.* The classic study of presidents tending to their own needs is Richard E. Neustadt, *Presidential Power* (New York: Mentor, 1964).

¹¹For discussions of this aspect of the Nixon personality, see Barber, *The Presidential Character,* Chapter 12, and Walter J. Hickel, *Who Owns America?* (Englewood Cliffs, N.J.: Prentice-Hall, Inc., 1971), especially Chapters 10 and 11.

¹²Senate, *Presidential Commissions,* p. 156.

¹³House, *Role and Effectiveness,* p. 6.

¹⁴House, *Presidential Advisory Committees,* p. 94.

¹⁵George E. Reedy, *The Twilight of the Presidency* (New York: New American Library, 1970), p. 4.

¹⁶Senate, *Presidential Commissions,* p. 208.

¹⁷Goodwin, private interview; also, Roche, private interview.

¹⁸Kearns, *Lyndon Johnson,* p. 299.

¹⁹McPherson, private interview.

²⁰Goodwin, private interview.

²¹Roche, private interview.

²²Johnson, *The Vantage Point,* p. 335.

²³*Ibid.*

²⁴McPherson, private interview.

²⁵Roche, private interview.

²⁶Lipsky and Olson, *Commission Politics,* p. 135.

²⁷*Ibid.,* pp. 135, 137.

²⁸See Neustadt, *Presidential Power,* pp. 142-45.

[29]Goodwin, private interview.

[30]Johnson, *The Vantage Point*, pp. 172-73.

[31]*Ibid.*, p. 173.

[32]*Ibid.*, p. 451.

[33]Marvin J. Weinbaum, "Congress and the Commissioners: A New Species of Oversight," in Philip Meranto, ed., *The Kerner Report Revisited* (Urbana, Ill.: Institute of Government and Public Affairs, University of Illinois, 1970), p. 129.

[34]Johnson, *The Vantage Point*, p. 173.

[35]Weinbaum, "Congress and the Commissioners," in Meranto, ed., *The Kerner Report Revisited*, p. 129.

[36]For one interpretation, see Lipsky and Olson, *Commission Politics*, pp. 133-35.

[37]*Commission on Civil Disorders*, pp. 91, 1.

[38]Kearns, *Lyndon Johnson*, p. 305, and pp. 304-307; also, Roche, private interview.

[39]Roger Wilkins, "The Kerner Report of 1968 Was One Element in a Year of Hope, Violence and Despair," *The New York Times*, February 27, 1978, p. A14.

[40]Goodwin, private interview.

[41]Richard Nixon, *RN: the Memoirs of Richard Nixon* (New York: Grosset and Dunlap, 1978).

[42]Senate, *Presidential Commissions*, p. 105.

[43]Eisenhower, private interview.

[44]Campbell, private interview.

[45]Quoted in Keating, "The Report That Shocked the Nation," pp. 39-40.

[46]Quoted by Sen. Strom Thurmond in Senate, *Presidential Commissions*, p. 96.

[47]"Pornography: The Oldest Debate," *Newsweek*, October 12, 1970, p. 37.

[48]Miller v. California, 413 U.S. 15 (1973); Paris Adult Theatre I v. Slaton, 413 U.S. 49 (1973); Kaplan v. California, 413 U.S. 115 (1973); United States v. 12 200-Ft. Reels of Super 8mm. Film *et al.*, 413 U.S. 123 (1973); United States v. Orito, 413 U.S. 139 (1973).

[49]*Commission on Campus Unrest*, p. 216.

[50]Derthick, "On Commissionship," p. 625.

[51]Jack Rosenthal, "Nixon Contests Scranton Report On Healing Rifts," *The New York Times*, December 13, 1970, p. 64.

[52]"Excerpts From Nixon's Letter on Campus Unrest," *The New York Times*, December 13, 1970, p. 64.

[53]*Ibid.*

[54]"The N.B.C. Nightly News," January 11, 1979.

[55]Quoted in Kenneth Crawford, "Pablum and Poison," *Newsweek*, October 12, 1970, p. 55.

[56]Derthick, "On Commissionship," p. 634.

[57]Senate, *Presidential Commissions*, p. 222.

[58]Quoted in John Kifner, "Scranton on Rebuff by Nixon: Pleased That He Read Report," *The New York Times*, December 15, 1970, p. 36C.

[59]*Ibid.*

[60]*Ibid.*

[61]Senate, *Presidential Commissions*, p. 216.

[62]Kifner, "Scranton on Rebuff," p. 36C.

[63]"Victimless Crime," *The New Republic*, July 3, 1971, p. 9.

[64]"Meet the Press," NBC telecast, April 9, 1972.

[65]Weaver, "U.S. Drug Study," p. 1.

[66]Shafer, private interview.

[67]"Population Growth and the American Future," PBS telecast, November 29, 1972.

[68]Shuman, "Behind the Scenes," reprinted in House, *Presidential Advisory Committees (Part 2)*, p. 145.

[69]Stewart Alsop, "Nixon and the Rancid Right," *Newsweek*, October 12, 1970, p. 132.

[70]Bradley H. Patterson, Jr., in House, *Presidential Advisory Committees*, p. 94.

[71]"New Criminal Code Asked," *Boston Herald Traveller*, January 17, 1971, sec. 2, p. 6.

Interestingly, the commission's recommended reforms included abolition of the death penalty, making possession of marijuana punishable only by fines, and prohibition of private hand gun ownership. There is no indication that Nixon endorsed these, specifically.

[72]On the unlikelihood of a positive Nixon response to the Kerner Report, see Wilkins, "The Kerner Report of 1968," p. A14. Presidential candidate Nixon was reported to have observed that the Kerner report "in effect blames everybody for the riots except the perpetrators." See "Guilty or Not?," *Newsweek*, March 18, 1968, p. 46.

[73]"Pornography: The Oldest Debate," p. 37.

[74]Eisenhower, private interview.

[75]Personal letter from Nicholas deB. Katzenbach, April 6, 1972.

[76]Neil Amdur, "U.S. Report Urges New Body To Direct Amateur Athletics," *The New York Times*, January 13, 1977, p. 1.

[77]Campbell, private interview.

[78]Marcy, *Presidential Commissions*, p. 41.

[79]Cronin, *The State of the Presidency*, p. 241.

[80]House, *Presidential Advisory Committee (Part 2)*, pp. 140-41.

[81]Ruth, "To Dust Shall Ye Return?," p. 833.

[82]Harris, "Mission Unaccomplished," p. 72.

[83]Senate, *Presidential Commissions*, pp. 8-9.

[84]Short, "The National Commission on the Causes and Prevention of Violence," in Komarovsky, ed., *Sociology and Public Policy*, p. 90.

[85]Letter from Henry E. Peterson, Assistant Attorney General, Criminal Division, U.S. Department of Justice, February 23, 1973. The case referred to was *United States* v. *Hamling, et al.*, Nos. 72-1892 through 72-1897, C.A. 9.

[86]*Commission on Obscenity and Pornography*, p. 62.

[87]Kifner, "Scranton on Rebuff," p. 36C.

[88]Senate, *Presidential Commissions*, pp. 185, 199.

[89]Personal letter from William W. Scranton, April 4, 1972.

# Chapter 6

[1]Richard F. Fenno, Jr., *Congressmen in Committees* (Boston: Little, Brown, 1973), p. 1.

[2]David R. Mayhew, *Congress: The Electoral Connection* (New Haven: Yale University Press, 1974), pp. 16, 81.

[3]*Ibid.*, pp. 47, 53, 130, 52-53, 115, 62.

[4]See Part 2, "Processes and Policies," in *Ibid*.

[5]Senate, *Presidential Commissions*, p. 177.

[6]Mayhew speaks of Congress' "servicing of the organized. . . . a deference toward nationally organized groups with enough widespread local clout to inspire favorable roll call positions on selected issues among a majority of members." *Congress: The Electoral Connection*, especially pp. 130-31.

[7]Eisenhower, private interview.

[8]Popper, *The President's Commissions*, p. 44; see pp. 44-45 on the greater likelihood of adoption of reforms regarding a "specific, concrete problem" rather than those of a social systemic nature.

[9]Silver, Introduction to *Commission on Law Enforcement*, p. 33.

[10]*Ibid.*, pp. 33-34.

[11]James Vorenberg, "The War On Crime: The First Five Years," *The Atlantic Monthly*, May, 1972, p. 67. In light of these developments, Nicholas Katzenbach now feels that if he had remained Attorney General, rather than taking a State Department position, "the impact of the Commission's work might well have been greater." Katzenbach, personal letter.

[12]Ohlin, "Report On the President's Commission," in Komarovsky, ed., *Sociology and Public Policy*, p. 113.

[13]*Ibid.*, pp. 113-14.

[14]See Senate, *Presidential Commissions*, p. 21, and Harris, "Mission Unaccomplished," p. 72.

[15]Lipsky and Olson, *Commission Politics*, p. 147.

[16]Weinbaum, "Congress and the Commissioners," in Meranto, ed., *The Kerner Report Revisited*, p. 126.

[17]*Ibid.*

[18]*Ibid.*, p. 127.

[19]*Ibid.*

[20]*Ibid.*, p. 128.

[21]Personal letter from Senator Philip A. Hart, April 6, 1972.

[22]Larsen, "The Commission on Obscenity and Pornography," in Komarovsky, ed., *Sociology and Public Policy*, p. 12.

[23]*Commission on Obscenity and Pornography*, p. 1.

[24]90th Cong., 1st Session (July 31, 1967).

[25]Quoted in Senate, *Presidential Commissions*, p. 29.

[26]Senate, *Presidential Commissions*, p. 29.

[27]Senator George McGovern, one of the five dissenters, has argued that this vote was taken without any of the participants' having read the commission's report. See George McGovern, *Grassroots: The Autobiography of George McGovern* (New York: Random House, 1977), p. 170.

[28]Reprinted in Senate, *Presidential Commissions*, pp. 96-97.

[29]Public Law 91-375, 91st Cong., 2nd Sess., 39 U.S.C. Sections 3010-3011; 18 U.S.C. Sections 1735-1737.

[30]See *Commission on Obscenity and Pornography*, pp. 68-69, and Larsen, "The Commission on Obscenity and Pornography," in Komarovsky, ed., *Sociology and Public Policy*, pp. 37-38.

[31]Larsen, "The Commission on Obscenity and Pornography," in Komarovsky, ed., *Sociology and Public Policy*, p. 22.

[32]Quoted in Joseph N. Bell, "Could Danish Smut Laws Work Here?," *Today's Health*, 48 (1970), p. 29.

[33]Shafer, personal interview.

[34]Personal letter from Charles F. Westoff, Director, Office of Population Research, Princeton University, November 28, 1977.

[35]Katzenbach, personal letter.

[36]Popper, *The President's Commissions*, p. 46.

[37]Personal letter from William B. Lockhart, Dean, University of Minnesota Law School, March 28, 1972.

[38]Senate, *Presidential Commissions*, p. 164.

[39]*Ibid.*

[40]Ohlin, "Report On the President's Commission," in Komarovsky, ed., *Sociology and Public Policy*, p. 113.

[41]Senate, *Presidential Commissions*, p. 164.

[42]Vorenberg, "The War On Crime," p. 67.

[43]See *Ibid.*, p. 64, for the material which follows.

[44]*Ibid.*

[45]*Ibid.*, p. 65.

[46]Personal letter from Otto Kerner, Circuit Judge, United States Court of Appeals, April 20, 1972.

[47]Lipsky and Olson, *Commission Politics*, p. 137.

[48]David Ginsburg, in Senate, *Presidential Commissions*, p. 16.

[49]Harris, "Mission Unaccomplished," p. 72.

[50]David Ginsburg, in Senate, *Presidential Commissions,* p. 16.

[51]Thomas Kitsos and Joseph Pisciotte, "State Legislative Reaction to the *Kerner Commission Report*: The Case of Illinois," in Meranto, ed., *The Kerner Report Revisisted,* p. 114.

[52]*Ibid.,* p. 115.

[53]*Ibid.,* p. 116.

[54]Senate, *Presidential Commissions,* p. 89.

[55]*Ibid.,* pp. 89-90, and Lockhart, personal letter.

[56]Larsen, "The Commission on Obscenity and Pornography," in Komarovsky, ed., *Sociology and Public Policy,* p. 40.

[57]Senate, *Presidential Commissions,* p. 90.

[58]Shafer, private interview.

[59]Harris, "Mission Unaccomplished," p. 72.

[60]*Ibid.*

[61]Lipsky and Olson, *Commission Politics,* p. 137.

[62]Walter Franke, "The Kerner Commission Recommendations Revisited: Employment," in Meranto, ed., *The Kerner Report Revisited,* pp. 23-24.

[63]McPherson, private interview.

[64]Kerner, personal letter.

[65]Short, "The National Commission on the Causes and Prevention of Violence," in Komarovsky, ed., *Sociology and Public Policy,* p. 89.

[66]Senate, *Presidential Commissions,* p. 148.

[67]*Ibid.,* p. 215.

[68]Scranton, personal letter.

[69]Senate, *Presidential Commissions,* p. 87.

[70]*Ibid.*

[71]*Ibid.*

[72]Ruth, "To Dust Shall Ye Return?," p. 830.

[73]*Ibid.*

[74]Popper, *The President's Commissions,* p. 42.

[75]Lipsky and Olson, *Commission Politics,* pp. 134-35.

[76]Gene Graham, "The Kerner Report and the Mass Media," in Meranto, ed., *The Kerner Report Revisited,* p. 92.

[77]See *Commission on Civil Disorders,* pp. 210-12.

[78]Graham, "Mass Media," in Meranto, ed., *The Kerner Report Revisited,* pp. 93-94.

[79]House, *Presidential Advisory Committees (Part 2),* p. 134.

[80]Senate, *Presidential Commissions,* p. 164.

[81]Lipsky and Olson, *Commission Politics,* p. 138.

[82]Harris, "Mission Unaccomplished."

[83]Lipsky and Olson, *Commission Politics,* p. 138.

[84]*Ibid.*

[85]Eisenhower, private interview.

[86]December 11, 1970.

[87]Senate, *Presidential Commissions,* p. 87.

[88]See Neil MacNeil and Howard W. Metz, *The Hoover Report, 1953-1955: What It Means to You as Citizen and Taxpayer* (New York: Macmillan Co., 1956).

[89]The National Urban Coalition and Urban America, Inc., *One Year Later* (New York: Praeger, 1969).

[90]*The State of the Cities: Report of the Commission on the Cities in the '70s* (Washington, D.C.: The National Urban Coalition, 1971).

[91]TRB from Washington (Strout), "Tick, Tick, Tick."

[92]Short, "The National Commission on the Causes and Prevention of Violence," in Komarovsky, ed., *Sociology and Public Policy,* p. 89.

[93]Eisenhower, private interview.

[94]"The People Problem," *The New York Times,* August 31, 1971, p. 30.

95House, *Role and Effectiveness,* p. 1.

96See House, *Presidential Advisory Committees* (the quotation is from p. 1), and House, *Presidential Advisory Committees (Part 2).*

97House, *Role and Effectiveness.*

98See House, *Advisory Committees* (Hearing on H.R. 4383); U.S., Congress, House, *Federal Advisory Committee Standards Act,* H.R. Rept. 92-1017 To Accompany H.R. 4383, 92d Cong., 2d sess., 1972; and U.S., Congress, House, *Executive Branch Advisory Committees,* Conference Rept. 92-1403 To Accompany H.R. 4383, 92d Cong., 2d sess., 1972. Pertinent dates are from letter from Richard L. Still, Staff Director, Special Studies Subcommittee of the Committee on Government Operations, U.S. House of Representatives, October 4, 1972.

99House, *Executive Branch Advisory Committees,* pp. 2-5, 7.

100By Executive Order 12024 (1977), President Jimmy Carter transferred the Committee Management Secretariat from the Office of Management and Budget to the General Services Administration. For this, and for a discussion of proposed amendments to the Federal Advisory Committee Act, see Stephanie Smith, *Advisory Committee Regulation and Reform,* Issue Brief Number IB77102, The Library of Congress, Congressional Research Service, Major Issues System, (Archived 10/06/78).

101Goodwin, private interview.

102See Senate, *Presidential Commissions.*

103*Ibid.,* pp. 4-5.

104Personal letter from Senator Edward M. Kennedy, October 30, 1972.

105See TRB from Washington (Richard Strout), "Tick, Tick, Tick," *The New Republic,* May 29, 1971; "Noncandidate Kennedy," *The New Republic,* June 5, 1971; "Crime Fighting," *The New Republic,* June 12, 1971; "Gun Toting," *The New Republic,* July 24 and 31, 1971. (Note: During this period, TRB columns were not assigned page numbers.)

106See John Herbers, "Black-White Split Persists A Decade After Warning," *The New York Times,* February 26, 1978, pp. 1, 28; Robert Reinhold, "Poll Indicates More Tolerance, Less Hope," *The New York Times,* February 26, 1978, p. 28; "Man Who Gave Name to Report Faced Scandal," *The New York Times,* February 26, 1978, p. 28; Jon Nordheimer, "1978 Race Relations: 3 Widely Divergent Views," *The New York Times,* February 27, 1978, pp. 1, A14; Roger Wilkins, "The Kerner Report of 1968 Was One Element in a Year of Hope, Violence and Despair," *The New York Times,* February 27, 1978, p. A14; Paul Delaney, "Middle-Class Gains Create Tension in Black Community," *The New York Times,* February 28, 1978, pp. 1, 22; Steve V. Roberts, "Black Progress and Poverty Are Underlined by Statistics," *The New York Times,* February 28, 1978, p. 22; Michael Sterne, "In Last Decade, Leaders Say, Harlem's Dreams Have Died," *The New York Times,* March 1, 1978, pp. 1, A13; William K. Stevens, "Since the 1967 Riots, Detroit Has Moved Painfully Toward a Modest Renaissance," *The New York Times,* March 1, 1978, p. A13; "Echoes," *The New York Times,* March 1, 1978, p. A26; Roger Wilkins, "Racial Outlook: Lack of Change Disturbs Blacks," *The New York Times,* March 3, 1978, p. A26; Roger Wilkins, "Blacks and Politics: Progress In a Decade of Disappointment," *The New York Times,* March 6, 1978, p. A12.

# Chapter 7

1Hart, personal letter.

2Marcy, *Presidential Commissions,* p. 42.

3Hart, personal letter.

4Katzenbach, personal letter.

5Popper, *The President's Commissions,* p. 11.

6*Ibid.*

7Harris, "Mission Unaccomplished," p. 72.

[8]Short, ''The National Commission on the Causes and Prevention of Violence,'' in Komarovsky, ed., *Sociology and Public Policy,* p. 90.

[9]Shafer, private interview.

[10]Short, ''The National Commission on the Causes and Prevention of Violence,'' in Komarovsky, ed., *Sociology and Public Policy,* p. 90.

[11]Westoff, personal letter.

[12]See Ohlin, ''Report On the President's Commission,'' in Komarovsky, ed., *Sociology and Public Policy,* p. 115.

[13]Ruth, ''To Dust Shall Ye Return?,'' p. 815.

[14]Information on Katzenbach Commission research is from *Ibid.,* pp. 825-26.

[15]House, *Presidential Advisory Committees (Part 2),* p. 127.

[16]Senate, *Presidential Commissions,* p. 88. See also, Larsen, ''The Commission on Obscenity and Pornography,'' in Komarovsky, ed., *Sociology and Public Policy,* pp. 33-34.

[17]*Commission on Obscenity and Pornography,* p. 26.

[18]*Ibid.*

[19]Senate, *Presidential Commissions,* p. 86.

[20]See Abraham H. Miller, Louis H. Bolce, and Mark R. Halligan, ''The New Urban Blacks,'' *Ethnicity* 3 (1976), pp. 338-67.

[21]Crawford, ''Pablum and Poison,'' p. 55.

[22]Martin Mayer, *About Television* (New York: Harper and Row, 1972), p. 221.

[23]See Daniel Bell, ''Comment: Government by Commission,'' *The Public Interest,* Number 3 (Spring, 1966), p. 6, and House, *Executive Branch Advisory Committees,* pp. 2, 3.

[24]Senate, *Presidential Commissions,* p. 117.

[25]Lipsky and Olson, *Commission Politics,* p. 135.

[26]Senate, *Presidential Commissions,* p. 104.

[27]Katzenbach, personal letter.

[28]Senate, *Presidential Commissions,* p. 165.

[29]Lipsky and Olson, *Commission Politics,* p. 137.

[30]Sulzner, ''The Policy Process,'' p. 443; see, also, Popper, *The President's Commissions,* p. 10.

[31]Harris, ''Mission Unaccomplished,'' p. 72.

[32]Katzenbach, personal letter.

[33]*Commission on Obscenity and Pornography,* p. xvii.

[34]Derthick, ''On Commissionship,'' p. 633.

[35]Senate, *Presidential Commissions,* p. 207.

[36]Johnson, *The Vantage Point,* p. 335.

[37]Shafer, private interview.

[38]See Harris, ''Mission Unaccomplished,'' p. 72, and Senate, *Presidential Commissions,* p. 148.

[39]Senate, *Presidential Commissions,* p. 198.

[40]Letters, *Newsweek,* March 25, 1968, pp. 4-5.

[41]Letters, *Time,* March 22, 1968, p. 5.

[42]*The New York Times,* November 3, 1970, p. 32M.

[43]Letters, *Time,* November 9, 1970, p. 10.

[44]Letters, *Newsweek,* October 19, 1970, p. 6.

[45]Indeed, it may be noted that the Louis Harris organization, to give one example, has never conducted a poll to gauge public reaction to the report of a Presidential commission. Letter from Louis Harris and Associates, Inc., October 20, 1977.

[46]See *Warren Commission,* pp. 4-5.

[47]*Ibid.,* pp. 37-43.

[48]For example, David W. Belin, Assistant Counsel to the Warren Commission, appeared on the NBC telecast ''Meet the Press'' (February 4, 1979) to dispute some of the Committee's methods and findings and to support the work of the Warren Commission. See David W. Belin, *November 22, 1963: You Are the Jury* (New York: Quadrangle, 1973). See, also, John Herbers,

"After 15 Years, Plot Theories Still Thicken," *The New York Times,* January 7, 1979, p. E5 (source of quotation); "Rush to Judgment," *Newsweek,* January 15, 1979, pp. 26-27; and "A Conspiracy," *The New York Times,* January 7, 1979, p. 18E.

[49]Herbers, "After 15 Years," p. E5.

[50]See Ohlin, "Report On the President's Commission," in Komarovsky, ed., *Sociology and Public Policy,*p. 94.

[51]Senate, *Presidential Commissions,* p. 163.

[52]See Lipsky and Olson, *Commission Politics,* pp. 110, 122-23; also, Senate, *Presidential Commissions,* p. 9.

[53]*Commission on Civil Disorders,* p. 89.

[54]Senate, *Presidential Commissions,* p. 9.

[55]James Campbell in *Ibid.,* p. 117.

[56]*Ibid.*

[57]Senate, *Presidential Commissions,* p. 87.

[58]*Ibid.*

[59]*Commission on Marijuana and Drug Abuse,* p. ix.

[60]"Meet the Press," NBC telecast, April 9, 1972.

[61]James M. Markham, "Calm Analysis Key to National Drug Report," *The New York Times,* March 23, 1973, p. 19.

[62]"Follow-Up on the News," p. 33.

[63]*Commission on Population Growth,* pp. 1, 3; also, PBS telecast, November 29, 1972.

[64]*Commission on Population Growth,* p. 7.

[65]Sulzner, "The Policy Process," p. 445.

[66]Popper, *The President's Commissions,* p. 13.

[67]Senate, *Presidential Commissions,* p. 105.

[68]Skolnick, "Violence Commission Violence," p. 38.

[69]*Commission on Civil Disorders,* pp. 5, 1.

[70]"Echoes," p. A26.

[71]Lipsky and Olson, *Commission Politics,* p. 144.

[72]Mack H. Jones, "The Kerner Commission: Errors and Omissions," in Meranto, ed., *The Kerner Report Revisited,* p. 155.

[73]Harris, "Mission Unaccomplished," p. 73.

[74]*Commission on Civil Disorders,* p. 230.

[75]Johnson, *The Vantage Point,* p. 173.

[76]*Commission on Civil Disorders,* p. 1.

[77]*Commission on the Causes and Prevention of Violence,* pp. xxxix-xi.

[78]*Commission on Campus Unrest,* p. 6.

[79]Lipsky and Olson, *Commission Politics,* p. 137.

[80]*Commission on Civil Disorders,* p. 2.

[81]Robert Curvin, "Remembering Martin Luther King," *The New York Times,* January 15, 1979, p. A18.

[82]"Good Morning America," ABC telecast, January 14, 1979.

[83]Lipsky and Olson, *Commission Politics,* p. 212.

[84]Graham, "Mass Media," in Meranto, ed., *The Kerner Report Revisited,* p. 92.

[85]See Reinhold, "Poll," p. 28, and George Gallup, "Bias Against Black As President Drops," *The Boston Globe,* August 27, 1978, p. 18.

[86]Regents of the University of California, Petitioner, v. Allan Bakke,—U.S.—, 57 L. Ed. 2d 750, 98 S.Ct. (1978).

[87]"A New Racial Poll," *Newsweek,* February 26, 1979, p. 53.

[88]*Ibid.* Some civil rights leaders disputed the findings of the Harris poll. See Thomas A. Johnson, "Survey Indicating Whites Favor Affirmative Action Is Questioned," *The New York Times,* February 21, 1979, p. A14.

[89]Gallup, "Bias," p. 18.

[90]Reinhold, "Poll," p. 28.

[91]*Ibid.*

[92]*Ibid.*

[93]*Ibid.*

[94]See *Ibid.*, and "A New Racial Poll," p. 53.

[95]Reinhold, "Poll," p. 28.

[96]Robert Lindsey, "Study Finds Wage Gap Between Races Narrowing," *The New York Times,* May 8, 1978, pp. A1, B15.

[97]Gallup, "Bias," p. 18, and Wilkins, "Blacks and Politics," p. A12. For an interesting comparison of the respective fates of prominent civil rights figures and segregationists of the 1950s and 1960s, see Neil Maxwell, "Mixed Fortunes: Black Leaders of the 1960s Have Come Out Better Than Segregationists," *The Wall Street Journal,* March 12, 1979, pp. 1, 25.

[98]William Brashler, "The Black Middle Class: Making It," *The New York Times Magazine,* December 3, 1978, p. 34.

[99]Delaney, "Middle-Class Gains," p. 1.

[100]*Commission on Civil Disorders,* p. 222.

[101]Brashler, "Making It," p. 35.

[102]*Ibid.,* pp. 35, 36.

[103]*Ibid.*

[104]*Ibid.,* p. 36.

[105]*Ibid.,*

[106]*Ibid.,* p. 35.

[107]*Ibid.,* p. 36 (emphasis added).

[108]A prominent treatment of this subject is William Julius Wilson, *The Declining Significance of Race: Blacks and Changing American Institutions* (Chicago: University of Chicago Press, 1978). See, also, the argument of black activist Rev. Jesse Jackson that government action has achieved most of what is possible and that blacks must now take responsibility for improvement of their lot; e.g. "Learning to Excel in School," *Newsweek,* July 10, 1978, pp. 45-46.

[109]Roberts, "Black Progress," p. 22.

[110]See Alan Baron, "Power," *Politics Today,* September/October, 1978, p. 6.

[111]Terence Smith, "President, in Atlanta, Asks Congress to Vote Holiday for Dr. King," *The New York Times,* January 15, 1979, p. 1.

[112]Howell Raines, "Wallace, at the Last, Tries to Erase, 'Unfair' Verdict," *The New York Times,* January 7, 1979, p. 16.

[113]*Ibid.*

[114]*Ibid.*

[115]Both excerpts are from " 'Segregation Forever,' " *The New York Times,* January 17, 1979, p. A22.

[116]Personal letter from Governor Fob James, Montgomery, Alabama, February 1, 1979. Gov. James took steps, once in office, which suggested a commitment to give substance to these sentiments. See Howell Raines, "5 New Southern Governors Seek Bold Changes Despite the Risks," *The New York Times,* February 25, 1979, pp. 1, 42.

[117]*Commission on Civil Disorders,* p. 1.

[118]*Ibid.,* pp. 1, 16.

[119]*Ibid.,* p. 16.

[120]Senate, *Presidential Commissions,* pp. 186-87 (emphasis added).

[121]*Ibid.,* p. 4.

[122]Gary T. Marx, "A Document," p. 56.

[123]Skolnick, "Violence Commission Violence," p. 38.

[124]Senate, *Presidential Commissions,* p. 150.

[125]*Ibid.,* p. 105.

[126]Hart, personal letter.

[127]Eisenhower, private interview.

[128]Lipsky and Olson, "Riot Commission Politics," p. 14.

[129]Eisenhower, private interview.

[130]*Ibid.*

# Chapter 8

[1]*Commission on Obscenity and Pornography,* p. 583.

[2]House, *Role and Effectiveness,* p. 5.

[3]Kennedy, personal letter.

[4]Cronin, *The State of the Presidency,* p. 21.

[5]Campbell, private interview.

[6]McPherson, private interview.

[7]James Q. Wilson, "Violence, Pornography, and Social Science," *The Public Interest,* 22 Winter, 1971, p. 61, quoted in Larsen, "The Commission on Obscenity and Pornography," in Komarovsky, ed., *Sociology and Public Policy,* p. 13.

[8]Ruth, "To Dust Shall Ye Return?," pp. 831-32.

[9]See Senate, *Presidential Commissions,* p. 15.

[10]*Ibid.,* p. 5.

[11]*Ibid.,* p. 186.

[12]*Ibid.,* p. 17.

[13]Goodwin, private interview.

[14]Campbell, private interview.

[15]Senate, *Presidential Commissions,* pp. 222-23.

[16]*Ibid.,* p. 20.

[17]William Lockhart, in *Ibid.,* p. 93.

[18]Lloyd Cutler, in House, *Presidential Advisory Committees (Part 2),* p. 134.

[19]Senate, *Presidential Commissions,* p. 87.

[20]H.Res. 784, S.Res. 271, 95th Cong., 1st sess., 1977.

[21]Senate, *Presidential Commissions,* p. 183.

[22]*Commission on Population Growth,* p. xvi. Interestingly, President Carter's commission to investigate the accident at the Three Mile Island nuclear power plant in Pennsylvania included among its membership a housewife from a community in the vicinity of the power plant. See Terence Smith, "Carter Picks Panel To Assess Accident At Atomic Facility," *The New York Times,* April 12, 1979, pp. 1, A20.

[23]House, *Advisory Committees* (Hearing on H.R. 4383), p. 85.

[24]Roche, private interview.

[25]See Lipsky and Olson, *Commission Politics,* Chapter 11; Introduction to Platt, ed., *The Politics of Riot Commissions;* Kopkind, "White on Black," in Boesel and Rossi, eds., *Cities Under Siege,* pp. 228, 252; and Popper, *The President's Commissions,* p. 34.

[26]McPherson, private interview.

[27]Norton E. Long, "Future Race Relations," in Meranto, ed., *The Kerner Report Revisited,* pp. 141, 139.

[28]See Stanley Kauffmann, "Stanley Kauffmann on Obscenity," *The New Republic,* October 17, 1970, p. 22.

[29]See Lyndon Johnson's comments on the unacceptability of violence, in his *The Vantage Point,* p. 172.

[30]William Stockton, "Celebrating Einstein," *The New York Times Magazine,* February 18, 1979, p. 52.

[31]Jerome R. Corsi, review of *Commission Politics: The Processing of Racial Crisis in America,* by Michael Lipsky and David J. Olson, in *The American Political Science Review,* Vol. 72 (December, 1978), p. 1424.

[32]"Rehabilitation," *The New York Times,* January 14, 1979, p. 20E.

[33]Clive Barnes, Special Introduction to *Commission on Obscenity and Pornography,* p. xvii.

[34]Senate, *Presidential Commissions,* p. 6.

[35]Crawford, "Pablum and Poison," p. 55.

# BIBLIOGRAPHY

# Bibliography

## Published Materials

"A Conspiracy." *The New York Times,* January 7, 1979, p. 18E.

Alsop, Stewart. "Nixon and the Rancid Right." *Newsweek,* October 12, 1970, p. 132.

Amdur, Neil. "U.S. Report Urges New Body To Direct Amateur Athletics." *The New York Times,* January 13, 1977, pp. 1, 42.

"A New Racial Poll." *Newsweek,* February 26, 1979, pp. 48, 53.

Barber, James David. *The Presidential Character: Predicting Performance in the White House.* Englewood Cliffs, N.J.: Prentice-Hall, 1972.

Baron, Alan. "Power." *Politics Today,* September/October, 1978, pp. 6-7.

Bauer, Raymond A.; de Sola Pool, Ithiel; and Dexter, Lewis Anthony. *American Business and Public Policy.* 2d ed. Chicago: Aldine Publishing Co., 1972.

Belin, David W. *November 22, 1963: You Are the Jury.* New York: Quadrangle, 1973.

Bell, Daniel. "Comment: Government by Commission." *The Public Interest,* Number 3 (Spring, 1966), pp. 3-9.

Bell, Joseph N. "Could Danish Smut Laws Work Here?" *Today's Health,* 48 (1970).

Boesel, David, and Rossi, Peter H., eds. *Cities Under Siege: An Anatomy of the Ghetto Riots, 1964-1968.* New York: Basic Books, 1971.

Brashler, William. "The Black Middle Class: Making It." *The New York Times Magazine,* December 3, 1978, pp. 34-36, 138-40, 144-57.

Braybrooke, David, and Lindblom, Charles E. *A Strategy of Decision.* New York: The Free Press, 1963.

*The Challenge of Crime in a Free Society: A Report of the President's Commission on Law Enforcement and the Administration of Justice.* New York: Avon Books, 1968.

Corsi, Jerome R. Review of *Commission Politics: The Processing of Racial Crisis in America,* by Michael Lipsky and David J. Olson. *The American Political Science Review,* Vol. 72 (December, 1978), pp. 1423-24.

Crawford, Kenneth. "Pablum and Poison." *Newsweek,* October 12, 1970, p. 55.

Cronin, Thomas E. *The State of the Presidency.* Boston: Little, Brown, 1975.

Curvin, Robert. "Remembering Martin Luther King." *The New York Times,* January 15, 1979, p. A18.

Delaney, Paul. "Middle-Class Gains Create Tension in Black Community." *The New York Times,* February 28, 1978, pp. 1, 22.

Derthick, Martha. "On Commissionship—Presidential Variety." Brookings Reprint No. 245. Washington, D.C.: Brookings Institution, 1972.

Drew, Elizabeth B. "On Giving Oneself a Hotfoot: Government by Commission." *The Atlantic,* May, 1968, pp. 45-49.

"Echoes." *The New York Times,* March 1, 1978, p. A26.

Edelman, Murray. *The Symbolic Uses of Politics.* Urbana, Ill.: University of Illinois Press, 1964.

Epstein, Edward Jay. *Inquest: The Warren Commission and the Establishment of Truth.* New York: The Viking Press, 1966.

"Excerpts From Nixon's Letter on Campus Unrest." *The New York Times,* December 13, 1970, p. 64.

Fenno, Richard F., Jr. *Congressmen in Committees.* Boston: Little, Brown, 1973.

"Follow-Up on the News: Marijuana Report." *The New York Times,* March 31, 1974, p. 33.

"489 Residents of Cities Questioned in Survey." *The New York Times,* February 26, 1978, p. 28.

Gallup, George. "Bias Against Black as President Drops." *The Boston Globe,* August 27, 1978, p. 18.

Gavin, James M., and Hadley, Arthur T. *Crisis Now.* New York: Vintage, 1968.

"Guilty or Not?" *Newsweek,* March 18, 1968, p. 46.

Harrington, Michael. *Socialism.* New York: Saturday Review Press, 1972.

Harris, Sen. Fred R. "Mission Unaccomplished." *LOOK,* March 18, 1969, pp. 72-73.

Herbers, John. "After 15 Years, Plot Theories Still Thicken," *The New York Times,* January 7, 1979, p. E5.

———. "Black-White Split Persists A Decade After Warning." *The New York Times,* February 26, 1978, pp. 1, 28.

Hickel, Walter J. *Who Owns America?.* Englewood Cliffs, N.J.: Prentice-Hall, Inc., 1971.

Holsendolph, Ernest. "Five-Day-a-Week Postal Deliveries And Increased Subsidies Proposed." *The New York Times,* April 19, 1977, pp. 1, 64.

Hughes, Emmet John. *The Living Presidency.* New York: Coward, McCann and Geoghegan, Inc., 1973.

Johnson, Lyndon Baines. *The Vantage Point—Perspectives of the Presidency, 1963-1969.* New York: Popular Library, 1971.

Johnson, Thomas A. "Survey Indicating Whites Favor Affirmative Action Is Questioned." *The New York Times,* February 21, 1979, p. A14.

Kauffmann, Stanley. "Stanley Kauffmann on Obscenity." *The New Republic,* October 17, 1970, pp. 22, 35.

Kearns, Doris. *Lyndon Johnson and the American Dream.* New York: Harper and Row, 1976.

Keating, Charles H., Jr. "The Report that Shocked the Nation," *The Reader's Digest,* January, 1971, pp. 37-41.

Kifner, John. "Scranton on Rebuff by Nixon: Pleased That He Read Report." *The New York Times,* December 15, 1970, p. 36C.

Komarovsky, Mirra, ed. *Sociology and Public Policy: The Case of Presidential Commissions.* New York: Elsevier, 1975.

Kopkind, Andrew. "White On Black: The Riot Commission and the Rhetoric of Reform." *Cities Under Siege: An Anatomy of the Ghetto Riots, 1964-1968.* Edited by David Boesel and Peter H. Rossi. New York: Basic Books, 1971.

Lane, Mark. *Rush to Judgment.* New York: Holt, Rinehart and Winston, 1966.

"Learning to Excel in School." *Newsweek,* July 10, 1978, pp. 45-46.

Letters, *Newsweek,* March 25, 1968, pp. 4-5.

Letters, *Newsweek,* October 19, 1970, p. 6.

Letters, *The New York Times,* November 3, 1970, p. 32M.

Letters, *Time,* March 22, 1968, p. 5.

Letters, *Time,* November 9, 1970, p. 10.

Lindsey, Robert. "Study Finds Wage Gap Between Races Narrowing." *The New York Times,* May 8, 1978, pp. 1, B15.

Lipsky, Michael, and Olson, David J. *Commission Politics: The Processing of Racial Crisis in America.* New Brunswick, N.J.: Transaction Books, 1977.

————. "Riot Commission Politics." *Trans-action,* VI (July/August, 1969), pp. 9-21.

McGovern, George. *Grassroots: The Autobiography of George McGovern.* New York: Random House, 1977.

MacNeil, Neil, and Metz, Howard W. *The Hoover Report, 1953-1955: What It Means To You As Citizen and Taxpayer.* New York: Macmillan Co., 1956.

"Man Who Gave Name to Report Faced Scandal." *The New York Times,* February 26, 1978, p. 28.

Marcy, Carl. *Presidential Commissions.* New York: King's Crown Press, 1945, reprinted in New York by Da Capo Press, 1973.

*Marijuana: A Signal of Misunderstanding. The Report of the National Commission on Marijuana and Drug Abuse.* New York: Signet, 1972.

Markham, James M. "Calm Analysis Key to National Drug Report." *The New York Times,* March 23, 1973, p. 19.

Marsh, Dave. "Singing For The World's Supper." *Rolling Stone,* April 6, 1978, pp. 32-37.

Marx, Gary T. "A Document with a Difference." Review of the *Report of the National Advisory Commission on Civil Disorders. Trans-Action,* V (September, 1968), pp. 56-58.

Mayer, Martin, *About Television.* New York: Harper and Row, 1972.

Mayhew, David R. *Congress: The Electoral Connection.* New Haven: Yale University Press, 1974.

Maxwell, Neil. "Mixed Fortunes: Black Leaders of 1960s Have Come Out Better Than Segregationists." *The Wall Street Journal,* March 12, 1979, pp. 1, 25.

Meranto, Philip, ed. *The Kerner Report Revisited.* Urbana, Ill.: Institute of Government and Public Affairs, University of Illinois, 1970.

Miller, Abraham H.; Bolce, Louis H.; and Halligan, Mark R. "The New Urban Blacks." *Ethnicity,* 3 (1976), pp. 338-367.

Morris, Richard B., ed. *Encyclopedia of American History.* New York: Harper and Brothers, 1953.

The National Urban Coalition and Urban America, Inc. *One Year Later.* New York: Praeger, 1969.

Neustadt, Richard E. *Presidential Power.* New York: Mentor, 1964.

"New Criminal Code Asked." *Boston Herald Traveller,* January 17, 1971, sec. 2, p. 6.

Nixon, Richard. *RN: The Memoirs of Richard Nixon.* New York: Grosset and Dunlap, 1978.

Nordheimer, Jon. "1978 Race Relations: 3 Widely Divergent Views." *The New York Times,* February 27, 1978, pp. 1, A14.

"The People Problem." *The New York Times,* August 31, 1971, p. 30.

Platt, Anthony, ed. *The Politics of Riot Commissions, 1917-1970.* New York: Collier Books, 1971.

*The Politics of Protest: A Report Submitted by Jerome H. Skolnick, Director, Task Force on Violent Aspects of Protest and Confrontation of the National Commission on the Causes and Prevention of Violence.* New York: Ballantine Books, 1969.

Popper, Frank. *The President's Commissions.* Millwood, N.Y.: Kraus Reprint Co., 1975 for the Twentieth Century Fund, 1970.

*Population and the American Future: The Report of the Commission on Population Growth and the American Future.* New York: Signet, 1972.

"Pornography: The Oldest Debate." *Newsweek,* October 12, 1970, pp. 37-38.

Raines, Howell. "5 New Southern Governors Seek Bold Changes Despite the Risks." *The New York Times,* February 25, 1979, pp. 1, 42.

———. "Wallace, at the Last, Tries to Erase 'Unfair' Verdict." *The New York Times,* January 7, 1979, p. 16.

Reedy, George E. "A Symbol Is Worth More Than a Thousand Words." *TV Guide,* December 31, 1977, pp. 2-5.

———. *The Twilight of the Presidency.* New York: New American Library, 1970.

"Rehabilitation." *The New York Times,* January 14, 1979, p. 20E.

Reinhold, Robert. "Poll Indicates More Tolerance, Less Hope." *The New York Times,* February 26, 1978, p. 28.

*Report of the Commission on Obscenity and Pornography.* New York: Bantam Books, 1970.

*Report of the National Advisory Commission on Civil Disorders.* Washington, D.C.: U.S. Government Printing Office, 1968.

*The Report of the President's Commission on Campus Unrest.* New York: Discus Books, 1971.

*Report of the Warren Commission on the Assassination of President Kennedy.* New York: Bantam Books, 1964.

*Rights In Conflict: A Report Submitted by Daniel Walker, Director of the Chicago Study Team, to the National Commission on the Causes and Prevention of Violence.* New York: Bantam Books, 1968.

Roberts, Steve V. "Black Progress and Poverty Are Underlined by Statistics." *The New York Times,* February 28, 1978, p. 22.

Rosenthal, Jack. "Nixon Contests Scranton Report On Healing Rifts." *The New York Times,* December 13, 1970, pp. 1, 64.

Roosevelt, Theodore. *An Autobiography. The Works of Theodore Roosevelt.* National Edition. Vol. XX. New York: Charles Scribners' Sons, 1926.

————. *State Papers as Governor and President, 1899-1909. The Works of Theodore Roosevelt.* National Edition. Vol. XV. New York: Charles Scribners' Sons, 1926.

"Rush to Judgment." *Newsweek,* January 15, 1979, pp. 26-27.

Ruth Henry S., Jr. "To Dust Shall Ye Return?." *Notre Dame Lawyer,* LXIII, No. 6 (1968), pp. 811-33.

Schlesinger, Arthur, Jr. *Violence: America in the Sixties.* New York: Signet, 1968.

" 'Segregation Forever.' " *The New York Times,* January 17, 1979, p. A22.

Shuman, Howard. "Behind the Scenes—And Under the Rug." *The Washington Monthly,* July, 1969. Reprinted in U.S. Congress. House. Committee on Government Operations. *Presidential Advisory Committees (Part 2), Hearings* before a subcommittee of the Committee on Government Operations, House of Representatives, 91st Cong., 2nd sess., 1970, pp. 143-49.

Silver, Alan. "Official Interpretations of Racial Riots." *Cities Under Siege: An Anatomy of the Ghetto Riots, 1964-1968.* Edited by David Boesel and Peter H. Rossi. New York: Basic Books, 1971.

Skolnick, Jerome H. "Violence Commission Violence." *Transaction,* Vol. 7, No. 12, (October, 1970), pp. 32-38.

Smith, Stephanie. *Advisory Committee Regulation and Reform.* Issue Brief Number IB77102, The Library of Congress, Congressional Research Service, Major Issues System, (Archived 10/06/78).

Smith, Terence. "Carter Picks Panel To Assess Accident At Atomic Facility." *The New York Times,* April 12, 1979, pp. 1, A20.

————. "President, in Atlanta, Asks Congress to Vote Holiday for Dr. King." *The New York Times,* January 15, 1979, pp. 1, A15.

*The State of the Cities: Report of the Commission on the Cities in the '70s.* Washington, D.C.: The National Urban Coalition, 1971.

Sterne, Michael. "In Last Decade, Leaders Say, Harlem's Dreams Have Died." *The New York Times,* March 1, 1978, pp. 1, A13.

Stevens, William K. "Since the 1967 Riots, Detroit Has Moved Painfully Toward a Modest Renaissance." *The New York Times,* March 1, 1978, p. A13.

Stockton, William. "Celebrating Einstein." *The New York Times Magazine,* February 18, 1979, p. 52.

Sulzner, George T. "The Policy Process and the Uses of National Governmental Study Commisions." *Western Political* Quarterly, XXIV (September, 1971), pp. 438-48.

Thompson, Josiah. *Six Seconds in Dallas: A Micro-Study of the Kennedy Assassination.* New York: Bernard Geis Associates, 1967.

*To Establish Justice, To Insure Domestic Tranquility: The Final Report of the National Commission on the Causes and Prevention of Violence.* New York: Bantam Books, 1970.

TRB from Washington. "Crime Fighting." *The New Republic,* June 12, 1971.
———. "Gun Toting." *The New Republic,* July 24 and 31, 1971.
———. "Noncandidate Kennedy." *The New Republic,* June 5, 1971.
———. "Tick, Tick, Tick." *The New Republic,* May 29, 1971.
U.S. Congress. House. Committee on Government Operations. *Advisory Commit-tees. Hearing* before a subcommittee of the Committee on Government Op-erations, House of Representatives, on H.R. 4383, 92d Cong., 1st sess., 1971.
U.S. Congress. House. Committee on Government Operations. *Presidential Advi-sory Committees. Hearings* before a subcommittee of the Committee on Gov-ernment Operations, House of Representatives, 91st Cong., 2d sess., 1970.
U.S. Congress. House. Committee on Government Operations. *Presidential Advi-sory Committees (Part 2). Hearings* before a subcommittee of the Committee on Government Operations, House of Representatives, 91st Cong., 2d sess., 1970.
U.S. Congress. House. Committee on Government Operations. *The Role and Ef-fectiveness of Federal Advisory Committees. Forty-third report* by the Committee on Government Operations, House of Representatives, 91st Cong., 2d sess., 1970.
U.S. Congress. House. *Executive Branch Advisory Committees.* Conference Rept. 92-1403 To Accompany H.R. 4383, 92d Cong., 2d sess., 1970.
U.S. Congress. House. *Federal Advisory Committee Standards Act.* H.R. Rept. 92-1017 To Accompany H.R. 4383, 92d Cong., 2d sess., 1972.
U.S. Congress. Senate. Committee on the Judiciary. *Presidential Commissions. Hear-ings* before the Subcommittee on Administrative Practice and Procedure of the Committee on the Judiciary, Senate, 92d Cong., 1st sess., 1971.
"Victimless Crime." *The New Republic,* July 3, 1971, p. 9.
Vorenberg, James. "The War On Crime: The First Five Years." *The Atlantic Monthly,* May, 1972, pp. 63-69.
Weaver, Warren, Jr. "U.S. Drug Study Stresses Treatment, Not Penalties." *The New York Times,* March 23, 1973, pp. 1, 19.
Wilensky, Harold L. *Organizational Intelligence.* New York: Basic Books, 1967.
Wilkins, Roger. "Blacks and Politics: Progress In a Decade of Disappointment." *The New York Times,* March 6, 1978, p. A12.
———. "The Kerner Report of 1968 Was One Element in a Year of Hope, Violence and Despair." *The New York Times,* February 27, 1978, p. A14.
———. "Racial Outlook: Lack of Change Disturbs Blacks." *The New York Times,* March 3, 1978, p. A26.
Wilson, James Q. "A Reader's Guide to the Crime Commission Reports." *The Public Interest,* 9 (Fall, 1967), pp. 64-82.
Wilson, William Julius. *The Declining Significance of Race: Blacks and Changing American Institutions.* Chicago: University of Chicago Press, 1978.
Wolanin, Thomas R. *Presidential Advisory Commissions, Truman to Nixon.* Mad-ison: University of Wisconsin Press, 1975.

## Unpublished Materials

Campbell, James S. Private interview. Washington, D.C., August, 1977.

Eisenhower, Milton S. Private interview. The Johns Hopkins University, Baltimore, Maryland, February, 1973.

Goodwin, Doris Kearns. Private interview by telephone. December, 1978.

McPherson, Harry C., Jr., Private interview. Washington, D.C.: February, 1978.

Roche, Professor John P. Private interview. The Fletcher School of Law and Diplomacy, Medford, Massachusetts, October, 1977.

Shafer, Governor Raymond P. Private interview by telephone. October, 1977.

Letter from Louis Harris and Associates, Inc., New York, New York, October 20, 1977.

Letter from Senator Philip A. Hart, Washington, D.C., April 6, 1972.

Letter from Governor Fob James, Montgomery, Alabama, February 1, 1979.

Letter from Nicholas deB. Katzenbach, Armonk, New York, April 6, 1972.

Letter from Senator Edward M. Kennedy, Washington, D.C., October 30, 1972.

Letter from Otto Kerner, Circuit Judge, United States Court of Appeals, Chicago, Illinois, April 20, 1972.

Letter from William B. Lockhart, Dean, University of Minnesota Law School, Minneapolis, Minnesota, March 28, 1972.

Letter from Henry E. Peterson, Assistant Attorney General, Criminal Division, U.S. Department of Justice, Washington, D.C., February 23, 1973.

Letter from William W. Scranton, Scranton, Pennsylvania, April 4, 1972.

Letter from Richard L. Still, Staff Director, Special Studies Subcommittee, Committee on Government Operations, U.S. House of Representatives, Washington, D.C., October 4, 1972.

Letter from Charles F. Westoff, Director, Office of Population Research, Princeton University, Princeton, New Jersey, November 28, 1977.

"The Dick Cavett Show" (Interview with W. Cody Wilson, Executive Director, Commission on Obscenity and Pornography.) ABC telecast, December 11, 1970.

"Good Morning America" (Interview with Andrew Young.) ABC telecast, January 14, 1979.

"Meet the Press" (Interview with members of the National Commission on Marijuana and Drug Abuse.) NBC telecast, April 9, 1972.

"Meet the Press" (Interview with David W. Belin, Assistant Counsel, Commission on the Assassination of President Kennedy.) NBC telecast, February 4, 1979.

"NBC Nightly News" (Interview with H. R. Haldeman.) NBC telecast, January 11, 1979.

"Population Growth and the American Future" PBS telecast, November 29, 1972.

# INDEX

# INDEX

ABC television network, 142
Abel, I. W., 75
Agnew, Spiro T., 114, 115
Ahern, James F., 17, 115-116, 189
Alabama, 171-173
Alsop, Stewart, 118
American Association of University
    Professors, 158
American Baptist Convention, 141
American Bar Association, 22
American Council on Education, 158
Anti-Defamation League, 140
Arizona, 138
Arno Press, 102
Avon Press, 102

Bakke decision (Supreme Court), 169
Bantam Books, 99, 101
Barnes, Clive, 37, 157, 194
B'nai B'rith Women, 139
Bolling, Richard, 28-29
Book-of-the-Month Club, 101
Boston, 137
*The Boston Globe*, 142
Brooke, Edward W., 48, 144
Bureau of Social Science Research, 74
cabinet *(see also,* individual departments
    and agencies),
    interference with commissions, 54-55,
    responses to commission reports, 122-125
Califano, Joseph A., Jr., 91
California, 136
Campbell, James S., 4, 26, 63, 64, 65, 66-
    67, 69, 71, 77, 88, 90, 91-92, 104-
    105, 113, 121, 156, 162, 183, 189
Carnegie Commission on Higher Education,
    158

Carter, Jimmy, 22, 105, 121, 171
CBS News, 149
CBS television network, 142
Center for the Study of Violence (Brandeis
    University), 136
Central Intelligence Agency, 69
*Challenger* (space shuttle), 23
Chapin, Harry, 22
Chicago Crime Commission, 72
Chicago Police Department, 72
*Chronicle of Higher Education*, 102
Citizens' Committee for the Hoover Report,
    144-145
Citizens for Decent Literature, Inc., 57
Civil Rights Act of 1964, 167, 174
Clesner, Herschel, 83
Coalition for a National Population Policy,
    145
Commercial Clearing House, 102
Commission on Departmental Methods, 13
Commission on Domestic and International
    Hunger and Malnutrition, 22, 190
Commission on Foreign Economic Policy,
    89
Commission on Mental Health, 105
Commission on More Effective Government,
    28-29
Commission on Obscenity and
    Pornography, 3, 29, 36-38, 43-44, 45,
    47, 56-58, 60, 64, 65, 71, 73-74, 76-
    77, 78, 87, 96-97, 104, 113-114, 119-
    120, 123-124, 132-134, 135, 138,
    141, 144, 154, 157, 159-160, 162,
    181, 182, 185-186, 188, 192, 194
Commission on Population Growth and the
    American Future, 29, 40-41, 45, 46,
    60, 64, 85, 86, 93, 96, 100, 118, 134,
    145, 153, 163, 191

*231*